ART AND KNOWLEDGE

Almost all of us would agree that the experience of art is deeply rewarding. However, why this is the case remains a puzzle: why do many of us find works of art much more important than other sources of pleasure? *Art and Knowledge* argues that the experience of art is so rewarding because it can be an important source of knowledge about ourselves and our relation to each other and to the world.

The view that art is a source of knowledge can be traced as far back as Aristotle and Horace. Artists as various as Tasso, Sidney, Pope, Shelley, Dylan Thomas, Reynolds, Constable, Trollope, Henry James and Mendelssohn have believed that art contributes to knowledge. As attractive as this view may be, it has never been satisfactorily defended, either by artists or by philosophers. *Art and Knowledge* reflects on the essence of art and argues that it ought to provide insight as well as pleasure. It argues that all the arts, including music, are importantly representational. This kind of representation is fundamentally different from that found in the sciences, but it can provide insights as important and profound as any available from the sciences. While science tries to exclude emotion, the emotional responses generated by artworks give them their cognitive value. Once we recognise that works of art can contribute to knowledge we can avoid thorough relativism about aesthetic value and we can be in a position to evaluate the avant-garde art of the past century.

Art and Knowledge is an exceptionally clear and interesting, as well as controversial, exploration of what art is and why it is valuable. It will be of interest to all philosophers of art, artists and art critics.

James O. Young is Professor of Philosophy at the University of Victoria. He is the author of *Global Anti-realism* (1995).

ART AND KNOWLEDGE

James O. Young

London and New York

First published 2001
by Routledge
11 New Fetter Lane, London EC4P 4EE

Simultaneously published in the USA and Canada
by Routledge
29 West 35th Street, New York, NY 10001

Routledge is an imprint of the Taylor & Francis Group

© 2001 James O. Young

Typeset in Times Roman by Rosemount Typing Services
Thornhill, Dumfriesshire
Printed and bound in Great Britain by
TJ International Ltd, Padstow, Cornwall

British Library Cataloguing in Publication Data
A catalogue record for this book is available
from the British Library

Library of Congress Cataloguing in Publication Data
Young, James O., 1957-
Art & Knowledge / James O. Young.
p. cm.
Includes bibliographical references and index.
1. Aesthetics. 2. Arts–Philosophy. 3. Knowledge, Theory of 4. Avant-garde
(Aesthetics) I. Title: Art and knowledge. II. Title.
BH39 .Y68 2001
111'.85–dc21   2001019640

ISBN 0-415-25646-1 hbk
ISBN 0-415-25647-X pbk

FOR MY WIFE

Art is not indifferent to truth; it is essentially the pursuit of truth.
R. G. Collingwood
Principles of Art, p. 288

I have no exquisite reason for't, but I have reason good enough.
Shakespeare
Twelfth Night, Act II, Scene 3

CONTENTS

PREFACE

Keats famously asserted that beauty is truth. I would not put the point in these terms (I am a philosopher, not a poet) but, roughly speaking, Keats was right. At least, he was right about the beauty frequently ascribed to works of art. We can mean many things when we call something beautiful, but sometimes when we say that a work of art is beautiful we mean that it provides insight into the truth. More generally, a work of art can be beautiful because it is a source of knowledge. I will call this Keats's hypothesis.

Keats has not been the only person to suggest that beauty and knowledge are intimately connected. Many other poets have maintained that readers can learn from their works. Horace, Tasso, Sidney, Pope, Shelley, and a host of others have held as much. Dylan Thomas once said that, 'A good poem ... helps to extend everyone's knowledge of himself and the world around him.' Painters (such as Reynolds and Constable), novelists (among them Trollope and James) and composers (Mendelssohn, for example) have made similar claims about their arts. Artists are not the only people who have endorsed Keats's hypothesis. Philosophers from Aristotle to Nelson Goodman and critics from Dr Johnson to F. R. Leavis have also done so.

Although Keats's hypothesis has had distinguished advocates, it remains controversial. The problem is that it has more frequently been asserted than defended. Philosophers have paid it insufficient attention. When they have considered the hypothesis, their defences have often been sketchy or unsuccessful. Many advocates of Keats's hypothesis have probably thought that it is obviously true. The hypothesis has obvious attractions. For example, it can explain why art is more important and valuable than either entertainment or decoration. The view that art, at its best, is a more important enterprise than the production of perfume or upholstery is not mere snobbery. Any enterprise that can provide knowledge will have an importance that entertainment and decoration cannot possess. Nevertheless, for all its intuitive appeal, Keats's hypothesis is in need of defence. This essay has been written in the hope of providing a more persuasive defence of the hypothesis than philosophers have hitherto presented.

Throughout this essay, I illustrate my arguments with examples of actual artworks. I have tried to choose examples that will be familiar to most of my readers. Of course, I have tended to refer to works that I most admire. Fortunately, my tastes in painting and literature are pretty standard. Most of my literary examples are drawn from the canon of English literature. The paintings that I mention are familiar masterpieces of European art. My tastes in music are a little more idiosyncratic, and I refer to works of the baroque period more often than is usual. Still, I think that most of the compositions I mention will be familiar to almost all readers.

I will draw examples from all of the fine arts, but I will speak mainly about music, literature and painting. Only occasionally will I mention architecture, sculpture, dance, film and other arts. This is partly because I know less about these arts and partly because I cannot mention everything. Nevertheless, I believe that Keats's hypothesis is true of all of the arts. Some people believe that only some arts can provide knowledge. I believe that all of them can.

One note on the format of this essay is required. It contains no footnotes or endnotes in the usual sense of the term. I find footnotes a distraction while I read, and this essay is designed to be read without reference to any notes. At the end of the book, readers will find a bibliographic note corresponding to most of the essay's twenty-seven sections. Readers who are curious about sources can consult these notes. I have also included a bibliography, probably the most extensive yet compiled on the topic of art and knowledge.

In the course of writing this essay, I profited from the comments and criticisms of many people. Most of all, I must thank my colleagues Colin Macleod and Jan Zwicky. They carefully read the entire manuscript and met with me to discuss it. I made fewer changes to the manuscript than they suggested, but their comments certainly helped me to improve it. My father-in-law, the Honourable Donald Bowman, also read an entire draft. I very much appreciated the comments of an informed non-philosopher, particularly one with the perceptiveness of an astute jurist. I participated in a session on literature and knowledge at the May 1998 meetings of the Canadian Philosophical Association. The paper I delivered on that occasion contained the germ of some material included in this essay. The other participants were David Davies, Peter Lamarque and Carl Matheson and they all made helpful comments on my contribution. Deborah Knight, who was in the audience on that occasion, also had useful criticisms. I read a paper on music as a source of knowledge at the University of Manitoba in March 1997 and I am grateful to the audience on that occasion for their probing questions and insightful comments. At the June 1997 Canadian Philosophical Association meetings Evan Kirchhoff and Carl Matheson gave a paper, to which I replied, in which they usefully criticised some of my early writings on art and knowledge. Correspondence with Dominic Lopes was of assistance when I was writing the passages dealing with art and moral knowledge. I had a brief but valuable conversation with Christopher Cordiner while in Melbourne for the 1999 Australasian Association of Philosophy Conference. Robert Ginsberg suggested many valuable stylistic improvements. I have also profited from the criticisms and suggestions of Jennifer Bates, Bill Barthelemy, Jeff Foss, Thomas Heyd, Duncan

MacIntosh, Justine Noel, Karen Shirley, Dick Simpson and Lana Simpson. The comments of two anonymous readers for Routledge were of great assistance as I revised this work for publication. I am grateful to Tony Bruce, the Routledge Philosophy Editor, and Muna Khogali, the Philosophy Editorial Assistant, for their assistance in seeing this book through the press.

This is the traditional place to thank one's wife for her assistance and encouragement. Unfortunately, my wife proved of virtually no practical assistance. She read next to nothing of the manuscript, and she would have laughed if I had suggested that she edit it or perform some similar wifely task. The fact that she gave birth to two children (Julia and Piers) while I was writing the book did not help matters at all. Still, Laurel is the light of my life, and to her this book is fondly dedicated.

Victoria, British Columbia, 2001

1

WHAT IS ART?

Definitions of art

I believe that every item properly classified as a work of art can contribute to human knowledge. In other words, I maintain that all artworks possess cognitive value. One might dispute this thesis in two ways. Some people will hold that no works of art have cognitive value. On their view, an artwork, unlike a work of history or science, is not the sort of thing from which one can learn. Alternatively, one might hold that, although some artworks have cognitive value, not all of them do. This second objection states that a satisfactory definition of art will not make reference to cognitive value. The bulk of this essay is designed to show that the first sort of objection is mistaken. This first chapter has the more modest goal of replying to the second objection. In this chapter, I assume that one can learn from at least some of the things which have been classified as works of art. I then argue that art ought to be defined in such a way that only items with cognitive value count as artworks.

This chapter is divided into four sections. The first section contains general reflections on how art is to be defined. I adopt the view that art is whatever is accepted as art by an artworld. In the second section I argue that art can be defined only relative to an artworld. Something never possesses arthood *tout court*. Rather it is an artwork for some artworld or other. The third section argues that an artworld can be given reasons for accepting only certain items as works of art. The fourth section reveals that these reasons indicate that an artworld ought to accept as art only works with cognitive value. The conclusions of this chapter are, in large part, independent of the general position adopted in the rest of this essay. Readers can deny that a definition of art ought to make reference to cognitive value. At the same time, they can accept that I give, in subsequent chapters, a sound argument for the conclusion that some artworks have cognitive value and that I explain how this is possible.

A few generations ago, writers on the epistemology of art typically began with the bald assertion that a *genuine* work of art is a source of knowledge. According to such authors, a work which is merely a source of delight or sensuous pleasure is not a work of art. Sometimes these writers implied that only decadent cultures and individuals have thought otherwise. I would like to be able to make such statements with impunity, but I cannot. Consequently, I am forced to begin this essay with a discussion of the definition of art. I will then be in a position to say that only works with cognitive value are works of art. I may even hint that anyone who disagrees is decadent.

A basic question often arises when we ask for the definition of a particular concept. A long time ago, Plato asked whether something is pious because the gods love it or whether the gods love something because it is pious. Similarly, we can ask whether something is art because the artworld accepts it, or whether the artworld accepts an object because it is art. (When the question is put in this way, another question arises: who counts as a member of the artworld? My answer is elegantly democratic. I count as an artworld member anyone who uses the word 'art'.) In other words, a question about the property of arthood needs to be addressed. It could be either a *relational property* or an *intrinsic property*. A relational property is a property an object possesses only in relation to another object. The property of being a father, for example, is a relational property. Someone possesses it only in relation to his children. The property of being beloved is another. An intrinsic property is a property an object possesses independently of any other. So, for example, the property of being spherical is an intrinsic property. If something is art because the artworld accepts it as such, then arthood is a relational property. If, on the other hand, the artworld accepts things as artworks because of properties they possess, then arthood is an intrinsic property.

Some philosophers have believed that arthood is an intrinsic property, others that it is relational. Some philosophers have believed that arthood is essentially the capacity to express or convey emotion. This capacity is an intrinsic property. Other philosophers have thought that artworks all possess certain formal properties, such as uniformity amid variety. These philosophers also believe that arthood is an intrinsic property. Still others hold that all arthood is the intrinsic property of being able to contribute to knowledge in some characteristic manner. (This last clause is important since many items with cognitive value are not works of art. The principal task of this essay is to identify the manner in which art contributes to knowledge.) Arthood has also been held to be a variety of relational properties. Some have held that arthood is the property of standing in some relation to the theories of an artworld. Another view, a version of the institutional definition of art, is that something possesses the property of arthood if and only

2

if it is accepted as art by the artworld. On this view, something possesses the property of arthood in relation to the artworld which accepts it as art.

The examples in the previous paragraph illustrate that the intrinsic properties artworks are thought to possess are usually taken to be functional properties. Arthood is often held, that is, to be the property of being able to perform some function. Works with the property of arthood may, for example, function to evoke emotion in an audience. Consequently, to say that arthood is an intrinsic property is not necessarily to say that it is a property completely independent of relations to an audience. Here an analogy to secondary qualities is helpful. Advocates of the view that arthood is an intrinsic property could hold that arthood is similar to secondary properties such as redness. Redness is never in objects in the same way that, say, rectangularity is. Nevertheless, redness is an intrinsic property in objects: a power to affect viewers. One might similarly hold that arthood is in objects as a power to affect audiences.

Given that I believe that all artworks possess cognitive value, I might be thought to hold that arthood is an intrinsic property. In particular, I might be expected to hold that arthood is a capacity to provide knowledge. Certainly, I can be expected to hold that not just anything the artworld accepts as a work of art is one. After all, it seems obvious that audiences have accepted as works of art items which have no cognitive value. Giving an example of such an item might prove controversial, but a huge variety of objects have been accepted as works of art. The suggestion that all of these objects have cognitive value is implausible. Nevertheless, I see no way to avoid the conclusion that arthood is a relational property.

Euthyphro was right: things are pious because loved by the gods. Piety is a relational property. In particular, it is an example of what might be called a *perspectival property*. A perspectival property is a relational property that does not exist independently of the perception of its existence. The nature of such properties is best appreciated by contrast with a non-perspectival property such as cubicalness. Something is cubical even if no one believes that it is. Even if every sentient being in the world disappeared, dice would continue to be cubical. Contrast this with piety. If no gods existed to love things, nothing could possess the property of being pious. In this way, piety depends on beings who perceive its existence. Similarly, a world without people who conceive of art is a world without art. Michelangelo's *David* would possess the property of being made from marble even if no one thought it was. It would not possess the property of arthood if people did not employ the concept of art. Arthood consequently depends on the perspective of an artworld. It is a perspectival property. As we shall see, if arthood depends on the perception of its existence, arthood is whatever an artworld conceives it to be. Should an artworld's conception change, so does arthood.

I seem, then, to be committed to a hopelessly inconsistent position. I accept that artworks are works accepted by an artworld and that items without cognitive value have been accepted as art. Apparently, I cannot consistently maintain that all artworks have cognitive value. The apparent inconsistency disappears once the relativity of arthood is recognised. Many writers have mistakenly assumed that only one artworld exists and that art is whatever this artworld accepts as art. In fact, as many artworlds exist as there are groups of people who are in general agreement about the membership of the class of artworks. The members of some artworld may accept as a work of art something without cognitive value. From this we cannot draw the unqualified conclusion that cognitive value is not a feature of all artworks. In other artworlds, only items with cognitive value are accepted as artworks. In these artworlds, the view that arthood is a perspectival property is not inconsistent with the view that all works of art have cognitive value. I am a member of an artworld which accepts as art only works with cognitive value. Consequently, I can consistently hold that arthood is a perspectival property and that all artworks have cognitive value.

The argument of the previous paragraph is plausible only if I can establish the existence of a multiplicity of artworlds and that arthood is relative to these worlds. As I have noted, virtually everyone who has employed the concept of an artworld in defining art has spoken of *the* artworld. The conjunction of the proposition that only a single artworld exists and the view that arthood depends on acceptance by an artworld quickly leads, however, to an absurdity. One way to avoid the absurdity is to reject the view that arthood is the perspectival property I have suggested it is. Since I believe that this would be misguided, I conclude that belief in a single artworld is mistaken. The relativity of arthood soon follows.

The relativity of arthood

It is helpful to begin the case for the relativity of arthood by returning to Plato's attempt to define piety. My definition of art, which I will call the *perspectival definition*, is parallel to Euthyphro's initial definition of piety. Early in their dialogue, Euthyphro tells Socrates that piety is what is agreeable to the gods. By Euthyphro's own admission, however, the gods quarrel among themselves. When they quarrel, they differ about what is good and what is bad. Since they love the good and abhor the bad, some things are loved by some of the gods, but hated by others. Socrates notes that Euthyphro is apparently committed to the conclusion that one thing can be both pious and impious, which is impossible. A similar argument can be advanced against the view that artworks are the items accepted as such by the artworld. Just as the gods disagree among themselves, so the members of the artworld have their differences. Consequently, it may seem that the perspectival definition of art, like Euthyphro's initial definition of piety, is reduced to absurdity. Since arthood is relative to an audience, however, this conclusion can be avoided.

It is easy to formulate the Socratic argument against the perspectival definition of art. We can imagine a situation where some people, all indisputably members of the artworld, disagree about whether some item is an artwork. Let us call these people Andy, Arthur, Clement and Peggy. Clement and Peggy, say, deny that some item is a work of art. Andy and Arthur, on the other hand, accept it as an artwork. Under these circumstances, it seems that the item in question both is and is not a work of art, which is impossible. Apparently, the perspectival definition is reduced to absurdity. Consequently, the perspectival definition must be rejected unless something is wrong with the Socratic argument.

A simple way to avoid this *reductio*, without accepting the relativity of arthood, immediately suggests itself. This response to the problem may be called the *simple response*. Defenders of the perspectival definition could hold that the arthood of any item does not depend on the unanimity of the artworld. Instead, they can maintain, some item is an artwork if even one member of the artworld accepts it as such. Imagine that an item is presented to Andy, Clement and Peggy, and none of them accepts it as a work of art. Subsequently, the item is presented to Arthur and he accepts it as an artwork. The simple response states that, given that Arthur is a member of the artworld, as soon as Arthur confers arthood upon the controversial item, it is an artwork. It is so whether or not the other members of the artworld recognise it as such. (They may not know that Arthur has accepted the item as an artwork.) According to the simple response, this is irrelevant. Even if some members of the artworld continue to believe that the work is not an artwork, it is. It may seem, then, that the simple response saves the perspectival definition from reduction to absurdity.

The simple response is unsatisfactory. The trouble is that when some members of the artworld decline to accept an item as an artwork, they thereby confer upon it non-arthood. That is, when someone has the power to confer arthood upon some item, but declines to do so, he thereby confers non-arthood upon it. So, when our controversial item is presented to Peggy, and she declines to accept it as an artwork, she *ipso facto* confers non-arthood on it. Arthur may try to persuade Peggy to accept the item as a work of art on the grounds that he has done so. Equally, however, Peggy can attempt to change Arthur's mind. Peggy might give in and admit that the item is an artwork, but she might continue to deny that the object is an artwork. In this situation, where the artworld is divided, the perspectival definition leads to the conclusion that something both is and is not a work of art. The *reductio* is as threatening as ever.

A move made by Euthyphro suggests another way to avoid the *reductio* without adopting relativism about arthood. This move may be called the *critical mass response*. According to the critical mass response, something possesses arthood only when some critical mass of the artworld accepts it as an artwork. Faced with Socrates' objection to his initial definition of piety, Euthyphro maintains that piety is what is loved by all of the gods. One could similarly suggest that art is what all of the members of the artworld accept as art. Euthyphro thus states that all of the Olympian world is the critical mass required to confer piety on something. The problem with this suggestion is that it is quite rare for the gods to agree. It is equally rare for an item to be unanimously accepted as a work of art. If unanimous acceptance by the artworld were a necessary condition of arthood, the class of artworks would be small. It might even be the empty set. It would be difficult to find a work whose arthood has not been denied by someone. Tolstoy by himself would decimate the class of artworks. Given that some objects are artworks, the critical mass needed for arthood cannot be the entire artworld.

One could maintain that something is a work of art when accepted as such by a sufficiently large segment of the artworld. Perhaps arthood is dependent on acceptance by a minimum percentage of the artworld. Alternatively, perhaps some minimum number of artworld members must accept something as a work of art. (Perhaps some of this number must come from each of the three estates: curators, critics and artists.) According to the critical mass response, whatever formula is adopted, once a specified critical mass of the artworld accepts something as an artwork, it is an artwork. Suppose that this is the case. We are still owed an account of the critical mass needed to confer arthood on an object.

Giving such an account will prove difficult. On some accounts of the critical mass necessary for arthood, the critical mass response fails for precisely the same reason that the simple response fails. Suppose that the critical mass necessary for arthood is set at a percentage of the artworld lower than 50 per cent. Suppose, moreover, that a similarly low percentage of the artworld can confer non-arthood on an item. In such a case, the critical mass needed to establish the arthood of some item and the critical mass needed to confer non-arthood could both be satisfied. Once again we would be left with a situation where an item could both be and not be a work of art.

This problem can be avoided by setting the critical mass for arthood in such a way that, if it is reached, the critical mass for non-arthood cannot be reached, and vice versa. Suppose that the critical mass required for arthood is set at 50 per cent plus one of the artworld, and the critical mass for non-arthood is set at the same percentage. In this case, a perspectival definition of art would never lead to the conclusion that some item both is and is not an artwork. Alternatively, the critical mass needed for arthood could be set at 10 per cent plus one of the artworld, and the critical mass required for non-arthood fixed at 90 per cent. In a limiting case, the critical mass necessary for arthood could be set as low as one member of the artworld, so long as the critical mass required for non-arthood is the entire artworld. In any of these cases, a work can never both be and not be an artwork.

The problems we face do not disappear when critical masses are judiciously set. We are still owed a defence of the settings. After all, it is not obvious that something is a work of art when accepted by 50 per cent of the artworld, but not when approved by only 40 per cent. More importantly, we need a defence of the suggestion that some segment of the artworld can override another segment. Without such a defence, we are back to the situation where Peggy sees no reason to accept some item as a work of art simply because Arthur does. Unfortunately, problems arise in attempting to argue for both high and low critical masses. The view that a small segment of the artworld can confer either arthood or non-arthood, and override a large segment of the artworld, cannot avoid the *reductio*. On the other hand, a new sort of problem arises if arthood requires the agreement of a large percentage of the artworld.

On the view to which I subscribe, the only justification for saying that something is an artwork is that members of the artworld classify it as an artwork. Similarly, the only justification for saying that something is not an artwork is that the members of the artworld decline to categorise it as art. Consequently, the only justification for setting the critical mass required for arthood is provided by the use members of the artworld make of the concept of art. Suppose now that someone says that a small critical mass is sufficient to establish the arthood of an item. The only way to assess this proposal is to examine the practice of the artworld. We need to ask whether members of the artworld accept that a novel item is an artwork when a small percentage of the artworld believes that it is. I suggest that this is not the practice of the artworld. Frequently, a small avant-garde will accept the arthood of some item. Equally frequently, the bulk of the artworld nevertheless refuses to recognise the item as an artwork. This was the case, for example, when Duchamp first began to exhibit his works. Although his readymades are now commonly accepted as works of art, we would do well to remember that this was not always the case. In the early twentieth century, influential but conservative critics such as Royal Cortissoz probably held the consensus opinion about the avant-garde art of the day. It is hard to know what to say in such a situation. If anything, it seems more reasonable to say that a small segment of the artworld cannot confer arthood. We could, however, say that the practice of a minority of the artworld is sufficient to establish the arthood of a controversial item. If we do so, a problem ensues: we apparently lack a principled reason for saying that a minority of the artworld cannot confer non-arthood. If a minority can confer arthood, the *reductio* then rears its ugly head.

Perhaps relativism can be avoided by saying that a large percentage of the artworld establishes the arthood of an object. When the acceptance of some item as an artwork is widespread, it is uncontroversially a work of art. When the segment of the artworld which accepts an object as art is sufficiently large, one is inclined to say that people who dissent are mistaken about the use of the concept of art. Such people may be said to have lost their franchise as members of the artworld. That is, they have lost the power to confer arthood. If widespread agreement about whether something is an artwork always existed, a *reductio* would not be a threat. Suppose that Andy, Clement, Peggy and a large number of other members of their artworld agree that some item is not an artwork. In the face of this consensus, Arthur must fail in his attempt to confer arthood upon the same item. There is no danger that the item both is and is not an artwork. The trouble is that widespread agreement does not always exist. When the artworld is roughly equally divided, the *reductio* remains a worry. Adopting a high critical mass faces, however, even more worrisome trouble.

The trouble is that, if a large percentage of the artworld must confer arthood on an item for it to be an artwork, avant-garde works would not be artworks, at least not at first. As a matter of historical fact, some of the controversial works of the early twentieth century were not widely accepted as artworks for many years. I would not be surprised to learn that a majority of artworld members still do not accept that Duchamp's readymades are artworks. After all, stodgy academicians, hidebound critics, conservative collectors and informed but fusty audience members are still members of the artworld. Consequently, the conditions for arthood were not met in the cases of many works, if these conditions involve widespread agreement in the artworld. Nevertheless, many people have the intuition that many avant-garde works became works of art either at, or very soon after, the time of their creation. We need, then, to choose between two incompatible claims. The first states that a controversial avant-garde work can have arthood conferred upon it immediately, or almost immediately. If this is the case, a small segment of the artworld can confer arthood on an object. The second is the proposition that if a small percentage of the artworld can confer arthood, a *reductio* cannot be avoided.

Once we recognise the existence of a plurality of artworlds, the puzzles about arthood disappear. Up to this point, I have spoken of *the* artworld, as if only one exists. This assumption must be rejected. A variety of artworlds exist and items are artworks in relation to some and not artworks in relation to others. Reflection on Marcel Duchamp's *Fountain* makes this clear. (This sculpture is, perhaps, the most influential artwork of the past century. It consists of a urinal, laid on its back and signed 'R. Mutt, 1917'.) *Fountain* did not exist in the sixteenth century, but it is fair to say that, if it had, it would not have been a work of art. The artworld of the Renaissance would have been completely unwilling to accept it as an artwork. Had a time-travelling Duchamp held that a bathroom fixture was an artwork, this would have been taken as evidence that he did not know how to use the concept of art. Today, however, Duchamp's readymade is widely accepted as an artwork. Relative to a contemporary artworld, *Fountain* is an artwork. Even though artworlds differ about the status of *Fountain*, it is not the case that it both is and is not an artwork. Rather, it is an artwork relative to a contemporary artworld and a non-artwork relative to a sixteenth-century artworld.

Just as a sixteenth-century artworld and a contemporary artworld disagree about the status of certain works, so different present-day artworlds disagree. Some groups of people accept *Fountain* as an artwork, and others (including Cortissoz) categorise it as a non-artwork. This difference of opinion should not lead us to conclude that the urinal in question both is and is not an artwork. After all, the difference of opinion between sixteenth-century and contemporary artworlds does not lead us to this conclusion. We should treat disagreement within our own times just as we treat disagreement between historical artworlds. We should relativise arthood to an artworld. Relative to one artworld, *Fountain* is an artwork. Relative to another artworld, it is not. Nothing is absurd in saying that something is art relative to one artworld and not art relative to another.

A simple thought-experiment will reinforce the conclusion of the previous paragraph. Imagine that a planet exists somewhere in the universe that is very much like ours in every respect. In particular, this planet (Twin Earth) has an art history much like that of Earth. Everyone on Earth has a *Doppelgänger* on Twin Earth. The *Doppelgängers* of the members of the artworld constitute twin artworld. The only difference between our artworld and twin artworld is that in ours an erstwhile urinal is accepted as an artwork, while in the twin this is not the case. If arthood is a relational property a work possesses when it is accepted as an artwork, in our artworld a urinal is an artwork. In twin artworld, however, no urinal is an artwork. This is the case despite the fact that the two artworlds exist simultaneously. If the members of twin artworld should learn of the existence of our artworld, they may not change their minds about their urinal. Likely, they will observe that on their planet a urinal is not an artwork, while on ours it is. Certainly, they will not accept that Earth's artworld can transform a urinal into an artwork in Twin Earth's artworld.

Fanciful as the story of artworld and twin artworld may seem, it reflects what happens in art circles on this planet. Earth is populated, not by a unified artworld, but by a number of mutually hostile and suspicious artworlds. The avant-garde artworld is one, and the *arrière-garde* artworld is another. The avant-garde artworld quite happily accepts Duchamp's readymades, Warhol's *Brillo Boxes* and similar works as artworks. Members of the *arrière-garde* artworld (to which I belong), refuse to accept as an artwork anything lacking a particular functional property. They hold that arthood involves being able to provide knowledge in a particular way. As far as they can see, many works by Duchamp and Warhol do not have this property. When another artworld accepts these works as artworks, members of the *arrière-garde* artworld do not feel compelled to grant that they are artworks. On the other hand, the avant-garde artworld counts as artworks only works that are quite unlike anything hitherto produced. When the *arrière-garde* artworld accepts as artworks contemporary figurative paintings, the avant-garde artworld can scarcely believe that people are so benighted. Its members will not accept the arthood of these paintings just because a rival artworld does.

Earlier we saw that if something is an artwork because it is accepted by an artworld, then we are threatened with a *reductio*. Now that we recognise the multiplicity of artworlds, we can see how to avoid the *reductio*. Arthood is relative to artworlds. The arthood with which objects are endowed cannot be transported across the boundaries of artworlds. If this is the case, the *reductio* is easily avoided. There is no absurdity in saying that some object is an artwork relative to one artworld, but not relative to another.

Having established the relativity of arthood, I can consistently accept that arthood is a relational property and hold that all artworks (in my artworld) have cognitive value. Something is an artwork if and only if accepted as such by an artworld, and items without cognitive value have been accepted by an artworld. Such items have not, however, been accepted as artworks by the artworld to which I belong. In this artworld, only objects which can contribute to knowledge in a certain way have been endowed with arthood. Arthood is not the property of having a kind of cognitive value, but all artworks happen to have this property, relative to some artworlds.

Defining art responsibly

I have shown that I am not required to accept the arthood of works without cognitive value. This is the case even if many people accept the arthood of items without cognitive value. Perhaps I should be content with this relativism, but I am not. I will argue that any artworld can be given reasons for holding that only works with cognitive value are works of art. An artworld has the power to transform into an artwork anything it likes. Ideally, however, an artworld will like only what has a valuable artistic function. Fortunately, any artworld can be given good practical reasons for accepting as artworks only works with a valuable function. An artworld should exercise responsibly its power to confer arthood.

In this section I will address an objection often levelled against positions, such as my perspectival account of arthood, which hold that arthood is a property which objects possess in relation to artworlds. According to this complaint, advocates of such positions lose sight of the value or function of art. An object is an artwork because accepted as such. Given this account of arthood, something can possess arthood even though it is of no particular value. This follows since nothing about an artwork, in and of itself, gives it arthood. That is, something can be a work of art even though it possesses no intrinsic property which anyone finds valuable. This section provides a response to this common objection. In responding, I bridge the gap between those who believe that arthood is a relational property and those who believe it is intrinsic. It is possible to give a reason for restricting arthood to works with an intrinsic functional property, even if objects are artworks because they have a relational property.

We need to begin by distinguishing between two sorts of reasons: evidential reasons and practical reasons. An evidential reason is a reason that provides a justification for some proposition. Consider, for example, the evidential reasons I can have for believing that snow is white. My reasons include memories of snow I have seen, beliefs about conditions of observation when I experienced snow, testimony from others about the colour of snow, and so on. A practical reason is a reason provided by desires or interests. My desire to stay dry, for example, gives me a reason to carry my umbrella on a rainy day. Similarly, an interest in good health provides people with a practical reason to exercise.

It is possible for someone to have reasons for believing that some object is a work of art. Imagine that you come across some new candidate for arthood. If arthood were an intrinsic property, you could have an evidential reason for classifying the novel item as an artwork. You could examine the object and acquire evidential reasons for believing that it is, say, an artifact which conveys emotion. If arthood is the property of being an artifact able to convey emotion, you would then have an evidential reason for believing that the object is an artwork. If, on the other hand, arthood is not an intrinsic property, it is not clear that you can have an evidential reason for classifying a novel item as an artwork. Before we can determine whether this is the case, we need to consider further the process by which an artworld confers arthood on objects.

An artworld can confer arthood by one of two processes. The first process an artworld can adopt is the fiat process. This is the process of considering objects one at a time and arbitrarily accepting them as artworks or, equally arbitrarily, rejecting them as non-art. The alternative to this process is the guideline process. If an artworld follows this process, it adopts a set of guidelines which determine membership in the class of artworks. In other words, the artworld adopts guidelines which determine the property of arthood. (I will refer to these as *art-defining guidelines* or, more simply, as *guidelines*. An artworld is composed of the people who share the same guidelines.) Once an artworld adopts a set of guidelines, all objects with the specified characteristics are transformed into works of art. On this view, an object can possess arthood even though it has not been examined by the artworld. An unexamined object is an artwork so long as it has the properties specified by an artworld's guidelines.

The process an artworld adopts will affect the reasons an artworld can have for classifying objects as artworks. If an artworld adopts the fiat process, a member of the artworld cannot have an evidential reason for accepting a novel item as an artwork. An inspection of the item cannot result in evidential reasons for thinking that something is art. This is the case since its intrinsic properties have nothing to do with its arthood. Even without any evidential reasons, however, an artworld which adopts the fiat process can classify novel items as artworks. An item can be classified as an artwork for no reason at all, on a whim. Nevertheless, people can have reasons for accepting something as an artwork, or refraining from doing so. These reasons can only be practical reasons. They will be precisely the sort of reasons an artworld can have for adopting a set of guidelines. I will examine the practical reasons for accepting, or declining to accept, something as an artwork in the context of my discussion of the guideline process.

The situation is different if an artworld adopts the guideline process. If the guideline process is adopted, a novel item will possess arthood if it possesses the properties specified in the guidelines. Moreover, an artworld can have evidential reasons for believing that an item is an artwork. Members of the artworld can examine the item and discover that it has the characteristics specified in the guidelines adopted by the artworld. If so, they have an evidential reason for believing that the item is an artwork. It is an artwork, however, only in relation to the artworld and its guidelines. Even though one can have evidential reasons for believing that an object is an artwork, one cannot have evidential reasons for adopting a set of guidelines. These must be adopted either by fiat or on the basis of practical reasons. Whichever process of conferring arthood members of an artworld adopt, complete evidential reasons cannot be given for accepting an object as an artwork. Either one cannot give evidential reasons at all or one cannot give evidential reasons for the guidelines which confer arthood.

For several reasons, the guideline process is and ought to be adopted by an artworld. We have already seen that adoption of this process makes it possible to preserve the intuition that an unexamined object can be an artwork. Perhaps the best reason for adopting the guideline process is that, by doing so, one can convincingly reply to a standard objection to the view that arthood is a matter of acceptance by an artworld. Opponents of the view that arthood is conferred by an artworld frequently ridicule the position. They complain that the artworld holds no meetings where the arthood of objects is discussed and determined. They conclude that arthood is not a relational property. If the guideline process is adopted, one can reply to this objection by saying that the practice of an artworld makes clear that it has adopted a set of guidelines. Consistent willingness to describe as art only objects with certain characteristics reveals an implicit acceptance of guidelines which circumscribe the class of artworks. From here on, I will assume any artworld adopts the guideline process.

The issue now is whether an artworld can have reasons for adopting one set of guidelines rather than another. As we have just seen, if one can have reasons, they must be practical reasons. Practical reasons are available. Members of an artworld have interests such as an interest in maximising the production of aesthetically valuable artworks. Moreover, most members of most artworlds find valuable only works with a certain range of characteristics. The adoption of some guidelines will encourage the production of works with the characteristics valued by most artworld members. Suppose an artworld adopts guidelines which state that only items with designated valuable characteristics are artworks. The adoption of such guidelines likely will maximise the probability that the artworld will be presented with works with these characteristics. If such guidelines are accepted, questions about the nature of art are not completely divorced from questions about value. Consequently, given their interests, members of any artworld have strong practical reasons for preferring some guidelines to others.

A few examples will illustrate how practical benefits can result from judiciously chosen guidelines. Here we are concerned with the guidelines which circumscribe the class of artworks. I will begin, however, with a couple of examples which illustrate how, in other contexts, one can have practical reasons for adopting one definition rather than another. (A definition of art is a specification of the membership of the class of artworks. Since a set of guidelines determines the membership in this class, to adopt a set of guidelines is to adopt a definition of art.) Practical reasons are similarly available when defining art.

Begin by considering the class of works of upholstery. Works do not group themselves together to form the class of works of upholstery. Instead, some people, call them the furnitureworld, identify a variety of objects (couches, sofas, divans, easy chairs, and so on) and class them as works of upholstery. The furnitureworld could sort through everything in the world one item at a time and decide whether to class each item as a work of upholstery. Probably, however, the furnitureworld will adopt guidelines which circumscribe the members of the class of works of upholstery. The furnitureworld cannot have evidential reasons for adopting a set of guidelines, but they can have practical reasons. The furnitureworld could say that something is a work of upholstery if it is produced by a recognised upholsterer for presentation to the furnitureworld. Such a guideline has, however, serious drawbacks. If it were adopted, it would be possible for something to be a work of upholstery even though one could not sit on it without risk to life or limb. Practical concerns about comfort and safety will probably lead the furnitureworld to adopt guidelines which confer upholsteryhood only upon items with a specific function. These guidelines will probably specify that works of upholstery are artifacts which provide a comfortable place to sit or recline.

Another example similarly illustrates how practical reasons can and should influence the choice of class-defining guidelines. Suppose that the scienceworld is trying to decide what counts as a work of science, that is, a scientific hypothesis. The scienceworld could adopt guidelines which restrict sciencehood to empirically supported and progressive hypotheses. Alternatively, the scienceworld could accept guidelines which confer sciencehood upon alchemy, astrology and phrenology. That is, guidelines can be accepted which classify as scientific positions which are unprogressive or not empirically supported. One cannot have evidential reasons for rejecting these guidelines. Good practical reasons can, however, be given for rejecting them. Everyone has a strong interest in encouraging the production of empirically supported and progressive hypotheses. This interest would not be served by classifying unsupported hypotheses as works of science. By doing so, a scienceworld would encourage the production of works unable to perform the functions it values. Scientists could produce theories which do not help cure diseases, keep bridges upright or prevent aircraft from crashing. Granting agencies could not refuse to fund a research programme simply on the ground that its hypotheses cannot be empirically supported. These are all undesirable outcomes. On the other hand, progressive, empirically supported hypotheses perform valuable functions. They assist scientists in predicting and controlling nature. Consequently, practical reasons can be given for adopting guidelines that limit the class of scientific hypotheses to ones with certain valuable functions.

Just as practical reasons can be given for restricting membership in the classes of works of upholstery and science, so reasons can be given for classifying as artworks only works with certain valuable functions. Artworld members obviously have an interest in encouraging the production of works which perform valuable functions. When an artworld adopts guidelines which confer arthood only on works with valuable functions, it encourages the production of such works. Art-defining guidelines provide guidance to aspiring artists. My experience, as someone who has taught aesthetics to art students, is that young aspiring artists are in dire need of guidance. Many of them have no clear idea about what they are trying to accomplish. Guidelines indicate to artists that, if they wish to produce works accepted as art, they must produce works with some (set of) functions. Likely, the desire to have works accepted as art will encourage people to produce works which meet the guidelines. A cachet is still associated with having one's works classified as art. If this inducement does not work, more drastic steps can be taken. Once an artworld has adopted guidelines which specify a valuable function, art students can be given failing grades if they submit works which do not perform it. Individuals who propose to create works which do not perform the function can be denied funding by granting agencies.

A failure to restrict arthood to works which perform a valuable function can have serious repercussions. Some artworlds have broken the link between arthood and the performance of valuable functions, and this has damaged the public standing of the arts. Many people regard artists as charlatans or worse. When artists and the arts are held in low regard, unfortunate results ensue. The audience for the arts shrinks, the arts become an attractive target for budget-cutting governments and young people, potentially talented artists, are more likely to seek alternative areas of endeavour. The desire to avoid any of these consequences provides an artworld with further practical reasons for rejecting some guidelines in favour of others. I am not suggesting that an artworld encourage artists to pander to an unsophisticated audience. I am saying that an artworld ought to be able to explain to any public why works of art are important. If the link between being art and having a valuable function is broken, this will be difficult and negative consequences will ensue. Artworlds have all the reasons in the world to choose guidelines responsibly.

An example of a specific ill-advised set of guidelines would be helpful. A possible set of guidelines states that anything is a work of art which is produced by recognised artists for presentation to an artworld. (These guidelines will need to specify who counts as a recognised artist.) If such guidelines were adopted, something could be an artwork even though it is completely without aesthetic value. This is the case because the guidelines make no reference to valuable aesthetic properties. Since an artworld has an interest in avoiding the production of worthless artworks, members of the artworld can be given a practical reason for not adopting these guidelines.

The reflections of this section might seem removed from the reality of what goes on in artworlds. An examination of the history of art reveals, however, that arthood is conferred when artworlds adopt guidelines. It also reveals that when an artworld adopts new guidelines, membership in the class of artworks changes. This has happened several times in the recent history of art. At one time, the academic artworld accepted as artworks only good imitations of nature. The guidelines of this artworld excluded African masks, fauvist paintings and a host of other works from the class of artworks. Within a few years, however, the academic artworld was happy to accept these as works of art. Nothing about the works themselves compelled this artworld to accept African masks as artworks. Remember, arthood is not an intrinsic property of works. People did not discover something about the mask which convinced them that masks are artworks after all. Rather, the artworld decided to accept new guidelines which classified as artworks objects expressive of emotion.

A further revision of the guidelines made it possible for a urinal, some reproductions of Brillo cartons and a variety of other items to count as artworks. Now the academic artworld is convinced that these are paradigms of artworks. (Nowadays, the academic artworld refers to itself as the avant-garde. What was once a radical view of art has become institutionalised.) The important difference between the artworld of the sixteenth century and today's academic artworld, is that they subscribe to different art-defining guidelines. As a result, *Fountain* could not have been an artwork in the sixteenth century. The Renaissance artworld did not have the right guidelines. Today, a widely held set of guidelines specifies that artworks expand and comment on the property of arthood. Such guidelines enfranchise works such as *Fountain*.

An artworld is free to adopt whatever guidelines it pleases. Certainly, some sets of guidelines are widely adopted at a given time, and fashion can be difficult to resist. It is also true that one set of guidelines may supersede another in a manner reminiscent of a revolutionary paradigm-shift in the sciences. That is, one set of guidelines may rapidly succeed another set. Nevertheless, guidelines are not imposed on artworlds, nor do they succeed each other with Hegelian inevitability. Only custom and fashion influence the choice of guidelines, and these do not deprive artworld members of the power to choose guidelines.

Nothing can stop the members of an artworld from changing their minds about guidelines. An artworld may, at one time, have adopted guidelines which confer arthood on a urinal. Having done so, nothing can stop the artworld from changing it back into a mere plumbing fixture. In order to effect this reversal, an artworld need only adopt a fresh set of guidelines and thereby draw anew the boundaries of the class of artworks. Most importantly, an artworld can have reasons for rejecting one set of guidelines and adopting another. I suggest that many commonly accepted guidelines are not serving the interests of artworld members. Convincing practical reasons can be given for accepting guidelines which restrict the class of artworks to works which perform a valuable function. The strongest reasons can be given for conferring arthood only on works with a cognitive function.

Why art ought to have cognitive value

We still need to address the question of which guidelines an artworld ought to adopt. Artworks can potentially perform several functions which serve the interests of artworld members. Artworks can arouse pleasurable emotions, entertain, delight and (I believe) enlighten. Consequently, one can have practical reasons for adopting several sets of art-defining guidelines. Moved by differing practical reasons, artworlds have adopted a variety of guidelines. The question now is whether artworlds can have stronger practical reasons for adopting guidelines which specify some functions rather than others. I believe that the strongest practical reasons can be given for restricting arthood to works with a cognitive function. In fact, the guidelines that I advocate have been widely accepted. Readers should not be surprised if this set of guidelines captures what they mean when they speak of art.

Before defending one set of guidelines, a potential worry should be addressed. It might be thought that my talk of art-defining guidelines could dangerously restrict the scope for artistic creativity. This is not a groundless worry. An artworld could adopt guidelines that state that all artworks must be painted in oils, composed in tonal harmony or written in rhyming couplets. Such guidelines could obviously restrict creativity, but guidelines need not be dangerously restrictive. The guidelines an artworld accepts should be as broad as possible, so that artists are encouraged to experiment. After all, any reasonable artworld has an interest in the production of innovative works of art. Nevertheless, a wide range of artworks perform a limited range of functions, and the guidelines should carefully specify the functions artworks are expected to perform.

When an artworld adopts a set of guidelines, it does not limit membership in the class of artworks to items which perform one or more functions well. Once guidelines have been adopted, a distinction still exists between the class of artworks and the class of good artworks. The good works of art are those which perform the specified functions well while the poor artworks perform them badly. Only items which do not perform the functions at all are excluded from the class of artworks.

One more preliminary point is necessary. When an artworld adopts a set of guidelines, it establishes the artistic functions of artworks. An artistic function is a function that something performs qua artwork. Artworks can have functions besides artistic functions. For example, statuettes can function as paperweights. When used in this manner, statuettes are functioning as heavy objects, not as artworks. From now on, when I speak of the function of art, I will be speaking of its functions qua art.

Let us begin to ask what artistic functions an artwork might have. I take it that any artworld will agree that the function of any artwork is to have an effect on an audience. (Perhaps the audience may be thought to be only the artist.) Artworks act on audiences by causing in them mental states. Consequently, artworks do not have intrinsic value. That is, they are not good in themselves. Rather, they have extrinsic value and are good because they have good effects. In particular, artworks are valuable because they produce valuable mental states. These mental states can be valuable for their own sake, valuable for the results they have, or both.

When a mental state is valuable for its own sake, it is pleasurable. A mental state with extrinsic value gives rise to mental states with intrinsic value. It can do this in one of two ways. The first way is directly to cause other mental states. It can directly cause states with intrinsic value or do so indirectly by causing states which ultimately cause a state with intrinsic value. A state of relaxation may, for example, cause a state of contentment. The second way is indirectly to cause mental states with intrinsic value. States with extrinsic value can do so by giving a person a capacity to act in such a way that he attains intrinsically valuable mental states. Pieces of knowledge are the most obvious examples of things that confer the capacity to achieve intrinsically valuable mental states. A person with knowledge is in a position to predict and control nature with a view to maximising human well-being. Humans also enjoy knowledge for its own sake, so possessing knowledge has both intrinsic and extrinsic value.

From the fact that artworks are valuable as causes of mental states, and the fact that mental states have either intrinsic or extrinsic value, I conclude that art can have at most two basic functions. An artwork can function to cause mental states with intrinsic value or states with extrinsic value which ultimately cause states with intrinsic value. If so, its function is to provide pleasure. Alternatively, it can lead to mental states which have extrinsic value because they provide a capacity to seek new mental states. In this case, the states caused are cognitive states. If art can cause them, it functions to provide knowledge. Both functions could be performed simultaneously, in which case art provides both pleasure and knowledge. Consequently, art can have hedonic value, cognitive value or both.

The claim that art ultimately functions to provide either pleasure or knowledge needs further defence. It might be objected that art often functions to express, arouse or convey emotion. These may seem to be functions over and above those I have identified. I have no desire to deny that artworks can express, arouse or convey emotion. If they can, however, no counter-example to my position has been provided. Suppose that art can, for example, arouse emotion. If so, we need to ask why audiences find valuable the arousal of emotion. The answer must be either that the audience finds the arousal of emotion enjoyable for its own sake, or that the arousal of emotion has extrinsic value. In the first case, art functions to cause pleasure. If the arousal of emotion has extrinsic value, it has so in one of

18

the two ways noted above. The first possibility is that arousal causes intrinsically valuable states, perhaps by a process of catharsis. The arousal of emotion could also have extrinsic value as a source of knowledge about emotion. Consequently, if art functions to arouse emotion, it functions to provide either pleasure or knowledge.

The capacity of art to arouse emotion is a source of some puzzles. It is puzzling that audiences freely view tragedies that apparently arouse unpleasant emotions. A willingness to view horror movies is also in need of explanation. Only two lines of explanation are available. The first explanation is that, contrary to appearances, tragedies and so on arouse pleasurable emotions. Alternatively, one can hold that audiences receive something that compensates them for the unpleasant emotions they receive. This compensation could take one of two forms. An audience could gain intrinsically valuable states in the long run. This will be the case if tragedy purges audiences of unpleasant feelings. The second possibility is that an audience gains insight. The existence of tragedies and horror movies, therefore, does not provide counter-examples to the view that art must have one of two basic functions.

Pleasures can be intellectual as well as sensory. The failure to take note of this might be the basis for scepticism about the claim that art can have only two functions. It is often said that our interest in music, for example, is an interest in musical forms. Suppose for the nonce that music is valuable because its formal properties are fascinating. The claim is that listeners find worthwhile the contemplation of patterns of sound. Someone might hold that this counts against the claim that works of art can have only two basic functions, but it does not. If the formalist is right about music, then music is valuable because it is a source of intellectual pleasure. Chess is similarly a source of intellectual pleasure.

Having shown that art can have two basic functions, I come to the central question of this section. We need to ask which of the functions should be specified in the art-defining guidelines adopted by an artworld. The strongest practical reasons are reasons for adopting guidelines which state that artworks have both a hedonic function and a cognitive one. In short, an artworld ought to adopt a traditional view of art, such as that advocated by Horace:

To teach – to please – comprise the poet's views,
Or else at once to profit and amuse.

Although Horace speaks only of poetry, his point can be generalised. All artists ought to teach and please. Here I will not bother to give reasons for assigning art a hedonic function. The reasons for doing so are sufficiently obvious. That an artworld has practical reasons for assigning art a cognitive function is less obvious, but compelling reasons for doing so can be given.

One reason for assigning art a cognitive function is that it becomes possible to avoid radical relativism about the value of artworks. A single work of art often causes different amounts of pleasure in two individuals. If the sole function of art is a hedonic function, then the work has one value relative to the first individual and another value relative to the second. If an artworld has an interest in avoiding such relativism, it has an interest in assigning artworks a cognitive function. I will return to this point in the first two sections of Chapter 4 (pp. 114–25), where I discuss the evaluation of art.

Another, and compelling, reason can be given for adopting guidelines which class as artworks only items with a cognitive function. An artworld has an interest in encouraging the production of works which are as valuable as possible. The guidelines it adopts should encourage artists to produce works with the maximum amount of aesthetic value. Certainly, it would be good to encourage artists to join vintners and upholsterers in the production of works with hedonic value. If novels, paintings, sonatas and so forth can do more than provide pleasure, however, then artists ought to be held to a higher standard than vintners. Artists ought to be encouraged to provide audiences with more than pleasure. An artworld will be better off if it is presented with works with both hedonic and cognitive value than it is if it receives only works with hedonic value. In my view, guidelines will not encourage artists to produce works with all the aesthetic value they can have unless the guidelines specify that artworks must have cognitive value. Consequently, artworld members have a practical reason for adopting guidelines which specify that art has a cognitive function.

One could object that artworks with cognitive and hedonic value do not, on average, have more aesthetic value than works with hedonic value alone. This is a possibility. Artworks with cognitive value may as a matter of empirical fact have, on average, less hedonic value than works without cognitive value. Perhaps the addition of cognitive value to a work is not able to compensate for an inevitable decline in hedonic value. Certainly, this may sometimes happen. The addition of a clumsy moral to an entertaining story may give it some cognitive value but lessen its hedonic value. Nevertheless, the possession of cognitive value is unlikely to detract, on average, from the total value of artworks. On the contrary, cognitive value will tend to enhance hedonic value. This is the case since knowledge is more than an instrumental good. People take delight in knowledge for its own sake. Consequently, cognitive value will tend to enhance hedonic value.

A common human interest provides an especially strong practical reason for the adoption of guidelines that encourage the production of artworks with cognitive value. I refer to a strong interest, not universal but widespread, in understanding ourselves, our emotions, our relations with each other and our place in nature. We have pragmatic reasons for wanting to understand these matters, but we also have an idle curiosity about them. Unfortunately, the sciences and other forms of inquiry have not been altogether successful in casting light on these subjects. I believe that some stories, paintings, musical compositions and so on have the capacity to provide audiences with extremely valuable insights into these matters. Many of these works are, I think, much more valuable than ones which perform only a hedonic function. The insights provided by these works are all the more valuable, I believe, because they are only obtainable by means of these works. If I am right, an artworld clearly has practical reasons for adopting art-defining guidelines which encourage the production of works with cognitive value.

These latest considerations should lead us to reflect again on the multiplicity of artworlds. Although many artworlds exist, only one ought to exist. Some people do not adopt guidelines of the sort that I recommend, but everyone has a practical reason to do so. As this essay unfolds, and the cognitive value of art becomes apparent, these reasons will become even more obvious. Earlier writers on the epistemology of art, who assumed that all genuine works of art have cognitive value, were not very far wrong. If everyone acted in his best interests, only one artworld would exist and all artworks would have cognitive value. (I take it that the decadent pursuit of sensory pleasure is in no one's best interests.) My hope is that, after reading this essay, more people will be disposed to join the ideal artworld I have in mind.

Some people will believe that much of this chapter has been an unnecessary digression. These are the people who believe that artworks share a functional property. In particular, they believe that all works of art have the capacity to contribute to human knowledge in some characteristic way. On this view, arthood is not a property works possess in relation to an artworld. If this should turn out to be the case, I would be delighted. People who believe that arthood is a functional property of the sort in question will hold that I have arrived at the right conclusion, even if they believe that the route I have adopted is circuitous and unnecessary. I have, as I indicated earlier, felt compelled to adopt this circuitous route. In answering the question, 'What is the definition of art?' only one sort of evidence ought to be consulted. This is evidence about how people use the concept of art. Unfortunately, the concept is variously employed. Practical reasons can be given for adopting one usage in preference to others, but this does not change the fact that different communities mean different things when they speak of art. Again, even if a single artworld ought to exist, many actually do.

I have come to the point where I can no longer assume that artworks can have cognitive value. I need to ask whether, how, and to what extent, works of art can perform a cognitive function. Only when I have demonstrated that art can perform a valuable cognitive function will it be apparent that an artworld has an interest in adopting the guidelines I recommend. In the meantime, I have shown that reasons can be given for restricting membership in the class of artworks. People dissatisfied with the current state of the arts, and inclined to cull the herd of things that are called artworks, can take some comfort from this conclusion.

2

ON REPRESENTATION

What is representation?

When I say that artworks have cognitive value, I mean that, like scientific hypotheses and historical narratives, artworks can provide an understanding of aspects of reality. If so, like science and history, art must represent the aspects of the world into which it provides insight. Reality can be represented in a variety of ways. Consequently, the epistemology of art involves an investigation of the types of representation and an account of the type employed in the arts. This chapter is designed to establish that the arts represent in ways quite different from those employed in the sciences. This is the first step towards showing that the arts and sciences contribute to knowledge in radically different ways.

The chapter is divided into seven sections. This introduction provides general remarks on representation. In 'Types of representation', which comes next, I distinguish two fundamentally different types of representation. One of these, which I will call illustrative representation, is characteristic of the arts. The other sort of representation is employed in the sciences. In 'The representation of types', I then address the question of whether fictions can represent and, if they do, what they represent. The final four sections are devoted to questions that arise with regard to representation in specific arts. The visual arts and literature certainly involve representation. Questions arise, however, about the type of representation they employ. The sections 'Visual art and semantic representation' and 'Representation in literature' are, respectively, devoted to showing that the visual arts and literature employ illustrative representation. The suggestion that music is importantly a representational art is more controversial. Two sections, both dealing with 'Representation in music', are required to show that it is.

Artworks need not be representations in order to be sources of knowledge. A great deal can be learned from an artwork qua example of art. A study of Bach's fugues, for example, will reveal much about counterpoint. A Bach fugue does not represent counterpoint. Rather, it is an example of contrapuntal composition.

From the study of artworks qua exemplars of art one can only learn about art. We can also learn from artworks qua historical or archaeological artifacts. The examination of an archaic bronze statue may reveal, for example, facts about the technology of the period and about how ancient Greeks dressed. I am not concerned with the possibility that works of art can be sources of knowledge qua historical artifact. Rather, I investigate the suggestion that artworks can, like scientific hypotheses, be sources of knowledge qua interpretations of reality. In order to be a source of knowledge in the sense of an interpretation of something other than itself, an artwork must be a representation. Having made this claim, a key challenge to my epistemology of art becomes apparent. I need to demonstrate that all artistic genres, including music, are importantly representational. The principal goal of this chapter is to meet this challenge.

Before we can proceed further, we need a general definition of representation. The concept of representation can be defined in a variety of ways, but as used here it is defined as follows:

> R is a representation of an object O if and only if R is intended by a subject S to stand for O and an audience A (where A is not identical to S) can recognise that R stands for O.

So defined, three necessary conditions are met when something is a representation. For a start, if something is a representation of some object, it must stand for the object. Next, representations must be intended to stand for something. This may be called the *intentionality condition*. The third condition may be called the *recognition condition*. According to this condition, nothing is a representation unless it can be recognised as standing for an object by someone other than the person (or persons) who intends that it represent the object. A few comments on each of these conditions are in order. In particular, an account is needed of what it is for something to stand for something else.

Let us begin by considering the intentionality condition. This condition states that representations are intentionally created. Nothing may accidentally be a representation. Bernini's bust of Louis XIV is a representation of the Sun King in part because Bernini intended that it represent him. Contrast this bust with a piece of marble which is eroded by the blind forces of nature into a form indistinguishable from Bernini's sculpture. The eroded rock is not a representation of Louis, no matter how closely it resembles him. Similarly, some cracks could spontaneously develop in a rock face and apparently spell out a passage from Voltaire's biography of Louis XIV. A passage from Voltaire's history can represent the Sun King. The cracks, however, would not be a representation of anything since they are not really sentences. The cracks resemble sentences but, since they are not intentional products of a language-user, they have no meanings and no truth-values.

The second condition is the recognition condition. It states that, if something is a representation, people other than the thing's creator must be able, in practice, to determine what is represented. This condition is necessary since the use of representations must be rule-governed and the criteria for the following of these rules must be public. Only if public criteria determine what something represents is it possible to determine what is represented. Representations cannot be private. It follows from the recognition condition that someone can intend to represent an object, but fail to do so. For example, I may make a drawing, or write a paragraph, with the intention of representing Jane Austen. If, however, other people cannot recognise that Austen is represented, then she is not.

The recognition condition does not require that, if something is a representation, everyone can determine what is represented. It is sufficient that suitably qualified audiences can recognise what is represented. Qualified audience members may need two sorts of knowledge. Many, perhaps all, representations are created in accordance with rules or conventions. Linguistic representation, for example, is entirely dependent on conventional rules and conventions are employed in drawing. An audience must be familiar with, say, the conventions of English before it can determine what is represented in a passage. Audience members will also require knowledge about the object represented, if they are to recognise that something is a representation. For example, audience members cannot recognise that a painting by Canaletto represents San Marco unless they know something about the appearance of the Venetian cathedral.

The third and most important condition that must be met, if something is to be a representation, is that it stand for something. The concept of aboutness is the key to understanding what it is for something to stand for something else. A representation is always about something. Something is about an object when it has the capacity to bring the object to the mind of a suitably qualified audience. So the painting by Canaletto stands for San Marco because it brings the cathedral to the minds of suitably qualified viewers. Similarly, someone who understands English, and has a rudimentary knowledge of British geography, will have the Thames brought to mind by passages from Jerome K. Jerome's *Three Men in a Boat*. We may say that these passages stand for the river. We can see, then, that if the intentionality and recognition conditions are met, the third condition is also met. That is, if someone creates a work with the intention of representing an object, and suitably qualified people can recognise that the object is represented (it is brought to their minds), then the work stands for the object. The work is a representation of the object.

Types of representation

A passage from *Three Men in a Boat*, another from *The History of Louis XIV*, a bust by Bernini and a painting by Canaletto have served as examples of representations. These examples demonstrate the existence of a wide variety of representations. In fact, representations are even more various than these examples indicate. We also find examples of representation in the arts of photography, dance, drama and (though this is controversial) music. More examples of representation are found in scientific theories and mathematical equations. Even mental states are said to be representations. Despite this apparently endless variety, it is possible to give a taxonomy of representations and the provision of such a taxonomy is an important part of the epistemology of art. We need to know what sort of representation is employed in the arts, and how it differs from the representation employed in other forms of inquiry, such as science and history.

Representations can be divided into two basic classes. The members of the first class may be called *semantic representations*. In the second class, we find *illustrative representations* (or *illustrations*). Semantic representations represent by being true. By way of contrast, truth is not a property of illustrative representations. Illustrations are not the sorts of things which can be true. For example, illustrations are found in music, but truth is not a property of musical compositions. As we will see, a representation can be true only when it represents by employing conventional semantic relations. Note that musical compositions, and other representations, can assist us in learning truths without themselves being true. Illustrations represent because an experience of the illustration has something in common with experience of the object represented. Some literary illustrations have elements, sentences, that may be true or false, but qua illustrations, even works of literature do not represent by being true. A brief discussion and a few examples will clarify what I mean when I talk of these types of representation.

Let us begin by clarifying the concept of semantic representation. A semantic representation is simply a true statement. The most familiar semantic representations are the true declarative sentences of a language. Such statements represent when they stand to specified objects in conventional semantic relations. Some of the component parts of these statements stand to objects in referential relations. A true statement as a whole stands in semantic relations to the conditions which make it true. The statement 'The cat is on the mat' is an example of a semantic representation. (Let us assume that the cat is on the mat.) This sentence represents the cat on the mat. It can do so because speakers of English have assigned to it and its component words specific uses. In English, 'the cat' refers to the cat, 'the mat' refers to the mat and 'is on' denotes the relation in which the cat stands to the mat. The conventions of English dictate that the sentence as a whole is true if and only if the cat is on the mat. Since the cat is on the mat, the sentence is true or, in other words, represents the cat on the mat. We can see, then, that what a statement represents is a function of two factors: what its component words mean and how the world is.

A semantic representation is completely conventional in the sense that without conventions, semantic representation is impossible. If English-speakers had not adopted suitable semantic conventions, 'The cat is on the mat' would represent nothing. If they had adopted other conventions (say, one according to which 'cat' denotes bats), it could represent something other than what it does represent. When speakers of English make a statement they intend that their interlocutors interpret it using the conventions of English. A knowledge of the conventions of English makes it possible for the interlocutors to understand the sentence, that is, to know what it can represent. Notice that nothing about the statement's phonetic or graphic form suits it to the representation of a cat on a mat. In illustrative representation, by way of contrast, the formal properties of representations are significant.

Semantic representation on a large scale is made possible by semantic compositionality. A method of representation is compositional when two conditions are met. The first condition is that all representations generated by the method are constructed using a finite set of basic elements. The second is that the significance of a given representation is a function of the significance of the elements of which it is composed. A natural language such as English possesses semantic compositionality since it contains a finite number of words and the literal meanings of statements of the language are a function of the meanings of the words of which they are composed. The beauty of semantic compositionality is that speakers of a language need not agree to conventions governing the meanings of all sentences. Since the number of statements in a natural language is infinite, this would, in any case, be impossible. Instead, each word is, by a convention, assigned a meaning and, where appropriate, a reference. Given these conventions, and rules for forming statements, an infinite number of semantic representations is possible.

Not all semantic representation depends on semantic compositionality. In some cases, a convention can be established for an entire statement. It could be held, for example, that a stylised picture of a worker digging, familiar to motorists, makes a statement. Displayed by the side of a road, the picture can be a semantic representation of the fact that roadwork is in progress. No conventions govern the use of the parts of the picture. Rather, a convention exists for the picture as a whole. In virtue of this convention, an instance of the sign can be used to state that roadwork is in progress. Usually, however, semantic representation depends on semantic compositionality. By way of contrast, as we will see, compositionality is not a feature of illustrative representation.

Statements in natural languages are not the only examples of semantic representations. As we have just seen, pictures may, in some circumstances, be used to make statements. Statements in the artificial languages of mathematics and logic also count as semantic representations. Many tables and graphs are other examples of semantic representations. A graph can represent, say, the growth of a city's population over time. It can do so only because certain conventions have been adopted. Without these conventions, it would not be possible to use the length of a bar on the graph to represent a city's population during a given year. Rules exist for transforming the information stored in a graph into statements. This indicates that graphs and linguistic statements are fundamentally akin forms of representation. By way of contrast, as we will see, no algorithms exist for transforming illustrations into statements.

Let us turn to a discussion of illustrative representation. As we have seen, an audience for a semantic representation is able to determine what is represented in a given case when its members have knowledge of semantic conventions. In the case of an illustration, an audience determines what is represented by noting a similarity between the experience of the representation and some aspect of the experience of the object represented. Perhaps the simplest form of illustration is exemplification. A paint chip, for example, illustrates a colour of paint by exemplifying (or possessing) it. The paint chip will not appear to be precisely the same colour as the paint in the tin. (Apparent colour depends on context.) Nevertheless, an experience of the paint chip is sufficiently and relevantly similar to the experience of the paint in the can. This similarity makes it possible for viewers to determine the object for which the paint chip stands. Consequently, the chip represents the colour of paint in the can.

More complex examples of illustrations are found in a snapshot of a baby and a watercolour of flowers. A snapshot is a representation of, say, my daughter Julia, since a qualified audience can notice a similarity between experience of the picture and experience of Julia. Likewise, the experience of the shape and colour of part of a painting and the experience of flowers can be similar. Given this similarity, a watercolour can be a representation of, say, a bouquet of yellow roses.

Illustrative representation requires more than just a similarity between two experiences. Convention also plays a role in illustrative representation. The conventions employed in illustration differ, however, from the conventions which govern semantic representation. In the case of semantic representation, conventions by themselves determine what a statement can represent. Semantic conventions arbitrarily associate statements or the components of statements with objects or sets of objects. Given these conventions, a statement can represent objects. Conventions similar to those employed in semantic representation cannot, by themselves, determine what all illustrations represent. This is the case because an infinite number of illustrative representations are possible and illustrations are not compositional. Consequently, we would need an infinite number of conventions to determine what illustrations represent. Needless to say, an infinite number of conventions cannot be established.

It might not be apparent that illustrations are not compositional in the way statements can be. If there were such a thing as illustrative compositionality, it would be like semantic compositionality. Illustrations would be formed using a finite set of illustration-components. What an illustration could represent would be a function of these components. The fact that illustrations are not compositional can be demonstrated by reflection on a familiar mode of illustrative representation, namely, drawing. Drawings are not composed from a finite set of basic components. They are composed of lines and the number of lines is potentially infinite. Consider any two lines whose properties differ in respect of length, thickness, saturation or contour. For any two such lines, a third line will exist whose length is intermediate between the lengths of the other two lines. A similar point could be made about any of the other properties of lines. Since the stock of pictorial components (lines) is infinite, we cannot develop a finite set of conventions which fix their illustrative properties.

Since illustrations are not compositional, the conventions of illustrative representation differ from those of semantic representation. An example of a convention found in illustrative representation will demonstrate this point. In drawing, a familiar convention states that lines represent edges or boundaries. This convention is nothing but a general principle which draughtsmen follow in producing drawings. Unlike the conventions which govern the meanings of sentences it does not, by itself, determine what can be represented by any given illustration generated in accordance with the convention. That is, knowledge of the convention will not, by itself, enable viewers to determine what an illustration represents. In order to see that this is the case one need only reflect that the same conventions are employed in drawings of shoes and ships and wombats. Something more is needed. Experience of the representation must also be similar to experience of the object.

Of course, audiences must be familiar with the conventions of illustrative representation. These conventions influence the experience of illustrations and, in this way, influence what is represented. It is a commonplace that people's experience is influenced by their knowledge. For example, only trained palaeontologists can notice certain features of a fossil. Similarly, only people with knowledge of a set of conventions will be able to experience an illustration in such a way that the experience is similar to the experience of the represented object. Someone may be, for example, ignorant of the conventions employed in drawing. That person will be unable to experience a drawing in such a way that experience of the drawing is similar to experience of the depicted object.

We need to be able to explain how an audience can recognise what any of a potentially infinite number of representations represents. Compositionality is important in semantic representation because it does just this. It explains how people can understand any number of statements of which they have had no previous knowledge. Speakers of a language need only master a finite set of conventions governing the elements of statements. People can also interpret an infinite number of illustrative representations. For example, qualified viewers can be presented with any of an infinite number of drawings, even ones they have never seen before. In such cases, they will be able to determine what is represented by the drawing. This is not because they have mastered a finite number of conventions governing the components of pictures. Rather, they are able to detect a similarity between experience of the drawing and experience of what it represents. Since people can detect an infinite number of resemblances between experiences, they have no difficulty in explaining how speakers can interpret an infinite number of illustrations.

All of my talk of the similarity between experience of an illustration and experience of an object can give rise to two concerns. Someone could object that we are owed an account of the ways in which experience of an illustration must be similar to experience of an object for one to be an illustrative representation of the other. One might also object that my account of illustration cannot be correct given that the experiences of representations and experiences of represented objects are generally quite dissimilar.

Let us consider the second of these objections. It is pointless to deny that experience of an illustration and experience of the object illustrated generally differ markedly. For example, experience of a snapshot of Julia differs dramatically from experience of Julia. The most obvious difference is that one is experienced as flat, while the other is experienced as three-dimensional. Nevertheless, they can still be similar in ways that make illustration possible. For all their differences, experience of the snapshot in my wallet and experience of Julia are similar in some respects. It would be surprising if this were not the case. After all, experience of anything is similar to experience of anything else in some respect. So long as audiences recognise what is represented in an illustration by noting a similarity in experiences, my account of illustrative representation is correct. Fortunately, people have the ability to pick up on certain similarities and ignore certain salient dissimilarities. This ability is probably, in part, our genetic inheritance. In part, it is probably due to training in the conventions of illustrative representation. In viewing photographs, for example, we have been trained to ignore the difference between the experience of something two-dimensional and something three-dimensional.

We come now to the question of the ways in which experiences of illustrations and objects must be similar. No general answer can be given to this question. Even within a mode of representation, such as painting, no general answer is available. Sometimes, a picture represents because viewers can recognise a similarity in colour. At other times, representation depends on the ability of viewers to recognise a similarity between the contour of a line and the contour of an object. The relevant similarity is, in part at least, determined by the convention employed by a mode of illustrative representation. When viewing drawings, for example, convention dictates that viewers should ignore the colour of drawings. Instead, they should focus on similarities of contour. One might ask about the degree to which experience of a representation must resemble experience of the object represented. All that can be said in reply to this question is that the degree must be sufficient for an audience to recognise what is represented.

The situation becomes even more complex when we recognise that illustrative representation can depend on similarities between non-visual experiences. All of the illustrations considered so far (photographs, drawings, representational paintings) involve similarities between visual experiences. Illustrative representation is much more various than these examples indicate. Illustrative representation can also involve similarities between auditory experiences and other similarities. In order to demonstrate this point, I will give a few examples of non-pictorial illustrative representation. In subsequent sections, more detailed and sophisticated examples of illustrative representation in the various arts will be provided.

Illustrative representations can involve similarities between auditory experiences. Simple examples of such illustrations are found when a little boy represents the motion of a bicycle by making a swooshing sound. Similarly, one could tap on a table with a pen to illustrate the way someone walked across the floor. Strangely, musical illustrative representation does not importantly involve similarities between auditory experiences. Sometimes, of course, music does represent in virtue of a similarity between experience of the music and experience of an object. For example, nightingales and cuckoos are represented in works such as Beethoven's *Pastoral Symphony* because certain motifs in the work sound like bird calls. In Handel's aria, 'Haste thee, nymph, and bring with thee' (from *L'Allegro, Il Penseroso ed il Moderato*), we find an illustrative representation of laughter. A similarity exists between the experience of the music and experience of laughter. Arthur Honegger's *Pacific 231* is said to sound like, and thereby to illustrate, a steam locomotive.

An important sort of illustrative representation involves similarities between the experience of representations and the experience of emotional states. This form of representation may be called *affective illustration*. In such illustration, emotions and other affective states are represented. Two forms of affective illustration can be identified: *introspective* and *extrospective*. In introspective affective illustration, an emotion is represented independently of its relations to objects. So, for example, experience of a representation may be like experience of sadness or joy. In such cases, an illustration of sadness or joy is possible. In extrospective affective representation, in contrast, an object is represented as the object of some emotion. Extrospective affective illustration is employed in conjunction with another mode of representation. A painter may, for example, represent an object. In doing so, the painter provides us with a pictorial illustration of the object. If experience of the painting involves something like an affective response to the object, the picture can also be an extrospective affective illustration. That is, such illustration involves the representation of affective responses to objects and situations.

Good examples of extrospective affective illustration are found in the novels of Dickens, especially in his descriptions of the Court of Chancery (in *Bleak House*) and debtor's prison (in *Little Dorrit*). The experience of reading these novels has an affective element. Readers experience a sensation akin to the anger or frustration that one might feel in response to an institution such as Chancery. Dickens's novels are able, as a result, to provide an illustration of an emotional response to such institutions. The section on 'Affective illustration and knowledge' in Chapter 3 (pp. 88–94) explores some of the techniques used by Dickens, and other artists, to give the experience of art an affective element.

Introspective affective illustration is quite common in lyric poetry. Tennyson's *Mariana* owes part of its capacity to represent despair to the fact that the experience of reading or hearing this poem is similar to the experience of despair itself. Likewise, many readers' experience of Matthew Arnold's *Dover Beach* resembles the experience of desolation. This similarity makes possible the illustration of desolation in the poem. Introspective affective illustration is particularly important in music. Debate rages about whether the experience of music evokes emotional responses in listeners. Some listeners report that emotions such as joy, melancholy and grief are aroused by music. Others swear that they experience no such emotional responses when listening to music. I will not take a side in this dispute. It seems incontrovertible, however, that some listeners do experience a similarity between the experience of music and the experience of emotion. This similarity makes possible the affective illustration of emotion in music. A fuller discussion of introspective affective representation in music is found in the final section of this chapter (pp. 60–4).

In the literary arts, we find several distinctive modes of illustrative representation. One might think that representation in literature is primarily semantic representation. After all, its medium, language, is employed in semantic representation. (The section on 'Representation in literature' later in this chapter considers in some detail the suggestion that literature employs semantic representation.) Nevertheless, illustrative representation is the principal form of representation in literature. This suggestion might seem odd given that the experience of words on a page and the experience of the objects represented by the words are so different. For all these differences, experience of a text's formal properties can have similarities to experiences of other objects. These similarities make possible illustrative representation in literature. Literary illustrative representation is also made possible by the fact that audiences can recognise a similarity between experience of a literary passage and experiences of ways in which objects can be described. This form of illustrative representation may be called *descriptive illustration*. A full discussion of the sorts of illustration found in literature is found in 'Representation in literature' (pp. 44–52).

Illustrative representation takes a different form in theatre from the form it takes in non-dramatic literature. The words actors speak can illustrate things people say off-stage. This illustration is not descriptive illustration since audiences can experience a similarity between what actors say and the things people say off-stage. Audiences are not simply noticing a similarity between a set of words and a possible description of some objects. In theatre more than spoken words are used to illustrate. Bodily movements are also employed. Audiences can experience a similarity between these movements and the ways people move in other contexts. In dance and mime, words are no longer employed and representation depends completely on illustration by means of bodily movement. Consider, for example, the case of a mime who brushes his hand across his eyes. In doing so, he does not wipe away a tear. Rather, he represents the action of wiping away a tear. The action is an illustrative representation since it represents in virtue of the ability of audiences to experience a similarity between the mime's action and the actions of people who wipe away tears.

One more piece of taxonomy needs to be introduced. We need to distinguish between *direct* and *indirect* illustrative representation. An illustration is direct when a similarity exists between experience of the representation and experience of the represented object itself. A portrait is a direct representation of the sitter's visage since the experience of the picture is relevantly similar to the experience of the sitter. Portraits, however, are often said to represent more than just a sitter's visage. For example, they are often said to represent characters. When they do, we have an instance of indirect representation. A portrait directly represents a person's visage, and indirectly represents the sitter's character. Indirect illustration is important because it makes possible the illustrative representation of objects (such as states of mind) that cannot be depicted.

Indirect representation is possible because of associations between what is directly represented and what is indirectly represented. These associations can take several forms. The appearance of a particular type of countenance can be associated in the minds of viewers with a type of character. As a result of such an association, a representation of the given sort of countenance can bring to the minds of viewers the character type. (Recall that, in order for something to be a representation, it need only be intended to stand for something else, and be recognisable as doing so.) Similarly, certain sorts of movement and certain states of mind can be associated. Joy, for example, is associated with light, skipping motion while melancholy is associated with slow, plodding movement. Consequently, someone (in dance or theatre) who is directly represented as frisking about is indirectly represented as joyful. As we will see in 'Representation in music: I', later in this chapter, indirect representation plays an important role in musical representation.

We now have a basic taxonomy of types of representation. As has already begun to emerge, I believe that the representation found in the arts is illustrative representation. On the other hand, the type of representation characteristic of the sciences, philosophy and history is semantic representation. This is significant since many attempts to criticise aesthetic cognitivism have been based on the assumption that art is a form of semantic representation. Before I can defend the suggestion that artistic representation is illustration, and indicate how illustrations can contribute to knowledge, an important problem needs to be addressed. As we saw in the introduction to this chapter, every representation is about something. The problem is that some works of art are not obviously about anything.

The representation of types

Some works of art obviously represent. A painting by Canaletto of San Marco and a photograph by Ansel Adams are both artworks and they certainly represent. Other cases are less clear. A novel is typically peopled by fictional characters and it is not obvious that such characters are representational. Similarly, paintings and other works of visual art often have as their subjects imaginary landscapes or mythical objects such as Venus. In short, works of art are often works of fiction. Since, on my view, the cognitive value of artworks depends on their being representations I have a problem if works of fiction cannot be representations. I could hold that works of fiction are not artworks. I would then be committed to holding that novels such as *Pride and Prejudice* and paintings such as *The Birth of Venus* are not works of art. This suggestion is unlikely to meet with much favour. In any case, it would decimate the class of artworks. Instead, I will argue that works of fiction can represent. In particular, they can be used to represent types of objects. This section will focus on literary works of fiction. The approach adopted applies, however, to works of fiction in the visual arts and elsewhere.

The problem about representation in works of fiction is a very real one. On the one hand, the claim that works of fiction do not represent fails to accord with most people's experience of fiction. Readers of novels, for example, commonly recognise features of themselves, or other people, in the characters of fiction. The behaviour of Mr Collins, the sanctimonious, toadying clergyman in *Pride and Prejudice*, may, for example, remind readers of their own behaviour, when they were young graduate students at a philosophy conference. Sometimes, then, fictions, like representations, bring objects to mind. Other characters strike them as artificial and contrived, as having nothing to do with real life. At the same time, saying that works of fiction represent does raise difficult questions. My definition of fiction entails that non-existent objects cannot be represented. Consequently, a passage concerning, say, Mr Collins cannot represent Mr Collins. After all, he never existed. In general, works of fiction cannot represent the objects they purport to be about.

One way to defend the claim that works of fiction represent is to note that sometimes particular real things are referred to in fiction. *Pride and Prejudice* and *Bleak House* both represent London, while *War and Peace* represents Napoleon. Some apparently fictional objects also represent things. For example, the character Harold Skimpole, in *Bleak House*, is a representation of Leigh Hunt. By his own account, Dickens intended to represent Hunt in the character of Harold Skimpole. People acquainted with Hunt apparently had little difficulty in recognising Skimpole as a representation of Hunt. Skimpole brought Hunt to the minds of such readers and all of the necessary conditions of representation are satisfied. Similarly, the Grand Academy of Lagado, described in Part III of *Gulliver's Travels*, is fictional, but nevertheless it is a representation of the Royal Society of Swift's day. In these cases, works of fiction represent individual objects, whether people, cities or institutions.

I cannot take much comfort from the reflections of the preceding paragraph. It establishes that descriptions of non-fictional objects and characters (such as London and Napoleon) in a work of fiction are representations. It also establishes that partially fictional objects and characters (such as Skimpole and the Grand Academy) are representational. Partially fictional objects are fictionalised representations of real individuals. Most of the objects and characters in most works of fiction (including Netherfield and Mr Collins) are, however, purely fictional. A purely fictional object is not based on any real individual. Nothing has been said to support the claim that purely fictional objects and characters are representations.

If purely fictional objects and characters cannot represent, I have a serious problem. Works of art are (I maintain) sources of knowledge only of the objects they represent. Suppose that only the non-fictional and partially fictional objects and characters in works of fiction represent. It would follow that *Pride and Prejudice*, for example, is only a source of knowledge of London and a few other particular things. The long passages concerned with purely fictional characters such as Darcy, Elizabeth and Mr Collins, if they do not represent anything, have no cognitive value. Most works of fiction, since they mainly contain purely fictional objects and characters, would have little cognitive value. Moreover, some works of fiction represent no particular persons or things, either overtly or covertly, in the manner of a *roman à clef*. It would follow that these works have no cognitive value at all. I find these conclusions completely implausible. We can learn a great deal about character by reading about, for example, Mr Collins. If so, then the character of Mr Collins represents something.

The class of objects represented in works of fiction needs to be expanded. We need to identify objects which are represented by purely fictional characters and objects. Perhaps we have been looking in the wrong place for these represented objects. Up to this point, we have assumed that the objects represented in works of fiction are particulars. Something can, however, be a representation without being a representation of a particular object. A representation can represent a type of object or (as nominalists prefer to say) a class of objects. In the *Poetics*, almost the earliest set of reflections on representation in works of fiction, Aristotle made this point with regard to poetry. This point can be generalised. Poetry is not the only sort of fiction that can represent types.

The representation of types is not in the least mysterious. For example, a statue of a soldier atop a memorial of the First World War is not usually a representation of an individual soldier. Rather, it is a representation of a type: say, the soldier who fought and died in the trenches. Similarly, a drawing of a wombat in an encyclopedia article does not only represent an individual marsupial. Rather, it represents the class of wombats. The drawing may be a portrait of an individual animal, but it may not. If it is not, it is, in a sense, a work of fiction. We would then have an example of a work of fiction which represents something in general. In these cases, the draughtsman and the sculptor intend to represent something other than an individual animal or person. They intend to represent members of a class. Audiences are able to recognise that the drawing or sculpture stands for members of a class. Readers of the encyclopedia, for example, do not think the drawing is a drawing of a particular animal. They recognise that it stands for all wombats. Consequently, the necessary conditions of representation are satisfied by the drawing and the sculpture, even if they are fictions.

The representation of types in literary fiction is similarly unproblematic. Consider Aesop's tale of the fox who could not reach the grapes hanging from a tree. This little work of fiction represents without representing a particular object. The fox represents the class of people who belittle goods they cannot attain. Audiences have no difficulty determining that this is what is represented. Note that the fox is representational despite being a purely fictional character. We find a similar sort of representation when we think again of Mr Collins. It is fair to assume that Austen intended to represent people of a certain type. Anthony Trollope quite explicitly stated that he had this intention in writing his novels. Certainly, many readers recognise Mr Collins as standing for a familiar type. (This is why he can remind them of people they have encountered.) Consequently, the recognition and intentionality conditions are met, and the character of Mr Collins is a representation.

Note that when a work of fiction represents individual things, it can simultaneously represent a type. Skimpole, for example, is a representation of Leigh Hunt. At the same time, Dickens represents persons like Skimpole: lazy people who affect an unworldliness, but who live comfortably at the expense of others. Similarly, a real city may be named and represented in a novel. At the same time, descriptions of this city could represent all cities of the same type. This type could be, say, large, dehumanising cities.

The types represented in works of fiction are real, or instantiated, types. I say this because non-existent objects cannot be represented and, I believe, uninstantiated types do not exist. An uninstantiated type is, at best, a mere possibility. I cannot, without recapitulating much of the history of metaphysics, fully defend my position on the ontological status of uninstantiated types. Even apart from metaphysical considerations, however, reasons can be given for saying that only instantiated types can be represented.

We lose sight of an important feature of representation in fiction if we allow that fictional characters can represent more than instantiated types. It is true that, if we allow that uninstantiated types can be represented, the problem of representation by purely fictional objects disappears. Every possible fictional object would represent a possible type. Only impossible fictional objects (such as the round square), which cannot be instantiated, would represent nothing. A character such as Mr Collins and a character from a trashy romance novel are, however, importantly different. Mr Collins is the result of careful observation of human nature and its types. Few people can read about him without being reminded of real people. Contrast him with a character from a bodice-ripper. Such a character might be a dissolute and withdrawn but wise and warm-hearted viscount who reforms his life and gives up his title to marry a shy, poetic factory girl with a degree in archaeology. This character is not based on a study of any real people. The erstwhile viscount could be said to represent a possibility. Unlike Mr Collins, however, the viscount does not bring to readers' minds anyone actual. On my definition of representation, only items which stand for, or bring to mind, real things (and types) count as representations.

The problem faced at the outset of this section was that of explaining how works of fiction can represent. This was a problem since we did not seem to have any objects which purely fictional characters and things could represent. Mr Collins cannot be represented because he does not exist. More generally, we have a problem finding something real to be represented by a purely fictional character. The problem disappears when we reflect that types, or classes, of objects really exist. When a class exists, something can represent it and purely fictional objects frequently do. Having established that fictions can represent, we need to return to the question of how artworks represent. I will begin with a discussion of representation in the visual arts.

Visual art and semantic representation

I have made clear that I believe that the arts employ illustrative representation. In the remainder of this chapter I will provide arguments designed to reinforce this conclusion. The visual arts are clearly often representational, but doubt has been expressed about the claim that they employ illustrative representation. This section will focus on arguments against the claim that the modes of representation employed in pictorial art are primarily forms of semantic representation. Many of the arguments provided in this section are, *mutatis mutandis*, arguments against the view that sculpture, film, dance and drama employ semantic representation.

One compelling reason has already been given for thinking that the visual arts do not employ semantic representation. As has been noted, drawing is a non-compositional mode of representation. Painting is similarly non-compositional. Paintings are not compounded from a finite set of colour patches any more than drawings are compounded from a finite set of lines. In general, pictorial modes of representation do not employ a basic stock of disjoint pictorial components. Since pictures are non-compositional, they are not suited to the making of statements. A similar point could be made about sculpture.

When a mode of representation is non-compositional, it can still be used to make statements. Conventions must exist, however, which govern the use of entire representations, rather than a basic stock of representation-components. In a few cases, these conventions exist. The picture of the digging worker has already been noted. Displayed by the side of the road, this picture states that roadwork is in progress. This picture is, however, anomalous. Conventions do not exist which would enable most pictures to function as statements. Indeed, such conventions could not possibly exist for every picture. If pictorial art is essentially a means of making statements, the number of required conventions is equal to the number of possible pictures. An infinite number of pictures are possible. Consequently, an infinite number of conventions would be required if all pictures make statements. Obviously, this is impossible. It follows that most pictorial art does not employ semantic representation.

One might reasonably think that this conclusion is hasty. Pictures can, in a few cases, be used to make statements even when conventions do not exist. Sometimes, a picture's context enables it to function as a statement. Imagine, for example, that I come across someone obviously in pain. In order to assist the person, I ask him where he is hurt. Rather than replying in words, the injured person displays a picture of a foot. Normally, this picture would not make a statement. Given the context provided by my query, however, the picture can make a statement. In the context, the picture clearly states that his foot hurts. In other words, the picture could be said to make the statement that the person's foot is injured. Assuming the foot is injured, the statement is true. Consequently, the picture may be said to be a semantic representation.

The picture just considered is anomalous. In most cases, what pictures, and particularly works of pictorial art, represent is completely independent of their contexts. I cannot think of any examples, but perhaps some works of pictorial art represent simply because of where they are, or what is happening in their vicinity. Such works would be unusual and they would certainly be semantic representations. A more typical picture would be Poussin's *Dance to the Music of Time*. Whatever it represents it represents, whether it is hanging in the Wallace Collection or in my living room. Whatever it represents, it illustrates. Again, a few pictures may make statements in virtue of context, as a few pictures make statements in virtue of a convention. This is no basis for thinking that many works of pictorial art are semantic representations.

These conclusions about the sort of representation found in pictorial art can be reinforced by a separate line of argument. The making of true statements is a method of conveying and storing information. That is, a true statement is a vehicle of information. If pictures (including works of pictorial art) are vehicles for the transmission of information, we would have evidence that they can be used to make statements. Initially, the claim that pictures are vehicles of information seems plausible. Unfortunately, it does not stand up to critical scrutiny. In fact, pictures are not suited to the storage and transmission of information. As such, they cannot be used to make statements and we have another proof that pictures, including works of pictorial art, are not semantic representations.

Before we can decide whether pictures can contain information, we need to know what information is. According to a standard definition, information is that commodity capable of yielding knowledge. On this definition, just about anything can store information. On this view, true statements are certainly one commodity capable of yielding information, but false statements can be so as well. For example, someone who knows I am lying can extract from my statement the information that I am dishonest, or that I wish to conceal something. Natural phenomena can also embody information. The light from a distant star can be said to contain information about its chemical composition. A fossilised dinosaur bone can be held to contain information about dinosaurs. On the standard definition, the claim that pictures contain information is uncontroversial. Pictures can certainly yield knowledge. An inspection of Karsh's photograph of Sir Winston Churchill yields the knowledge that Churchill had a nose. Similarly, a painting by Canaletto can yield the knowledge that San Marco is domed. It seems that pictures contain information and they may be used to make statements. The only trouble with this conclusion is that it is based on a flawed definition of information.

On my view, the concept of information is closely linked to the concept of propositional knowledge. We would normally say, for example, that someone who knows that Jane Austen was born in 1775 possesses some information. Similarly, the propositional knowledge that the earth revolves around the sun is a piece of information. Knowledge that something is the case seems, then, to be the basic sense of information. Sometimes, however, when we speak of information this is not knowledge. When we speak of information in this sense we are speaking about data stored in propositional form, or stored in a form which can be algorithmically transformed into propositional form. Consider a history book which no living reader has examined. No one has knowledge of the contents of the book, but it contains data stored in a propositional form. Even though no one has propositional knowledge of the contents of the book, it may be said to contain information. Information need not, however, be stored in propositional form. Consider, for example, the case of an automated telescope which makes a record of the sort of radiation emitted by a star. The telescope, say, generates a collection of numbers, arranged in a table or graph. The numbers are data about the wavelengths of light measurable at certain points in the heavens and these data are information. This is the case since astronomers can, by following an algorithm, transform the data into propositional form. Part of this algorithm may state that, if a range of numbers occurs at a point in the recorded data, then a given star emits ultraviolet radiation. Information in this sense is potential propositional knowledge.

Good conceptual reasons can be given for defining the concept of information in terms of propositional knowledge. For a start, not just any knowledge counts as information. We do not say that someone who possesses knowledge of how to do something possesses information. For example, being able to ride a bicycle or play the harpsichord is not a matter of possessing information. People who can play the harpsichord do possess some information. They know, for example, that one plucks the strings by depressing the keys. Their ability to play the harpsichord is, however, not exhausted by such information. More importantly, a world without knowledge is a world without information. Consider a world without minds. In such a world, the sun would still exist and the earth would keep its accustomed path. However, the information that the earth revolves around the sun would not exist. The concept of information is applicable only in relation to knowers. The concept of information, then, is tied to the concept of propositional knowledge.

Now that we have an analysis of the concept of information, we can return to the question of whether pictures can contain information and so be semantic representations. On the face of it, we have no reason for thinking that information cannot be stored in pictorial form. It is plausible that Karsh's photograph contains the information that Churchill had a nose. Reflection on the nature of information will reveal, however, that it cannot be stored in pictorial form. Information can be derived from pictures, but not stored in pictures.

We can begin to see that pictures do not contain information when we recognise that we get information from them in the same way as we get information from natural objects. A fossilised dinosaur bone, for example, contains no information. Had intelligent life never evolved after the extinction of dinosaurs, the fossil would have existed, but not information about it. Nevertheless, information can be derived from fossils. An examination of a fossil may lead palaeontologists to the conclusion that dinosaurs were cold-blooded. The scientists reach this conclusion, not by extracting stored information, but by using observations of the fossil as evidence for hypotheses. Consider now a photograph of the fossil. Palaeontologists would acquire information from it in precisely the way in which they acquire it from the fossil. Stored information is not extracted from the photograph. Rather, the photograph is used to generate information. If this is not obvious, consider the case of a photograph of a fossil which a palaeontologist mistakes for a real fossil. The scientist uses observations of the picture to support the conclusion that some creature was cold-blooded. The conclusion is information, but it is new information rather than information extracted from the photograph.

Another argument reinforces the conclusion that pictures do not contain information. The key premiss in this argument states that information has not been stored unless it can be extracted in a determinate manner. That is, if propositional knowledge is stored in some medium, then it must be possible to extract precisely the same propositional knowledge. Suppose I know that Jane Austen was born in 1775. Afraid that I will forget this information, I make a note of the year of her birth. Subsequently I do forget, and I consult my notes. Unless my note enables me to know that she was born in 1775, it does not contain this information. The note need not be propositional in form. It might simply say, 'Jane Austen, 1775–1817'. It must, however, be possible to generate the proposition with which I began. This will be done by following a rule or algorithm. In this case, the rule followed says that the first date following a name is the date of birth. Similarly, information stored in a graph or table can be algorithmically transformed into propositional form.

These reflections on the storage of information are important because we lack algorithms for transforming pictures into propositions. This point is anticipated in the *Philosophical Investigations* in the discussion of the picture of the boxer. Suppose we are presented with a picture of a boxer in a particular stance. The picture might be thought to state that some boxer stood in a particular way. It could equally easily be thought to state that the represented stance is the one favoured by boxing instructors, or that it is not a stance recommended by pugilists. The point is that we have no general rule for determining what propositions are stored in this (or any other) picture. Since something is a vehicle of information only if propositional knowledge can be determinately extracted from it, pictures are not vehicles of information.

This point is even more obvious when we consider works of pictorial art. One might reasonably think that a painting by Canaletto of San Marco contains the information that the cathedral looks a certain way. Even if this is the case (which I deny), we clearly have no rule for extracting information from other pictures. It is frequently suggested, for example, that Picasso's *Guernica* provides insight into the evil of fascism and the horrors of modern war. Perhaps it does, but not because it contains the information that fascism is evil. Viewers lack a rule that will enable them to derive the proposition that fascism is evil from the painting. At most, *Guernica* may be said to contain the information that some people were dismembered. One cannot, however, validly infer from this information the conclusion that fascism is evil.

In spite of these arguments, pictures might seem to contain information. Someone might hold that a photograph of Churchill contains the information that he had a nose. One could say, in defence of this view, that rules exist for the interpretation of such a picture. Given these rules, one might argue, it is possible to say that the picture states that Churchill had a nose. In responding to this argument, we need to recall the difference between deriving information from an object and extracting stored propositional knowledge. Nothing I have said should be taken to deny that information can be derived from pictures. Neither do I deny that rules may exist for deriving information from pictures. I simply deny that pictures contain information and that viewers can extract it. We know how to examine Churchill in such a way that we can acquire the information that he has a nose. It does not follow from this that Churchill contains information. Similarly, we know how, by following a rule, to examine photographs and acquire information from them. This does not entail that photographs contain information. Rather, as we have seen, information is derived from pictures, while it is extracted from books and data bases.

One might think that the claim that pictures cannot contain information is inconsistent with my admission that pictures can sometimes function as statements. Recall that I earlier allowed that a picture of a digging worker and a picture of a foot can be used to make a statement. In fact, however, no inconsistency exists. Consider first the case where context makes it possible for pictures to function as statements. In the case I described, the picture of the foot does not contain the information that the foot is sore. Shown the picture in context, I would come to the conclusion that a foot is hurt. I would do so, however, in much the same way as I would if a person pointed to her foot while grimacing. In neither case do I extract information from a vehicle of information. This conclusion is reinforced by the following reflection. Imagine that I see the picture of the foot in a context other than the one described, say, in a gallery. In this context, it does not contain the information that someone's foot is sore. Since the picture is the same in both contexts, it does not contain this information in either.

The street sign with the digging worker may be said to contain the information that roadwork is in progress. However, the sign does not contain this information qua picture. Rather, it contains the information qua conventional sign. Given the right convention, a sign marked with a purple circle would serve just as well to state that roadwork is in progress. A simple consideration shows that the street sign is not functioning as a picture. The picture of the digging worker differs somewhat from jurisdiction to jurisdiction. The signs in each jurisdiction, however, contain precisely the same information. If the signs were functioning qua pictures, they would have somewhat different content. This is the case since pictorial modes of representation are syntactically replete. To say that a mode of representation is syntactically replete is to say that every variation in a representation is significant. Drawing, for example, is syntactically replete. Every variation in the contour, thickness, and length of a line affects what is represented. By way of contrast, the mode of representation employed by an electrocardiogram is not replete. Here, the colour and thickness of lines are insignificant. Consequently, if the various pictures on the street signs were functioning qua pictures, they would represent different objects. On the contrary, however, they represent precisely the same state of affairs. Hence, they are functioning qua conventional signs.

Since statements are vehicles of information, and pictures are not, pictures are not statements. Since pictures in general are not statements, works of pictorial art in particular are not statements. A painting by Canaletto of San Marco, for example, represents San Marco, but it does not make any statements about the Venetian cathedral. In other words, the picture is not a semantic representation. If it represents at all, it is an illustrative representation. This point is quite general. Many paintings, drawings and other works of visual art are clearly representational. Since they are not semantic representations, they must be illustrations. Even if works of visual art are illustrations, however, one might think that the other arts do not employ illustrative representation. The coming sections are designed to show that they do.

Representation in literature

Of all the arts, the literary arts seem most likely to yield examples of semantic representation. Their medium is language, and language is the medium of semantic representation *par excellence*. Counting against this consideration is the fact that most of the sentences in most works of literature are false and falsehoods cannot be semantic representations. Although most sentences in works of literature are false, perhaps they nevertheless state truths. According to one proposal, works of literature, including novels, poems and short stories, obliquely make statements. That is, the falsehoods of which they are composed somehow imply true statements. An alternative proposal suggests that literal falsehoods can be true in another, non-literal sense. If so, a collection of false sentences might still amount to a semantic representation. Neither of these proposals is acceptable. Illustration is the primary form of representation in the literary arts.

Let us begin with the proposal that sentences in works of literature are true in a non-literal sense. This suggestion is frequently heard in discussions of metaphor. It is suggested, for example, that 'Juliet is the sun' is literally false but metaphorically true. The sentence is literally false since Juliet is not a huge, super-heated ball of luminous gasses. Still, many people think, the sentence can be used to make a true statement. Something similar might be said about the sentences that compose works of literature. One might think that these sentences can have two truth-values: literal falsehood but non-literal truth. So, for example, sentences in *Pride and Prejudice* literally (and falsely) state that Elizabeth Bennet was slighted by Fitzwilliam Darcy at a ball. These same sentences may non-literally (and truly) state that first impressions are a poor guide to a person's character. On this view, literature can employ semantic representation even if it employs mainly literally false sentences.

If a sentence has two truth-values, it must have two meanings: a literal meaning and a non-literal meaning. This is the case since the truth-value of a sentence is a function of two factors. The truth-value of a sentence depends on how the world is, but also on what the sentence means. In order to see that this is the case, consider again the sentence, 'The cat is on the mat.' (Assume that the cat, and nothing else, is on the mat.) This sentence would be false if the world were, in certain respects, otherwise than how it is. In particular, it would be false if the cat were not on the mat. The sentence would also be false if it meant something other than what it does. If, for example, it meant that the bat is on the mat, it would be false. In general, the truth-value of any sentence depends on what it means. Consequently, a sentence with two truth-values has two meanings.

A sentence can certainly have two meanings and two truth-values. Any ambiguous sentence will serve as an example. Consider the sentence, 'This elevator stops on the third floor only during business hours.' It means that only during business hours does the elevator stop on the third floor. It also means that, during business hours, it stops only on the third floor. In one sense, the sentence can be true, while in the other it is false. Perhaps sentences in works of literature are like ambiguous statements. Perhaps they have literal and non-literal meanings and, consequently, can be literally false but non-literally true. In fact, however, the only meanings sentences in works of literature possess are literal meanings. Consequently, they cannot be non-literally true. We cannot appeal to such truths in the effort to claim that literature employs semantic representation.

We need only reflect on the nature of meanings to see that literal meanings are the only meanings. Any meaning a sentence possesses is the product of semantic conventions. Without fixed, publicly acknowledged rules, meaning cannot exist. As we have seen, semantic rules or conventions typically concern the parts of sentences. This is so since the rules must be finite in number, even though speakers of a language can understand an infinite number of sentences. Let us keep in mind the phenomenon of semantic compositionality, because it is incompatible with the existence of non-literal meanings. The literal meanings of sentences are fixed by ordinary semantic conventions such as the one that tells us that 'cat' means cats. The existence of literal meanings is not in the least puzzling. The existence of non-literal meanings, however, is puzzling. A second set of semantic conventions, which determine non-literal meanings, would have to exist. A finite set of such conventions could not exist.

In order to see that this is the case, consider a work of literature in which 'The cat is on the mat' occurs. Suppose that, in the context of this work, this sentence does not just mean that the cat is on the mat. Its additional meaning is not fixed by the conventions which specify that 'cat' means cat, and so on. An additional set of conventions must determine what 'cat' and the other words in the sentence mean. But now consider that 'The cat is on the mat' can be included in any number of literary works. Presumably, in each of these works it can have a different non-literal meaning. In one work it may contribute to the fact that the work as a whole states that first impressions are a poor guide to character. In another, it makes it possible for the work to state, say, that the best laid plans often go awry. For each of these works, a different set of conventions would be required. The number of literary works in which a sentence can be used is potentially infinite. If sentences in works of literature can have non-literal meanings, a sentence can have a different meaning in each work. An infinite number of conventions are needed to account for the infinite number of non-literal meanings of a sentence such as 'The cat is on the mat.' This is impossible, and I conclude that sentences in literary works have only literal meanings.

One could object that readers of literature grasp what a work means (and states) without employing conventions. Perhaps readers grasp what authors intend and recognise what works state without a knowledge of semantic conventions. Since readers must rely on their knowledge of semantic conventions to discover what authors intend to say, this is an implausible suggestion. Still, a couple of linguistic phenomena suggest that grasping what a sentence states is a matter of grasping the author's intentions. The first of these phenomena is irony, while the other is the existence of malapropisms. We can understand what people are saying when they speak ironically or employ malapropisms. In doing so, it seems, we do not employ semantic conventions. Malapropisms and ironical statements apparently mean something besides what they literally mean. Instead, understanding these statements seems to be a matter of grasping a speaker's or author's intentions. Perhaps something similar happens when we read literature.

Let us consider whether the existence of malapropisms and their meanings supports the view that sentences in works of literature can have additional, non-literal meanings. An example of a malapropism will be useful. A student once said to one of my friends, a punctilious, demanding teacher of English, and a woman of unimpeachable character, 'You are nothing but a pederast!' It took a second, but my friend soon recognised that the student meant that she is a pedant. The student's sentence literally means that my friend is a pederast. It seems to mean, in addition, that my friend is a pedant.

One might think that the existence of malapropisms supports the view that non-literal meanings exist in literature. Grant that malapropisms have additional, non-literal meanings. Even if this is so, grasping the additional meaning is not a matter of divining a speaker's intentions. Rather, when we understand what the producer of a malapropism means, we rely on our knowledge of the same semantic conventions that enable us to understand any sentence. Consider how my friend, the English teacher, probably discerned what the student meant. She noted that it is unlikely that a student would accuse her of pederasty. Next, she recalled that 'pederasty' sounds quite like 'pedantry' and decided that the student had confounded the two words. In order to figure out what the student meant, my friend did not need to posit a new semantic convention, according to which 'pederast' means pedant. She simply proceeded on the assumption that the student meant to say 'pedant' and interpreted his utterance using the convention which states that 'pedant' means pedants. 'Pederast' and 'pedant' have only their usual meanings.

Reflection on malapropisms does not support the view that, in works of literature, sentences have non-literal meanings. If sentences in literature have secondary meanings, it must be possible for readers to grasp these meanings. Moreover, speakers must be able to grasp these meanings using their knowledge of existing semantic conventions, as my friend did when she grasped what the student meant. Unfortunately, this cannot be done. 'Pederasty' resembles 'pedantry' and the student plainly did not mean that my friend is a pederast. This tipped her off to the semantic conventions which reveal the additional meaning of the student's malapropism. Nothing about sentences in works of literature similarly tips off readers to the semantic conventions they need to employ in grasping non-literal meanings. The sentences in works of literature are false, but readers expect them to be false. Readers understand perfectly well the convention of telling stories composed of false sentences. The fact that sentences are obviously false does not set readers off on a quest to find additional meanings. These sentences typically do not resemble other sentences. Taken in their literal senses, they are perfectly appropriate in their contexts. Readers have no grounds for using any semantic conventions but the obvious ones when they grasp the meanings of sentences in literature. Suppose, for example, readers come across the sentence, 'A hungry fox tried to reach clusters of grapes which he saw hanging from a vine trained on a tree, but they were too high.' Readers grasp the meaning of this sentence using conventions that specify that 'fox' means foxes, 'grapes' means grapes, and so on. In general, only ordinary semantic conventions are employed in grasping the meanings of sentences in works of literature.

Irony is another phenomenon which might seem to support the view that sentences in literary works have an additional meaning. Ironical statements do have meanings besides their literal meanings. Imagine that I find in my mailbox another idiotic memo from the Academic Vice-President. (Perhaps my department is directed to teach its course on Hume with an Asia-Pacific focus.) 'That is just wonderful', I exclaim. My statement literally means that the memo is wonderful. Obviously, my words are meant ironically. They also mean, roughly, that the memo is not wonderful. It might be thought that, like ironical statements, sentences in works of literature have two meanings. In fact, however, the existence of ironical meanings provides no grounds for belief in additional meanings in literature.

In order to see this, let us reflect on how ironical statements have additional meanings. For a start, the ironical meaning of a statement is generally the opposite of its literal meaning. My exclamation, for example, means that the Vice-President's memo is wonderful and means that it is not wonderful. Ironical statements are able to have opposite meanings because of a simple semantic convention. It states that when a sentence is spoken in a sarcastic tone of voice, or when speakers say just the opposite of what they could reasonably be expected to say, then a sentence means the opposite of what it literally means. As we have seen, however, no semantic conventions exist to provide literary statements with additional, non-literal meanings. Once again, in the absence of such conventions, statements appearing in works of literature have no non-literal, literary meaning.

Some ironical statements are illustrations, not semantic representations. Imagine that a university is thinking about hiring our former Academic Vice-President. A friend at this university asks what sort of administrator he is. I reply by saying, 'He has neat handwriting.' In such a context, I am not simply stating that he has neat handwriting. I am not even saying that he does not have neat handwriting. He probably does. If one asks whether my utterance is true or false, one has lost sight of its import. The utterance is not really a semantic representation at all. Rather, it illustrates the best that can be said about the incompetent individual in question.

Even if literature does not involve semantic representation, more needs to be said in defence of the claim that it employs illustration. We can make the case for the literary use of illustration by reflecting that ordinary uses of language afford examples of illustrative representation. I will consider three examples of illustration in ordinary linguistic usage.

For a start, I can use quotation to illustrate rather than to state something. Suppose I want to convey to you that the former Academic Vice-President is an ass. I could just state that he is. Alternatively, I could say, 'Well, he has solemnly asserted that "Students are our clients and partners" and then went on to say that this is linked to "Asia-Pacific initiatives".' It is absurd to suppose that students (qua students) can be both the clients and partners of their teachers, and not much less silly to suppose that they are either. Moreover, it is ridiculous to suppose views about the status of students are tied to Asia-Pacific initiatives, whatever they might be. I have not, however, asserted that the Vice-President is an ass for believing such twaddle. My utterance is not a semantic representation of his state of mind. Rather, I represent his idiocy simply by giving illustrations of the sorts of things he says.

Consider now the second sort of illustration found in ordinary usage. Sometimes language is used to represent an object, not by describing it, but by describing something like it. This sort of representation is found in parables and other contexts. Suppose that someone asks me whether the former Academic Vice-President of my university was seriously incompetent and I reply by saying, 'Let me put it this way. That is like asking whether the Pope is a Roman Catholic.' I have illustrated one of the Vice-President's salient characteristics even though I have made no statements about it.

Finally, the way words look and sound can be used, in ordinary conversation, to illustrate objects. Examples of this sort have been mentioned in passing. Recall the child who illustrates the motion of a bicycle by saying, 'It just went *swoosh*.' This sentence is a statement, but it also illustrates the motion of the bicycle. Here the formal properties, in this case how words sound, are used to illustrate.

We find in works of literature illustrative representations similar to all three of the cases just described. I do not mean to suggest that these sorts of representation are exclusive. They can simultaneously be employed by a single work of literature. Neither do I claim that these types of illustrative representation are exhaustive of the sorts of illustration found in literature. (I have already noted that affective illustration is common in literature.) They are, however, three common and important forms of literary illustration. I will call the first sort of illustration *verbal illustration*. In this form of illustration, words are used to directly represent utterances and types of utterances. Such illustrations can also indirectly represent characters, character-types or states of mind. The second form of literary illustration will be called *descriptive illustration*. In descriptive illustration, descriptions are not employed to make statements about an object. Rather, descriptions represent since audiences can recognise a similarity between them and descriptions of the objects represented. I will call the final sort of literary illustration, *formal illustration*. Works which employ this technique represent since experience of the work has something in common with experience of the object represented. A few examples will clarify each of these types of illustration.

For an example of verbal illustration in literature, consider a rudimentary work of literature such as Scott Adams's comic strip, *Dilbert*. Adams frequently uses verbal illustration to represent the idiocy of the pointy-haired boss. In one strip, the pointy-haired boss announces at a meeting, 'Ten of our finest executives got together and created a statement of our core values.' In the next frame, the boss reads from this statement: 'We help the community and the world by producing state-of-the-art business solutions.' The difference between my illustration of the Academic Vice-President and Adams's representation of the boss is that I represented a real university administrator, but the pointy-haired boss does not exist. Adams can only represent a type of manager, which is certainly what he intends to do. Adams does not assert that people like the pointy-haired boss are silly twits for taking such empty verbiage seriously. Instead, he gives an example of the sort of thing such people say and thereby provides an illustrative representation of such people and of their cluelessness.

More sophisticated examples of verbal illustration than can be culled from *Dilbert* can be found in Dickens. In *Bleak House*, for instance, examples of the Reverend Mr Chadband's utterances are used to represent the things said by a character of an unctuously sanctimonious type. The character-type itself is indirectly represented. Mr Chadband, sermonising on the subject of 'Terewth', says (in Chapter 25) 'Say not to me that it is *not* the lamp of lamps. I say to you, it is. I say to you, a million times over, it is. It is. I say to you that I will proclaim it to you, whether you like it or not.' In this passage, Dickens gives a wonderful representation of a character-type I can see every Sunday morning on television. In this example, not only what is said, but how it is said determines what is depicted. Notice that Dickens does not assert that people like Mr Chadband are silly and sanctimonious. Instead, examples of their discourse illustrate them in such a way that this becomes apparent.

Almost all representation in dramatic works (considered as works of literature) involves verbal illustration. When a play is representational, it consists almost entirely of instances of the sorts of things people say and it involves verbal illustration. Verbal illustration is not the only type of representation found in drama. On the contrary, most good plays simultaneously employ other forms of illustration. Moreover, once dramatic works are staged, other forms of illustrative representation are introduced.

A couple of examples will illustrate the use of descriptive illustration. A simple case of such illustration is found in Aesop's tale of the fox and the sour grapes. Any qualified reader immediately recognises that, in two sentences, Aesop represents people who belittle the objects they cannot attain. The fable illustrates certain people only because audiences can notice a similarity between descriptions of them and the description of the fabulous fox. Likewise, Dickens's descriptions of Coketown represent industrial cities of the Midlands of England. He plainly intended to represent such cities and minimally qualified readers immediately recognise a similarity between Dickens's description of Coketown and descriptions of real cities. In virtue of such similarities, a passage can be a descriptive illustration.

Notice the difference between descriptive illustration and semantic representation. A statement does not represent because speakers can notice a similarity between it and something else. It represents because speakers have adopted the convention that the statement is to be asserted only when certain conditions obtain, and the conditions obtain. In short, a statement represents because it is true. By way of contrast, descriptive illustrations can represent even though they are false. Both of the sentences in Aesop's fable of the sour grapes are false, but it still represents a certain kind of person.

Formal illustration involves a resemblance between experience of the formal characteristics of a text (often a poetical text) and experience of the object represented. Good examples of such depiction are found in Shakespeare's Sonnet CXXIX. In this sonnet, Shakespeare represents impetuous lust and the effect of such an emotion on the mind. The lines of the sonnet are experienced as impulsive, rude and fractured:

> The expense of spirit in a waste of shame
> Is lust in action; and till action, lust
> Is perjured, murderous, bloody, full of blame,
> Savage, extreme, rude, cruel, not to trust.

These lines represent lust, in part at least, because, like these lines, it is experienced as an impulsive and rude passion. A few lines later, the repeated hs, especially in line 10, ('Had, having, and in quest to have, ...') make the poem resemble panting. On the face of it, this poem is a series of (very possibly true) statements, but the semantic properties of the poem are incidental to its capacity to represent a particular state of mind. Instead, certain formal properties are used to illustrate a passion.

All of this said, it might still seem that semantic representation is crucial to literature. After all, as the sonnet just considered illustrates, some works of literature, including many lyric poems, are composed of true statements. Another example of such a work is provided by Wordsworth's *Tintern Abbey*. Consider the opening lines of this poem:

> Five years have past; five summers, with the length
> Of five long winters! and I hear
> These waters, rolling from their mountain-springs
> With a soft inland murmur.

This sentence is true (apart, perhaps, from the bit about mountains). Five years had elapsed between the time when Wordsworth last visited the Wye valley and when he wrote this sentence. He did hear the Wye murmur as its waters rolled from their springs. As a true statement, the quoted sentence is a semantic representation. Wordsworth's poem is not, however, merely a semantic representation. The fact that the sentence is true is largely irrelevant. If Wordsworth were mistaken about where he was or when he had last been there, the poem would still be a descriptive representation. Even if Wordsworth had created an imaginary river valley, the poem would be a descriptive illustration of a type of country and, more importantly, a descriptive illustration of a perspective on nature.

Sometimes the use of true sentences plays a role in illustrative representation. For example, *Moby Dick*, even apart from the chapters which are effectively essays on whaling, contains many true sentences about the whaling trade. I assume that it is (or was) true that, 'When in the Southern Fishery, a captured Sperm Whale, after long and weary toil, is brought alongside late at night, it is not, as a general thing at least, customary to proceed at once to the business of cutting him in' (Chapter LXV). Similarly, Arnold Bennett's *Anna of the Five Towns* contains many true sentences about the production of pottery. The use of true sentences in this manner is not important qua semantic representation. Rather, the use of true sentences can contribute to the realism of a work. True sentences give the work, that is, an air of verisimilitude. In this way, realism is a technique employed to assist an audience to recognise a similarity between the events narrated in a work and the objects which the work descriptively illustrates. Realism of this sort is, however, only one of many techniques of illustrative representation.

I conclude from these reflections that literature is a representational art, but not because it somehow makes true statements. Rather, literary works employ various forms of illustrative representation. I would go so far as to suggest that literary works may be distinguished from non-literary works on this basis. Works of literature are the texts which employ illustrative representation. Notice that, on this definition of literature, some works of non-fiction count as works of literature.

Representation in music: I

The claim that the visual arts and literature are representational is not uncontroversial. The claim that musical compositions represent is vastly more controversial. Compositions with a text are generally allowed to represent, but only in virtue of the text. A few pieces of programme music are also admitted to be representational, but only in conjunction with the programme. In general, however, widespread scepticism, even incredulity, greets the suggestion that representation is common and important in music without a text or programme. At the risk of incurring ridicule I will, in this section, challenge this widespread belief about music. I believe that many musical works are works of art and that artworks have cognitive value. Since I believe that artworks have cognitive value only when they represent, I am forced to argue that musical works of art, including works without a text or programme, are representational.

Before beginning my discussion of representation in music, I want to make three preliminary points. For a start, I believe that more musical compositions are representational than is often recognised, but I am not committed to the view that all are. Many compositions are purely decorative. That is, they are enjoyable sonic patterns. It follows from my general position that these compositions are not works of art. Fortunately, few, if any, of the works usually regarded as the masterpieces of musical art are purely decorative. I am also not committed to the view that all of every musical composition is representational. On the contrary, even some of the greatest works of musical art contain decorative elements. The second point is that I will not speak here of music as expressing emotions. This may seem an oversight since talk of expressiveness features centrally in contemporary debates in philosophy of music. I believe, however, that talk of representation in music is a more precise way of capturing what people mean when they say that music is expressive. That is, to say that a composition expresses an emotion is an unsatisfactory way of saying that it represents an emotion. Finally, I could be right in holding that music has cognitive value, even if my account of representation in music is unsatisfactory. Another, more satisfactory, account of representation in music may be available. I mention this because I am painfully aware that the following account of representation in music is, at best, incomplete.

I will not argue at length for the conclusion that music does not employ semantic representation. The suggestion that music has a language is still occasionally heard, but at this stage in the history of philosophy of music little purpose would be served by rehashing the arguments against this suggestion. I will just note that it might be thought that music is compositional in a way that would make semantic representation possible. All musical compositions are, it could be argued, compounds of a finite number of audible pitches. In fact, however, music is not compositional in anything like the way in which a natural language is. For a start, the claim that all compositions are compounded from a finite number of pitches is dubious. This claim overlooks the fact that microtones are employed in some musical styles. The octave is infinitely divisible. Even if only a finite number of pitches can be discerned, it is far from obvious that compositions are compounded from a finite number of discernible elements. Even when two notes have the same pitch, they can have different timbres or different durations. This is significant since the timbres and durations of notes plausibly play a role in musical representation, but timbres and note durations are infinitely various. Even if musical compositions shared a finite number of components, music is not compositional in the manner of natural languages. The problem is that individual notes, or short combinations of notes, do not have a significance in the way in which words do. The significance of a composition is not a function of the significance of its components. Consequently, the claim that music is a form of semantic representation is implausible. If music represents, it illustrates.

Nevertheless, it is not easy to see how many compositions can illustrate. Music can illustrate, as has already been noted, if experience of music resembles auditory experience of the represented objects. If this is the only way in which music can represent, few compositions are representational. Certainly, some compositions sound like (and illustrate) objects as various as birdsong, bagpipes and trains, but most do not. (Recall, for example, the illustration of the cuckoo's call in the second movement of Beethoven's *Pastoral Symphony*, and in innumerable baroque compositions.) This approach will, however, not take us very far. If music can only represent by sounding like things, very little music is representational. Most music simply does not sound at all like anything it might be supposed to represent.

The attempt to demonstrate that music represents by illustration is complicated by the fact that music is often said to represent emotions. The trouble is that emotions and other affects do not have a sound. Consequently, music cannot illustrate emotions by sounding like them. Certainly, emotions can cause or be otherwise associated with certain sounds. A person stricken with grief, for example, may groan or sigh while a happy person is likely to laugh. The sounds associated with emotions are sometimes illustrated in music. I have already referred to Handel's representation of laughter, and sighs were commonly represented in baroque music. Still, even when we count these works, we will have identified comparatively few representational compositions. If music is importantly a representational art, it must somehow represent without sounding like the represented objects.

The argument for the conclusion that music is importantly a representational art is not a simple one. The problem is that no simple and unitary account of musical representation is available. Indeed, some attempts to give an account of musical representation have been hobbled by the assumption that a single explanation is available. In fact, however, music represents in a variety of ways. Several of the forms of representation described earlier in this section are found in music. In particular, affective illustration plays an important role in music and it will be discussed in the next section. The balance of the current section is devoted to an investigation of another way in which music can represent emotion. Music can represent emotion indirectly. Experience of music more often resembles experience of motion than it resembles auditory experience. When experience of music resembles experience of motion, music can directly represent motion. It can simultaneously indirectly represent the emotional states associated with various forms of motion.

Before I can argue that music indirectly represents affects, I need to provide a defence of the claim that music can directly represent motion. It is often remarked that music does not literally move. This is true in the sense that it does not involve the movement of objects through space. Nevertheless, music does, in a sense, move. Movement can be temporal as well as spatial and a series of notes literally does move through time. We certainly experience the series as moving. In fact, tempo is almost the first thing we notice about performances and we describe them as quick or slow, spritely or lethargic. These descriptions are not metaphors. There is a literal sense in which an allegro performance of a piece moves more quickly than one taken allegretto. The notes move through time more quickly in the allegro performance. The experience of the movement of a series of notes through time can, by itself, account for the fact that music can illustrate motion of objects. Since the experience of music resembles the experience of moving objects, a musical passage can potentially illustrate moving objects. Nevertheless, the types of motion represented in music are amazingly various and I need to say something more about how this is possible.

Music is experienced as accelerating and decelerating, sinking and rising, striding and quavering, darting and flowing, surging and ebbing, and as moving in a variety of other ways. Even to experience a composition as graceful is to experience it as moving. In such cases, 'graceful' is a predicate which applies to movement. Again, I do not think that a simple, unified explanation is available of the fact that our experience of music resembles our experience of movement. Part of the explanation of this resemblance is found, however, in an examination of the effect of music on the bodies of listeners. In part, the contours of musical lines suit them for the representation of movement.

Let us begin with the suggestion that the effect of music on bodies contributes to its representational possibilities. Music often inspires movement in our bodies. While listening to music, people sway back and forth, tap their feet and so on. In the privacy of my own home, I have been known to 'air conduct' while listening to recordings, and I am certain that others do so as well. It is particularly important to note the intimate connection between music and dance. An enormous amount of music is closely tied to the dance. The baroque suite, even examples never intended for dancing, is usually a collection of dance movements (allemand, courante, saraband and gigue in Germany, and more heterogeneous collections in England and France). In the classical period, dance movements (including minuets and rondos) continued to appear in chamber works, concerti and symphonies. It is worth remembering that, even as late as Haydn's time, audiences would frequently dance to the minuet of a symphony. The use of dance movements extends into the romantic period, as the polonaises and waltzes of Chopin attest. Much of this dance music inspires movement in the body, or recalls the movement of a dancer, even when listeners do not actually dance.

Even when listeners do not actually move, as when they sit in a concert hall, the effect of music on the body is significant. It does not follow from the fact that listeners do not dance or otherwise move to the music that the music has no effect on their bodies. On the contrary, it is sometimes difficult to sit motionless. Given the effect of music on the body, listeners can easily imagine how they would move, if they were to move in time to the music. No one dances to Beethoven's Seventh Symphony, but Wagner could still call it the apotheosis of dance. It is easy to feel what sort of motion it inspires.

For present purposes, the effect of music on the body is important since it affects listeners' experience of the music. When, for example, a composition inspires a stately motion in listeners, the music is experienced as moving in a stately fashion. Experience of the music then has something in common with experience of objects moving in a stately manner. It is possible, then, that one illustrates the other. If listeners can recognise what a composition stands for by noticing a similarity between experience of the composition and experience of some object, then (assuming a composer intended to represent the object) the object is illustrated. In fact, I suggest, this is precisely what happens in the case of a work such as the 'Dead March' from Handel's *Saul*. This work inspires a feeling of stately motion and, as a result, is able to illustrate stately motion.

Let us turn now to the suggestion that the very form of musical lines suits them to the illustration of movement. Even apart from music's effect on the body, experience of music can resemble experience of motion. This is partly due to the fact that a musical line has a direction. A line has a direction through time, but as it moves through time, its pitch rises and falls. Experience of changes of pitch frequently resembles experience of change of direction of an object. For example, experience of rapid changes of pitch, over large intervals, resembles experience of darting motion. Examples of such experience are frequently provided by the violin concerti of Vivaldi. It is hard not to experience such works in a way that resembles experience of frenzied, darting motion. Experience of regular, stepwise change of pitch, on the other hand, resembles experience of walking motion.

An unchanging pitch is experienced as rest. In Handel's *Joshua*, for example, the violas play a single note for an extended series of bars and thereby represent the sun, held stationary so that the Israelites could get on with the slaughter. An interesting case of musical motion is provided by the fifth movement of Telemann's Paris Quartet No. 6 in E Minor. In this movement, episodes of rapid alternation between two widely separated notes are interspersed with passages where one of the melody instruments plays a long note. A good performance of this movement sounds, for all the world, like periods of darting, panicky motion interrupted by periods of paralysed indecision.

The experience of music is related to the experience of movement in ways besides those I have noted. I would suggest that an increase in the volume of music is frequently experienced as motion towards the listener. Diminution is experienced as motion away from the listener. Dynamics are also important in that larger volumes of sound are experienced as the motion of larger bodies. These claims might prove controversial, but the general point has been established: the experience of music often resembles the experience of motion.

Two phenomena reinforce the tendency of listeners to experience the alterations of a musical line as like the motion of bodies. The first of these is the human capacity to hear something as something else. The human predilection for seeing something as something else is frequently noted. We can scarcely help ourselves, for example, from seeing billowing clouds as images of various objects. We have a tendency to hear in a similar manner. We hear, for example, the clacking of a train as repeated words. Similarly, listeners can hear the changes of a musical line as movement of bodies. As a result, experience of music can increasingly resemble experience of moving objects. The movable objects with which we are most intimately acquainted are human bodies and it will be natural to hear changing musical lines as the movement of bodies.

The second of the phenomena is the capacity to listen with imagination. When we listen to music with imagination, we ask ourselves, 'What is this like?' Listeners can simply delight in the formal patterns of music. No one can force an audience to listen with imagination. Nevertheless, listening with imagination is an option. When this option is exercised, experience of music can increasingly resemble the motion of objects. Music becomes, as a result, increasingly suited to the illustration of motion.

A knowledge of musical conventions can influence the experience of music and affect its capacity for illustrative representation. In order to see that this is the case, reflect on the difference between Matthew Locke's incidental music to *The Tempest* and the storm passage from Beethoven's *Pastoral Symphony*. Neither of these works, by itself, represents a storm. Nevertheless, both represent impetuous, violent motion. They do so in spite of quite dramatic differences. By the standards of the late seventeenth century, Locke's work is characterised by daring irregularity and forcefulness. By the standards of romantic music, however, the work is rather tame. An audience needs to bring a knowledge of the standards, or conventions, of composition to listening. Otherwise, it may be difficult for them to hear the music as representative of what the composer intended.

Even if the present account of the representation of motion is accepted, it might seem to be an unduly limited account of what can be represented in music.

Music is often said to represent directly things besides motion and sounds. Most famously, Vivaldi's *Four Seasons* are supposed to represent everything from sleeping dogs and gentle breezes to fleeing stags and thunderstorms. The sonnet accompanying the Autumn concerto indicates that the violin in the third movement represents a fleeing stag. The sonnet corresponding to the Spring concerto suggests that a particular passage represents a sleeping goatherd and his dog. The claim that Vivaldi represents these objects is, however, questionable. Someone unfamiliar with the companion sonnets would be unable to recognise what the works represent. (I take it that the sonnets are not part of the works.) The Autumn concerto could just as well represent a harried fox as a fleeing stag. Similarly, without a knowledge of the programme, it would be difficult to say why the Spring concerto represents a sleeping goatherd and a dog. It might just as well be a resting shepherd and a somnolent ruminant. Vivaldi may have intended to represent stags and swineherds, but the recognition condition is not satisfied.

Still, I would say, works such as the *Four Seasons* are representational. The only things directly represented in these concerti are, however, types of motion. In the third movement of the Autumn concerto, the solo violin line moves rapidly, with many abrupt and unexpected changes of direction. As such, it is easy to hear as a good representation of rapid, darting, impulsive and haphazard motion. The lines of the goatherd passage, on the other hand, have slow tempi, long note values and gentle curves. As such, experience of the passage resembles experience of the slow, gentle movement of a body in relaxed repose. A programme can lead listeners to imagine that the represented motion belongs to some particular objects, but music by itself cannot represent those objects. Here I have concentrated on Vivaldi's *Four Seasons*, but similar points can be made about other works which supposedly directly represent things besides motion.

Suppose that I have shown that direct representation in music is primarily the representation of motion. I really want to show that music can represent emotions and we are still a way from understanding how this is possible. After all, emotions no more move than they have sounds. Saying that music can represent emotions by representing motion might seem a little like saying that one can represent apples by painting oranges. The puzzle begins to disappear once we recognise that emotions are often indirectly represented in music. The distinction between direct and indirect representation was introduced in 'Types of representation' (pp. 26–34). We saw that a portrait can directly represent a sitter's countenance, and indirectly represent his character. This will be the case when certain physical characteristics are associated with certain character traits. In a similar manner, certain associations make possible the indirect representation of emotion in music.

The indirect representation of emotion in music is possible since certain patterns of movement are associated with certain affects. Carefree insouciance, for example, is associated with light, skipping motion. Sobriety, on the other hand, is associated with steady, regular and even motion. Motion is always the motion of something and when motion is represented something is represented as moving. The moving object is usually imagined to be a person. Consequently, when an object is represented as possessing a certain sort of motion, the object is represented as possessing the affect associated with the motion. Something represented as moving in a light, skipping motion, for example, is represented as carefree, while something represented as moving with a steady, even motion is represented as sober.

Associations between types of motion and types of emotions exist because certain forms of human expressive behaviour are consistently conjoined with certain sorts of motion. Happy people walk with a bounce in their steps. Melancholy people, on the other hand, share a slow, dragging gait. Calm people move evenly. Associations also exist between types of emotions and patterns of vocal expression. The voice of a grief-stricken person, for example, moves in characteristic ways. They sigh, their voices move in a broken fashion and so on. (The characteristic sigh motif, so common in baroque music, does not really sound like a sigh. Rather, it reflects a certain pattern of movement: a rise followed by a slower fall.) The voices of happy people, by way of contrast, move with a lilt.

A couple of examples will illustrate how such associations make possible the indirect representation of emotions in music. As has already been noted, the solo violin line in the final movement of Vivaldi's Autumn concerto represents darting, impulsive and haphazard motion. This is precisely the sort of motion expected from something pursued by baying hounds. More importantly, desperate panic is the effect associated with such motion. To the ears of many listeners, this is precisely what is indirectly represented in this concerto. Vivaldi apparently wanted to represent such panic, specifically the panic of a hunted stag. His concerto certainly brings this emotion to the minds of listeners, via the representation of the motion of someone in the grip of panic. It is, then, a representation of panic. By way of contrast, the third movement (adagio) of Haydn's Symphony No. 44 in E Minor represents calm. Its lines move with a placid grace, like leaves in a gentle breeze. Such motion is associated with the state of mind of someone calm and at peace. By representing such motion, Haydn's composition certainly brings to the minds of listeners, and indirectly represents, such a state of mind.

Music can also indirectly represent emotions by representing the movement of voices. 'Questi i campi di Tracia' from Monteverdi's Orfeo (the first aria after the second death of Eurydice) does not directly represent the sort of grief experienced by the twice-widowed singer. Rather, it only directly represents the motion characteristic of a voice under the influence of grief. Like such a voice, it sinks and moves irregularly. At the same time, however, Monteverdi indirectly represents the sort of distress Orpheus is imagined to feel. Everything said so far is, however, at best part of the story about representation in music. For the remainder of the story, we have to consider the use of affective representation in music.

Representation in music: II

In the section 'Types of representation', I introduced the concept of affective illustration and indicated that this form of representation is common in music. Affective illustration is, unlike the sort of representation of emotions discussed in the previous section, a direct representation of emotions. In affective illustration, music illustrates an emotion since experience of the music itself resembles experience of the emotion. The resemblance between experience of music and experience of emotion enables listeners to recognise what is represented in a given composition.

By claiming that music can employ affective illustration, I am committed to the claim that listeners have an affective response to music. That is, I am committed to the view that music can arouse affective states in listeners. This claim is a matter of considerable controversy. Certainly, musical compositions arouse some affects in listeners. At the very least, great works inspire in us feelings of awe and wonder, and poor works are a cause of boredom and irritation. The real question is whether music can arouse emotions such as sadness, joy, hope, longing and triumph.

At least two problems confront the suggestion that music arouses such emotions. For a start, it has been argued that emotions have an object. For example, when one is sad, one is sad about something and when one is joyful, one is joyful about something. This view is reinforced by the belief that emotions cannot be distinguished solely by means of their phenomenological properties. The distinction between one emotion and another is partly that they have different objects. Part of the difference between fear and sadness, for example, is that the object of one is possible future pain, while that of the other is something distressing in the past. One often hears that, in hearing music, listeners are not, say, sad or joyful about some object. People conclude that music does not arouse emotions. This argument is reinforced by a second set of reflections. Emotions have behavioural correlates. If something is a source of sorrow or fear, for example, one tries to avoid it. In fact, however, people listening to music fail to display much of the characteristic behaviour associated with emotions. For example, they willingly listen to music which is supposed to evoke sorrow or fear.

These are serious and worrisome problems. Nevertheless, I believe that the experience of music can resemble the experience of various emotional states. Most listeners report that they have an affective response to some music. These listeners include some of the greatest performing artists, critics and composers. Frequently they will report that these are experiences of emotions such as sadness and joy. Perhaps listeners actually do experience these emotions. In light of the many competent and apparently sincere reports of affective responses to music, the denial of this claim seems frankly incredible. I am, however, only committed to saying that the experience of music can resemble the experience of such emotions. This could be the case even if music does not arouse fully-fledged emotions. If I am right, the experience of music still has an affective element. Music does arouse something in listeners. If this is not emotions, it is something the experience of which is like the experience of emotion. At the same time, we have to respect the sincerity of those who maintain that they have no affective response to music. Confronted with such reports of listeners who do experience an affective response to music we must allow, as did Hume in another context, that experience may differ and that people might be essentially different in this particular.

Experience of music can be like experience of emotions in (at least) three ways and for three reasons. The first way is related to a point we have already noted. As we have already seen, music frequently inspires the body to movement. Failing that, music can make listeners aware of how they would move to the music. The experience of moving in certain ways, even an awareness of how the body would move in time to a composition, can have a great deal in common with the experience of certain emotions. As well, experience of music can resemble experience of emotions because of the ways listeners react to the formal properties of music. A brief discussion and a few examples will illustrate and clarify each of the ways in which experience of music can resemble experience of emotions. Finally, conventional associations between aspects of music and emotional responses can give the experience of music an affective aspect.

Let us begin by considering how music's effects on the body gives rise to experience like the experience of emotions. Listeners anything like me find a good performance of 'In the Mood' eminently and infectiously danceable. If they get up and dance to such a performance, or even if they do not, they feel their spirits rise. That is, moving to the music, or even the inspiration to move in a certain way, is accompanied by an experience of elation. (I leave it to psychologists to explain precisely why this is the case.) We might want to say that the performance arouses exuberance and gaiety in these listeners. Even if we do not, it is scarcely deniable that the experience of the music, via its effect on the body, has much in common with the experience of such emotions.

Marches are the source of many good examples which illustrate the present point. Marches definitely inspire bodily movement. The 'Dead March' from *Saul*, as we have seen, inspires a slow, stately movement. People moving in this fashion often feel (something like) restrained, dignified mourning. Consequently, via the inspiration of a certain sort of movement, the experience of this march resembles the experience of restrained, dignified mourning. The *Marcia funebre* from Beethoven's *Eroica* Symphony inspires a less restrained sort of movement than does Handel's work. Even someone who merely imagines moving to this march can feel (something like) a bitter sorrow. Again, the experience of the music, given its effect on the body, can be similar to experience of sorrow.

Turn now to the second way in which experience of music can be like experience of emotions. The conventions of tonal harmony and other musical practices lead listeners to form expectations about the forms compositions will assume. When listeners are aware of these conventions, patterns of sound can surprise and soothe, raise and disappoint expectations. Musical forms can satisfy or intrigue. These simple affective responses to music can resemble simple emotions. In combination these simple responses can resemble more complex emotions. A couple of examples will illustrate how experience of a composition's formal properties can resemble experience of emotions.

The first example is from Paul Hindemith's *Trauermusik*, a work composed on the occasion of the death of King George VI. The fourth movement of this piece ends with a quite unexpected cadence. The melody of this movement is taken from the Lutheran hymn, '*Herr Gott, dich loben alle wir*'. (This melody is known in the English-speaking world as the tune of the Old Hundredth.) Most harmonisations of this hymn (including Bach's) end with a perfect cadence: a chord based on the dominant of the scale is resolved to a chord on the tonic. This is the most familiar of all cadences. Hindemith's final cadence, however, involves the movement from an inverted triad on the sixth degree of the scale to a chord on the tonic (A). A remarkable feature of this conclusion is that the B in the melody makes a penultimate chord of E-G#-B and a perfect cadence difficult to avoid. Given all of our previous experience of tonal harmony, this is the expected chord, but it does not materialise. Moreover, listeners hear the final chord on the tonic without ever having heard the leading tone (G#). Careful listeners cannot help but be surprised by the unexpected cadence. They feel that something is missing. This feeling is reinforced by the experience of the absence of the leading tone. A feeling of absence is part of the experience of sorrow. Consequently, the experience of *Trauermusik* is like a feeling of sorrow.

Another example of how experience of musical form can resemble experience of an emotion is provided by Handel's cantata *Apollo e Daphne*. Most of the arias in this cantata are in standard da capo form, but one aria is a notable exception. In the climactic aria ('*Mie piante correte*'), Apollo chases Daphne through the A and B sections of what seems to be another da capo aria. However, just at the moment when listeners expect the return of the A section, Daphne metamorphoses into a laurel bush. The expected A section never reappears. Instead, a brief, confused accompagnato ensues. Denied the expected repeat, listeners feel a kind of surprise and frustration. As a result, experience of the music resembles what someone in Apollo's position might be expected to feel when frustrated by a sudden, unexpected escape. Consequently, Handel's cantata can provide an affective illustration of frustration and disappointment.

The experience of a piece such as the adagio from Haydn's Symphony No. 44 provides another good illustration. The experience of hearing a good performance of this movement is very satisfying. The classical perfection of the piece is experienced as being just right. It seems to unfold just as it should. Nothing in the work is jarring or unexpected. For reasons that, once again, can be left to psychologists, experience of Haydn's work is like experience of a state of serenity. Contrast this with the experience of the roughly contemporary Fantasia in F# Minor (Wq. 67) by C. P. E. Bach. This work is characterised by considerable tonal, melodic and rhythmic instability. Listeners never hear a pattern systematically developing. Plodding, meandering lines are succeeded by rapid, whirling passages. Tempi, rhythms, and thematic material change rapidly and unpredictably. The experience of hearing this music is profoundly unsettling. As such, experience of the music is like the unsettled feeling characteristic of brooding, distracted melancholy.

These examples provide, incidentally, the basis of a response to the claim that music cannot arouse emotions because emotions must have an object. Listeners' responses to music do have an object. These objects are provided by the music itself. Listeners can be pleased about, frustrated by, or have a variety of other reactions to, formal properties of compositions.

Finally, conventional relations between music and emotional responses can affect the way music is experienced and give it an affective element. For example, the incorporation of a chorale into a composition can give it a range of associations. Similarly, trumpets, the key of D major and 2/2 time are associated with the military. Many people cannot listen to many compositions with these characteristics without experiencing something like martial ardour, though I am not committed to the claim that people actually feel martial ardour. Perhaps some of Hume's terminology is useful here. We might say that an experience of martial ardour is an impression, that is, a lively and forceful perception. The experience of music arouses in listeners the idea of such ardour, that is, a less lively perception. In any case, some associations certainly affect listeners' experience while listening to music.

Sometimes one can determine only with difficulty whether listeners have been affected by conventional associations, or by something inherent in the formal properties of a composition. For example, one would be hard-pressed to say why experience of many compositions in minor keys is somehow like experience of dark emotions. Perhaps the similarity is the result of a conventional association between minor tonality and dark emotions. Perhaps, however, something about the formal properties of triads based on a minor third leads audiences to experience them as unsettling.

I conclude from this discussion that, for a variety of reasons, the experience of music can be like experience of emotions. In a sense, music does arouse affective responses in listeners. Most importantly for present purposes, it follows that affective illustration in music is possible. The affective illustration in music is generally introspective. That is, music represents emotions on their own, not in relation to a particular object. Extrospective affective illustration in music must be rare because this form of representation is found in conjunction with other sorts of representation and music has a strictly limited capacity for non-affective illustration.

The general conclusion of this chapter is that the visual arts, literature and music all employ forms of illustrative representation. I have not devoted much attention to arts such as theatre, opera, film and dance. Since these arts are composites of the other arts, I believe that representation in these arts is illustrative representation. I have not argued for the conclusion that representation in the sciences, history and philosophy, is generally semantic representation. However, I take this conclusion to be sufficiently obvious. An investigation of the forms of representation employed in the arts is only the first step in the epistemology of art. The epistemology of art must go on to show how illustrative representations, and specifically those found in the arts, can be a source of knowledge. Let us turn now to an investigation of the ways in which various forms of representation can have cognitive value.

3

ART AS INQUIRY

Ways to knowledge

Advocates and opponents of the view that art has cognitive value tend to agree on one point. They agree that, if art is a source of knowledge, it is so in the same way as science is. Since science has been the paradigm of inquiry for centuries, this agreement is not surprising. Nevertheless, although both art and science can contribute to our knowledge, they do so in radically different ways. Each of these fundamentally distinct forms of inquiry corresponds to a basic sort of representation. Semantic representations (employed in the sciences) help us understand the world in a way very different from the way illustrations (characteristic of the arts) do. Many of the arguments against the claim that art has cognitive value are directed against the view that art aids understanding in the same way as science does. Once this misconception is rejected, many of the arguments against the view that art has cognitive value are seen to be baseless.

This chapter is divided into six sections. This introductory section indicates that a representation can be a source of knowledge by performing either of two functions. This section goes on to indicate that the types of representation identified in the previous chapter (illustrative and semantic) perform these functions in quite different ways. In 'Rejected alternatives', prior to investigating the ways in which the illustrative representations found in the arts contribute to knowledge, I consider and reject the principal alternatives to my epistemology of art. The next two sections present the positive case for my position. Affective illustrations provide knowledge in ways quite different from the ways other illustrations do. The contributions of affective illustration to knowledge are investigated in 'Affective illustration and knowledge'. Other forms of illustration are addressed in the section on 'Interpretive illustration'. Works of art can provide knowledge, but not just any knowledge. The scope and limits of the knowledge which can be derived from the arts are examined in 'What can be learned from art?'. Even after the case for my position has been presented, some concerns may remain. The most pressing worries about my epistemology of art are considered in 'Replies to objections'. The final section demonstrates that my epistemology of art carries with it some important bonuses. Once it is adopted, several otherwise inexplicable features of the experience of art can be easily explained.

The sciences and the arts are not completely dissimilar forms of inquiry. Art and empirical science have a common foundation: both begin with careful observation. Before artists or scientists can represent anything, they must observe aspects of the world. If their representations have cognitive value, they are grounded in careful observation. Just as scientists conduct experiments and gather observations prior to constructing theories, so (good) artists make a careful study of the objects they intend to represent. Scientific observations are typically made quite deliberately in laboratories and other formal contexts, while artists frequently make their observations in the course of ordinary life. However, even this difference does not always hold. Renaissance painters and sculptors, for example, made careful, systematic studies of human anatomy before representing the body. Similarly, novelists frequently undertake considerable historical research before writing. The arts and sciences resemble each other in another respect. They both represent objects in such a way that, ideally, insight is provided into the objects represented. Despite these similarities, the ways in which the arts and sciences represent and contribute to knowledge are quite different.

The representations produced by the arts and sciences can each contribute to knowledge of some matter in two ways. That is, the representations these modes of inquiry produce have two cognitive functions. They may provide testimony about objects and they may interpret objects. Testimony is simply a record of observations. Interpretation is the attempt to understand this record, either by means of theories or in some other way. (Of course, as is well-known from philosophy of science, theory and observation cannot always be kept completely distinct. For present purposes, this point can be ignored.) Since arts and sciences employ different sorts of representation, they perform each of the cognitive functions in different ways.

Let us begin by considering the testimonial function and the ways in which art and science perform it. We may identify *semantic testimony* and *illustrative testimony*. To provide testimony is simply to provide information. The sciences frequently provide information by means of statements. (A true statement, as we saw in the section on 'Visual art and semantic representation' (pp. 38–44), is a vehicle of information.) So, for example, scientists provide testimony when they report the data they have collected. (These reports used to be called observation statements.) The testimony in works of art, on the other hand, is provided by means of illustrations from which information can be derived. So, for example, a painting by Canaletto is testimony about the appearance of San Marco. It is an illustration from which viewers can derive the information that the cathedral is domed. Semantic testimony is not exclusive to the sciences, nor is illustrative testimony confined to the arts. Sometimes, works of art contain semantic testimony. We have noted, for example, the case of *Tintern Abbey* where Wordsworth testifies that he visited the Wye valley five years prior to writing the poem. On the other hand, instances of illustrative testimony, including photographs, drawings and sound recordings, are common in the sciences.

Testimony, whether semantic or illustrative, can be a source of knowledge. One can learn from the testimony in Darwin's journals, Wordsworth's poems or Canaletto's paintings. A bare statement or an unsupported illustration is not, however, by itself, a source of knowledge. Statements can be false, illustrations deceptive and justification is a necessary condition of propositional knowledge. Testimony can, however, be justified by the reliability of the person who produces it or by the reliability of the process in accordance with which the documentation of testimony is produced. After examining Karsh's photograph of Churchill, for example, I am justified in believing that he had a nose. This justification is provided by my knowledge of the reliability of the photographic process and by information about Karsh's reputation as a reputable photographer. As a result, after examining the photograph, I may be said to know that Churchill had a nose.

Although a great deal of what goes on in the arts and sciences is testimony, they owe only a small part of their cognitive value to the fact that they provide testimony. An important part of both scientific and artistic inquiry is the interpretation of the objects which are documented in testimony. The sciences and the arts interpret objects in quite different ways. The sciences interpret objects by means of theories or models. The arts, on the other hand, do not. This is one of the fundamental differences between forms of inquiry which employ illustrative representation and those which employ semantic representation. Instead, the arts provide what I will call a *perspective* on objects. A perspective is a way of conceiving of an object that can enhance the understanding of the object. A simple example will clarify what I mean by a perspective. Suppose someone is puzzled by a *trompe-l'oeil* and I point and say, 'If you see those things as the eyes, and those as the ears, you will see that it is a face.' In so saying and gesturing, I have provided the person with an interpretation of the painting. I have suggested that it be thought of as a face. I have, in other words, provided a perspective on the *trompe-l'oeil*.

Both scientific theories and the perspectives provided by the arts are in need of justification. They ought not to be accepted on the word of a scientist or an artist. In other words, theories and perspectives need to be demonstrated and a great deal of what goes on in the arts and sciences is demonstration. Semantic representations and illustrative representations can both be used in demonstrations, but demonstration by means of semantic representations is quite different from demonstration by means of illustrative representations. Consequently, the way in which scientists demonstrate a theory is different from the way in which artists can demonstrate a perspective. An analysis of demonstration, and the form it takes in the arts, is an important part of the epistemology of art.

We need to begin by distinguishing between two quite different sorts of demonstration. I will call the first type *illustrative demonstration* or *showing*. The second sort may be called *rational demonstration*. Rational demonstration is demonstration by means of an argument. Illustrative demonstration, on the other hand, is non-rational. That is, such a demonstration does not provide one with an argument for some proposition. Rather, an illustrative demonstration places one in a position where one can recognise something. A few examples will indicate the difference between the two forms of demonstration.

Suppose that Colin wants me to demonstrate to him the colour of the pencil on my desk. I provide him with an illustrative demonstration if I lead him into my office and point to the pencil. I have not given Colin an argument. Instead, I have put him in a position to recognise that the pencil is orange. In short, I have shown him the colour of the pencil. Jan, on the other hand, wants to know whether all ravens are black. Providing her with an illustrative demonstration is not an option. I cannot show her all ravens, and that they are all black. Instead, I will give her a series of reports about ravens. I must also provide some reason to suppose that the reports are reliable and that a representative sample of ravens has been surveyed. These reports must support the hypothesis that all ravens are black. In short, in order to demonstrate that all ravens are black, I will provide Jan with an inductive argument. This argument is a rational demonstration.

The distinction between these forms of demonstration is significant since they correspond to the types of representation identified in the section 'What is representation?' in Chapter 2 (pp. 23–5). Semantic representations provide rational demonstrations while illustrations are used to show. An argument is a series of statements designed to support a conclusion. Artworks, as we have seen, employ illustrative representation. They do not make statements. Consequently, an artwork cannot provide an argument. Other forms of inquiry, including the sciences, which employ semantic representation, provide rational demonstrations. Scientific inquiry is essentially a process of marshalling evidence, expressible in statements, for certain conclusions. The only way to demonstrate, for example, the theory of evolution, is by means of an argument. The premises in this argument are statements about the fossil record, the beaks of finches in the Galapagos Islands, or a related matter. The argument is designed to prove that the theory is true.

Artworks cannot provide rational demonstrations of perspectives, but they can provide illustrative demonstrations of the rightness of a perspective. That is, artworks can put audiences in a position to recognise the rightness of a perspective. In *Pride and Prejudice*, Jane Austen does not argue for a perspective on first impressions (that they are a poor guide to character) or on inflexible pride (that it is a failing). Neither does Picasso's *Guernica* constitute an argument for a perspective on the aerial bombardment of civilian populations (that it is indefensibly horrible). Nevertheless, both of these artworks present demonstrations just as surely as the theory of evolution does. They show or provide illustrative demonstrations. They represent objects (human relations or modern war) in such a way that audiences are put in a position where they recognise the rightness of a perspective on some matter.

Notice that I spoke in the previous paragraph of the rightness of perspectives. A perspective is not the sort of thing that can be true or false. Truth and falsity are properties of statements or beliefs only and a perspective is neither. It is a way of looking at objects. Still, an epistemic virtue (rightness) distinguishes some perspectives and not others. A few words will clarify what I mean by 'rightness'. A set of instructions for finding something is never true, but it might be right. Suppose, for example, you want to know the colour of my new computer and I give you a set of instructions for finding it. I may say, 'Go down the corridor, take the first left and go through the second door on the right. Then look on the desk.' This set of instructions is not true. (Imperative sentences cannot be true.) If the set of instructions assists in acquisition of knowledge, however, it is right. More generally, a perspective is right when it aids people who adopt it in the acquisition of knowledge. So, for example, my perspective on the former Academic Vice-President of my university is neither true nor false. If my perspective on him is right, however, it will assist me in acquiring the knowledge that he is incompetent, malicious, pompous and so on. When perspectives are not right, they are not false. Rather, they are wrong or mistaken. A mistaken perspective tends to hinder the acquisition of knowledge.

The claim that perspectives are neither true nor false may seem to be contentious since I apparently believe that works of art can provide propositional knowledge. I have suggested, for example, that readers can learn from *Pride and Prejudice* that 'First impressions are a poor guide to character' is true. The fact that perspectives can provide propositional knowledge is no reason to believe that they are either true or false. A glance at my computer provides the propositional knowledge that my computer is blue. The glance is neither true nor false. It is simply a means of apprehending the truth. Similarly, perspectives are means of apprehending the truth of certain propositions. (As I will argue, perspectives can also be the source of non-propositional knowledge.)

The principal task of this chapter is to investigate the ways in which artworks such as *Pride and Prejudice* and *Guernica* can provide an illustrative demonstration of the rightness of a perspective. I will begin this task in the next section but one. Before I defend my position on illustrative demonstration in the arts, however, I need to consider and refute some alternatives to the epistemology of art advocated in this essay.

Rejected alternatives

Two important and influential accounts of how artworks perform their cognitive function need to be considered. The first is the propositional theory of art, while the second may be called the exemplification hypothesis. The propositional theory is probably the most venerable epistemology of art. Nevertheless, in light of what has already been said, it can be quickly dispatched. While the position is clearly a non-starter, it needs to be explicitly rejected. This is the case since opponents of aesthetic cognitivism often attack the propositional theory and think that they have shown that art has little or no cognitive value. The exemplification hypothesis is less obviously mistaken and deserves a more careful assessment.

On the propositional theory of art, works of art have cognitive value qua informative statements. Artworks rarely make statements explicitly and advocates of the propositional theory recognise this. They suggest that artworks somehow implicitly make statements or imply them. The propositional theory is most often applied to works of literary arts, but it need not be so limited. Some advocates of the theory have applied it to works of visual art and even to music. Some defenders of the position even maintain that artworks make statements that cannot otherwise be made.

The propositional theory has some unfortunate consequences. Notice that if the theory were correct, artworks would primarily have cognitive value qua testimony (in the sense identified in the previous section). This is, by itself, the basis of an objection to the propositional theory. People who believe that art has cognitive value typically hold that it is the source of important and controversial insights into complex matters. Bare assertions about such matters have little cognitive value. Opponents of the propositional theory can object that the mere word of an artist, no matter how reliable, is not sufficient justification for statements about such matters. Consequently, if artworks just made statements about controversial and important matters, they would not be an important source of knowledge. A demonstration is required of any statement about such complex and controversial matters. If artworks make statements, possibly they can be used to provide rational demonstrations. No one has argued that artworks provide arguments, and the suggestion is implausible. The suggestion that works of literature provide arguments may, in a few instances, be remotely plausible. The suggestion that paintings, sculptures, works of architecture and musical compositions provide arguments is, however, frankly incredible.

Even without this problem, the propositional theory need not be considered in any detail. The position has already been undermined by the reflections of Chapter 2. Artworks are essentially illustrations, not semantic representations. Only occasionally, in instances such as those noted in 'Visual art and semantic representation' (pp. 38–44), do pictures and other illustrative representations make statements. The propositional theory does not even work in the case of literature. Sentences in works of literature are not statements. Most of them just are not products of the right sort of speech act. That is, authors typically are not making assertions. More importantly, as argued in 'Representation in literature' (pp. 44–52), the only meanings possessed by sentences in literary works are literal meanings. Even if sentences in literary works are statements, they are literally false. This is a problem for the propositional theory since collections of falsehoods do not have much cognitive value qua statements.

The exemplification hypothesis is a more serious alternative to the position defended in this essay. It is certainly the most influential epistemology of art of recent times. According to this hypothesis, the concept of exemplification is the key to understanding how artworks have cognitive value. Exemplification is a form of reference to, or as I would prefer to say, a type of representation of, properties. The claim is that artworks can exemplify properties and this capacity accounts for art's cognitive value. Up to a point this is right, but the cognitive value of artworks cannot be completely, or even largely, explained by the fact that they can exemplify properties. If artworks owed all of their cognitive value to the fact that they can exemplify properties, art would not be an important source of knowledge.

In assessing the exemplification hypothesis, we should begin by giving an analysis of the concept of exemplification. Exemplification is often defined as reference by means of a sample (or an exemplar). As we saw in 'Types of representation' (pp. 26–34), a paint chip is an instance of an exemplar. In the right circumstances, however, just about anything can serve as an exemplar. Suppose, for example, someone asks me what a banana is and I proffer one. In this instance, the banana is an exemplar. This seems clear enough, but a couple of questions ought to be clarified. For a start, we need to ask what is exemplified by an exemplar. As well, a question arises about the relationship between an exemplar and what is exemplified. That is, we need to identify the sense in which exemplars refer.

Let us begin with a few words about the first of these questions. Advocates of the exemplification hypothesis sometimes speak of the exemplification of (or reference to) labels. On this view, the paint chip exemplifies (and denotes) the label 'is teal' while the banana exemplifies (and denotes) 'is a banana' (or 'is bananoid'). This account of what exemplars denote seems odd. One would have thought that, if an exemplar denotes anything, it denotes the extension of a label. Advocates of the exemplification hypothesis were moved, however, by some technical considerations (which need not concern us) to prefer the view that exemplars refer to labels. In the end, talk about exemplars referring to labels does not differ from talk about them referring to extensions. This is the case since when an object refers to a label it also and indirectly refers to objects in the label's extension. In fact, advocates of the exemplification hypothesis often say that an exemplar denotes objects in the extension of a label. Most commonly, the label denotes properties. For the purposes of this essay, we can afford to speak with the vulgar and say that properties are exemplified. Nothing will turn on this terminological convenience, especially since advocates of the exemplification hypothesis frequently talk of the exemplification of properties.

Let us turn now to the relation between exemplars and the properties they exemplify. Usually, as noted above, the relationship between exemplar and exemplified is described as reference. I would prefer to reserve the term 'reference' for the relation between names ('Plato'), natural kind terms ('gold') and descriptions ('the teacher of Aristotle') and the objects they denote. No violence is done to the exemplification hypothesis if we say that exemplification is a matter of standing for or representing properties. The colour of a paint chip stands for all other instances of the same colour. More generally, an exemplar stands for some property by possessing the property.

Now we need to ask what properties exemplars can exemplify. At first this question seems to be easy to answer. One might think that the answer is that an item can exemplify whatever properties it possesses. So, for example, some paint chip is teal and, consequently, can exemplify the property of being teal. The banana possesses and can exemplify the property of bananahood. Unfortunately, this glib answer is inadequate. For a start, mere possession of a property is not sufficient to make something an exemplar which stands for the property. In other words, an object does not exemplify all of the properties it possesses. The banana mentioned above, for example, exemplifies the property of bananahood, but not the property of being grown in Guatemala (even if it was grown there). So the question becomes that of which of its properties something exemplifies. The answer to this question is that interpretation of an artwork (or another exemplar) reveals what it exemplifies. In particular, attention to context will reveal a good deal about what something exemplifies. Imagine, for example, that someone asks me about the exports of Guatemala and I produce a banana. In this context, the banana would exemplify the property of being a product of Guatemala, not the property of bananahood.

A pressing question about what properties an object can exemplify remains to be considered. Art is generally supposed to provide insight into things such as emotions, social circumstances, human relations and so on. If the exemplification hypothesis is correct, art does so by exemplifying, for example, emotional states. The trouble is that artworks possess a fairly limited range of properties. Musical compositions, for example, possess properties such as pitches, rhythms, durations and so on. They do not possess emotional states. If artworks provide knowledge about properties by possessing them, apparently they cannot provide knowledge of emotions. Advocates of the exemplification hypothesis try to get around this difficulty by holding that an object can exemplify properties besides those it literally possesses. The suggestion is that an object can also exemplify properties that it metaphorically possesses. The claim that an object can metaphorically possess properties is questionable. Unless, however, it can be established, the exemplification hypothesis is in great difficulty.

Ordinary, non-metaphorical, exemplification is unproblematic. All of the instances of exemplification considered so far are non-metaphorical. The paint chip literally can exemplify the property of being teal since it literally is teal. The banana literally exemplifies bananahood since it really is bananoid. Similarly, literal exemplification in the arts is not in the least mysterious. Malevich's painting, *Red Square,* consists of a red square on a white ground. It literally exemplifies the property of redness. Paintings by Morris Louis and other members of the Washington School are flat and literally exemplify flatness. Mozart's *Musical Joke* (K 522) literally exemplifies dissonance and crude chord progressions. Other alleged cases of exemplification are more problematic. Some properties seem unsuited for literal exemplification by artworks. A painting is unfeeling, so it cannot literally exemplify the property of having some feeling. No emotion can be found in a sonata, so it cannot literally exemplify the property of, say, yearning. Nevertheless, advocates of the exemplification hypothesis want to hold that works of art can exemplify feelings, emotions, attitudes and other properties they cannot literally possess. The concept of metaphorical exemplification is introduced in an effort to explain how this is possible.

The concept of metaphorical exemplification is in need of careful examination. Advocates of the exemplification hypothesis need to maintain that an object can metaphorically possess certain properties. They can then argue that the object can metaphorically exemplify the properties that it metaphorically possesses. This position is motivated almost entirely by the use of examples. A mathematical proof might literally be a *reductio* and, consequently, it can literally exemplify the property of being a *reductio*. The same proof might be described as elegant. Adherents of the exemplification hypothesis suggest that the proof is not literally elegant. It metaphorically possesses the property of elegance. If so, it can metaphorically exemplify elegance. Likewise, a musical work could literally possess, and literally exemplify, sonata form. At the same time it could be metaphorically graceful and able to metaphorically exemplify grace. A final sort of example is used to motivate the idea of metaphorical exemplification. A painting might literally exemplify the property of redness. The same painting might turn out to be a sound investment. Such a painting is not literally a gold-mine, but perhaps it is a metaphorical gold-mine. As such it is supposed to be able to exemplify metaphorically the property of being a gold-mine. Similarly, the painting is not literally frenzied, but it might be metaphorically frenzied and able to exemplify frenzy metaphorically.

Those who believe in metaphorical exemplification are deeply confused. This confusion has at least two sources. For a start, the concept of metaphorical exemplification has an application only if metaphorical properties exist, but they do not. The only properties are literal properties. Even if, however, there were instances of metaphorical exemplification, the advocates of the exemplification hypothesis would still be deeply confused. They identify as cases of metaphorical exemplification, cases that, even by their own account, ought not to count as such. Worse, some of these instances are treated as paradigm cases of metaphorical exemplification and are used to motivate belief in such exemplification. Since the cases that are held to be paradigms of metaphorical exemplification turn out to be nothing of the sort, we are left without grounds for belief in such exemplification.

Let us begin by considering the first sort of reason for thinking that the concept of metaphorical exemplification is confused. Metaphorical exemplification does not exist since metaphorical properties do not. Advocates of the exemplification hypothesis apparently believe that a metaphor creates a property in an object, but this is not the case. When one uses a metaphor to describe an object, one does not create new, metaphorical properties in the object. Rather, one describes in a new way literal properties the object always had. Consider the case of the painting which is a sound investment. Imagine that a metaphor is used to describe this painting: someone calls it a gold-mine. When a valuable painting is described as a gold-mine, a metaphor is used to describe a property the painting literally possesses, namely the property of being a sound investment. When the painting is so described, it does not acquire any new properties. In particular, it does not acquire the property of being a pit from which gold ore is extracted. Considered from a financial perspective, the painting can only exemplify the property of being a sound investment. This property might be described as the property of being a gold-mine, but it is the same property.

74

In the previous paragraph I said that the use of a metaphor does not endow an object with new properties. Strictly speaking, this is not true. When a metaphor is used to describe an object, it acquires the property of being described by a metaphor. Perhaps the object also acquires the property of being better understood by an audience. (In this respect, metaphorical descriptions do not differ from literal ones. All descriptions endow objects with the property of being described.) The point, however, is that metaphorical descriptions do not endow objects with new intrinsic properties. The objects only acquire relational properties such as the property of being described by someone. Such relational properties are not the sorts of properties advocates of the exemplification hypothesis take artworks to exemplify.

Advocates of the exemplification hypothesis pass from cases such as that of the painting that is a gold-mine to cases where works of art are described as graceful or elegant. When a work exemplifies grace or elegance, they believe, we have another case of metaphorical exemplification. Here is an instance where defenders of the hypothesis are confused about what counts, even on their own terms, as metaphorical exemplification. Even if the concept of metaphorical properties has an application, it would not apply to the grace or elegance of an artwork. Consider an elegant sonata. The description of this work as elegant is not a metaphorical description. In this respect the case of the elegant sonata differs from that of the painting described as a gold-mine. The painting is not literally a gold-mine but the composition literally is elegant. It literally is, that is, tasteful and refined. In short, the sonata's property of elegance is a literal property. If the sonata exemplifies elegance, it does so because it possesses the literal property of elegance. Since we have no metaphorical property, and even no metaphor, we can have no metaphorical exemplification of elegance.

These reflections on exemplification are important because advocates of the exemplification hypothesis motivate the idea of metaphorical exemplification by using examples such as those just discussed. The only case they provide for thinking that a work of art can metaphorically exemplify, say, bitter-sweetness, is found in the supposedly uncontroversial examples of metaphorical exemplification. However, neither the gold-mine of a painting, nor the elegant sonata, provides an example of metaphorical exemplification. Consequently, they do not provide any basis for thinking that other such cases can be found. In particular, they provide no basis for thinking that works of art can metaphorically exemplify properties such as being frenzied or bitter-sweet.

In any case, as we have seen, the whole concept of metaphorical exemplification is suspect. Without the existence of metaphorical properties, metaphorical exemplification cannot exist. In particular, works of art cannot possess, say, the metaphorical properties of bitter-sweetness, yearning or frenzy.

Neither can works of art literally possess these properties. Since artworks do not have minds, they cannot literally yearn or be excited and agitated. Consequently, they cannot in any sense exemplify such properties.

It might still be thought that a work of art can exemplify a property such as the property of being frenzied. Consider, for example, Vivaldi's concerto, *La tempesta di mare* (RV 253). This work can be described as frenzied and this might be thought to be grounds for thinking that, in some fashion, the concerto exemplifies frenzy. Anyone who thinks this is mistaken. The fact that a work is accurately described as frenzied is not grounds for thinking that it exemplifies frenzy. The fact remains that frenzy is a state of mind and works of art do not have such states. Not possessing the property of frenzy, a concerto cannot exemplify it. The question of why the concerto is described as frenzied remains. To say that the concerto is frenzied is simply an elliptical way of saying that it represents frenzy. In this case, frenzy is not represented by exemplification. Rather, it is represented in the ways discussed in the two sections on 'Representation in music' in Chapter 2 (pp. 52–64).

Now that we have an appreciation of exemplification and the sorts of properties that can be exemplified by artworks, we can turn to the crucial question. We need to ask how artworks, qua exemplars, are supposed to contribute to knowledge. The exemplification hypothesis is nowhere developed as fully or as systematically as one might like, but the general picture emerges clearly enough. The claim is that the examination of exemplars can open up new perspectives on aspects of the world. For a start, an exemplar focuses an audience's attention on the property exemplified. When we focus on some property, we can acquire a better knowledge of its characteristics. More importantly, advocates of the hypothesis suggest, once we have a clearer conception of some property, we can use our conception to interpret our experience and enhance our knowledge of the world. I see no reason to doubt that this is true. However, as we have seen, works of art cannot metaphorically exemplify any properties. This conclusion is a key premiss in the argument for the conclusion that only a small part of the cognitive value of art can be explained by appeal to art's capacity for exemplification.

A few examples will illustrate how exemplars can contribute to knowledge. Consider, for example, Jackson Pollock's *Number One*. This painting draws attention to the viscosity of paint by exemplifying this viscosity. (A painting by Botticelli also employs a viscous medium, but it does not exemplify the viscosity of paint since it does not refer to this property.) Having had our attention drawn to the viscosity of paint by *Number One*, we can become aware of a feature of other paintings. Paintings by Barnett Newman and by members of the Washington School, particularly those of Louis, exemplify flatness. They thereby draw the attention of an audience to the flatness of paintings. This is a good use of exemplification because the exemplification of flatness enhances our understanding of the painting. We see more clearly that it is flat. More importantly, the exemplified property can be 'projected' on to other aspects of our experience. The result is that we become aware of the flatness of other paintings. In other words, we are presented with a perspective (in the sense identified in 'Ways to knowledge', pp. 65–70) on paintings.

All of the examples of artistic exemplification in the previous paragraph have something in common. The knowledge that can be gained from each case of exemplification is pretty trivial and, in any case, already possessed by most people. Some advocates of the exemplification hypothesis seem to think that something interesting can be learned from paintings that exemplify properties such as the viscosity of paint or flatness. They also appear to think that a great deal is to be learned about redness and squareness from Malevich's *Red Square*, which exemplifies redness and squareness. The fact of the matter, however, is that the information that pictures are flat, that red looks a certain way, and so on has comparatively little cognitive value. It is of little value when compared with the important knowledge unquestionably provided by the sciences. It is also of little value when compared with the profound insights the arts are often thought to be able to provide. (I realise that not everyone, and especially not every painter and critic, will agree with my estimate of the value of the knowledge, say, that paintings are flat. Still, I believe it is an accurate estimate.)

Now the important question comes to be that of whether artworks can provide any knowledge besides the comparative trivialities just discussed. When people talk about the cognitive value of art, they usually have in mind deep insights into the emotions, human nature, human relations, humanity's place in nature and so on. They do not have in mind the knowledge that paintings are flat or that paint is viscous. Defenders of the exemplification hypothesis believe that works of art can, by exemplifying properties, provide knowledge of such important matters. Perhaps, for example, Ibsen's *A Doll's House* (metaphorically) exemplifies Nora's discontent. The suggestion is that this exemplar draws attention to a property commonly found in women in certain situations. Audiences can then recognise that women can feel and, indeed, be trapped even when their circumstances are comfortable. Picasso's *Guernica* may similarly be thought to provide insight by exemplifying certain emotional states. One might hold that its image of the mother holding her dead child (metaphorically) exemplifies a certain form of grief. The suggestion is that, when we are presented with an exemplar of such grief, we are able to see more clearly how this shade of mourning is distinct from others, such as sorrow. Information about women's lives and the shades of emotions, unlike information about the dimensionality of paintings, is certainly not trivial. The suggestion is that *A Doll's House* and *Guernica*, qua exemplars, provide perspectives on (respectively) women's lives and grief.

The question is whether knowledge about social circumstances or emotions can be gained via the metaphorical exemplification of properties by artworks. Unfortunately, the answer to this question is 'no'. If artworks can only have cognitive value by exemplifying properties, the only knowledge to be gained from art is of the comparatively trivial variety. This conclusion follows from the reflections on exemplification with which this section began.

If we want to know what we can learn from an artwork qua exemplar, we need to ask what properties it possesses. A work of art (or anything else) can only exemplify the properties that it literally possesses. Works of art can literally possess only a limited range of properties. Works such as paintings and sculptures, are instantiated in material objects. These works possess what we might call material properties. These properties include mass, viscosity, colour, shape, texture and so on. Such works can also possess formal properties. A formal property is a structure or pattern. Symmetry is an example of such a property. Other works of art, such as literary and musical works, do not possess material properties. They do possess formal properties such as having tones or words ordered in certain ways. Certain aesthetic properties can supervene on the material and formal properties of artworks. As a result of such supervenience, works of art can possess properties such as elegance, grace and so on. Artworks also possess representational properties.

An exemplar (qua exemplar) is a source of knowledge concerning only those properties which it exemplifies. Consequently, works of art, in so far as they function as exemplars, can only provide insight into material, representational, formal and aesthetic properties. When works of art exemplify a material property such as viscosity, we can learn that paint is viscous. Similarly, since works of art can be symmetrical or elegant, they can exemplify such properties and thereby provide knowledge of these properties. The exemplification of a property, as we have seen, can influence our perception, and enhance our understanding, of the property as it is found in other objects. So, for example, we might find symmetry in objects where we had never noticed it before. Since works of art have representational properties, they can exemplify being a representation of various sorts. We can learn from a work of art, qua exemplar of representation, that works of art can represent, and something about how they do so. This is, however, the extent of the sort of knowledge to be gained from artworks qua exemplars.

The corollary of the point stated in the previous paragraph is that works of art cannot, qua exemplars, provide knowledge of properties they do not and cannot possess. In particular, artworks possess no affective properties and, consequently, they cannot exemplify affective properties or, by exemplifying them, provide insight into them. A similar line of reasoning leads to the conclusion that artworks cannot, simply by exemplifying properties they possess, help audiences understand affective states, human nature, society and other important matters. So, for example, we cannot learn about women's lives from the properties *A Doll's House* exemplifies. Nor does any property *Guernica* exemplifies give us insight into grief. Such matters and similar ones are, however, precisely those into which art is often said to provide insight. They are also the matters about which we might most hope to learn something from art.

One of two conclusions follows from what has been said so far in this section. The first possibility is that art has much less cognitive value than advocates of the exemplification hypothesis (and I) believe it has. Perhaps, that is, artworks have cognitive value only qua exemplars and art can only inform us about comparatively trivial matters, such as the viscosity of paint. The other possibility is that the exemplification hypothesis provides, at best, an incomplete account of the cognitive value of art. Obviously, I favour the second of these alternatives. In my view, forms of representation besides exemplification must be considered if we are to account for the cognitive value of art. Subsequent sections are devoted to providing an argument for this view. In the remainder of this section, I want to indicate that the exemplification hypothesis is not completely mistaken.

Sometimes what a work of art represents, and how, is influenced by what properties it exemplifies. Sometimes this is trivially true. The fact that a picture of a banana exemplifies yellowness partly determines that it represents a banana. In other cases, the properties an artwork exemplifies contribute more subtly to what it represents. In Handel's sereneta, *Aci, Galatea e Polifemo*, when Polyphemus appears, he blusters and rages to the accompaniment of the full orchestra, including trumpets. Galatea's subsequent aria, '*S'agita in mezzo all'onde*', is accompanied only by harpsichord. Particularly in this context, the music of this aria is literally quiet and easily overwhelmed and it exemplifies this property. Since the aria exemplifies this property, it is better able to represent the vulnerability of people in the position of Acis and Galatea. Since, as I will argue, such representation has cognitive value, the concept of exemplification has a role in explaining the cognitive value of art.

A role for exemplification is not all that survives of the position of defenders of the exemplification hypothesis. A lot of what they say about the cognitive role of exemplification applies to the cognitive role of representation in general. *A Doll's House*, for example, does not exemplify discontent, but it does represent it. (More precisely, the play directly represents a woman and her situation and, indirectly, her mental state.) This representation plays very much the cognitive role assigned by the exemplification hypothesis to exemplification. Nora's situation is presented in such a way that audiences are put in a position to recognise something about woman's lot. The discontent represented can be recognised in the lives of other women. In other words, the suggestion is that *A Doll's House* presents a perspective on women's lives. Similarly, *Guernica* represents (among other things) grief. The painting does not exemplify it. This representation can contribute to knowledge in much the same way as an exemplification is supposed to. It presents and demonstrates a perspective. Defenders of the exemplification hypothesis have, however, not said nearly enough about how representations can be a source of knowledge. This is the central task of an epistemology of art. We return to it now.

Interpretive illustration

As already indicated, illustrative demonstration (or showing) is the sort of demonstration we can expect to find in any form of illustrative representation. I have also foreshadowed a principal conclusion of this essay: artworks that provide illustrative demonstrations open perspectives on objects so that audiences may achieve a fuller understanding of them. Like any other sort of showing, illustrative demonstration guides audiences to a position from which they can recognise the rightness of a perspective on something. Different types of illustrations manoeuvre audiences into position in different ways. This section is primarily concerned with a form of illustration that I will call *interpretive illustration*. A variety of techniques are employed in interpretive illustration and make illustrative demonstrations possible. Some of the more important of these techniques are discussed in this section.

Before I can argue that illustrative representations can demonstrate a perspective, it needs to be shown that they can present a perspective. Different sorts of illustrations present perspectives in somewhat different ways. Let us begin by considering extrospective affective illustration. Some perspectives on objects involve affective attitudes towards the objects. After all, emotions can have a cognitive component. As a result, the very act of representing, in extrospective affective illustrations, something as the object of some emotion is to present a perspective on the object. Imagine, for example, that my university's former Academic Vice-President is represented in such a way that one feels that he is ridiculous. This representation presents the perspective that he is ridiculous. Similarly, Dickens presents a perspective on the Court of Chancery when he makes us feel outrage about that institution. Dickens's representation presents readers with the perspective that Chancery is an institution about which one ought to be angry.

The case of introspective affective illustration is somewhat different. In such representation, a work of art can present a perspective on an affective state. One might argue that many of Mozart's compositions present a perspective on pleasure. In listening to these works one feels something like pure, invigorating delight. As such the music can be an introspective affective illustration of such an affect, and also provides a perspective on it. On this perspective, pure delight is to be thought of as something to be relished. When pleasure is viewed in this way, it is not trivial or something about which one ought to feel guilty. It is somehow essential to being human. In other cases, an introspective affective illustration may simply present the perspective that some emotion is possible. The existence of some emotion (disinterested love, for example) might be controversial. The introspective affective illustration of such an emotion presents the perspective that it is possible. Introspective affective illustration does, however, more than present perspectives on affects. A great deal of such illustration is testimony. Affective illustration is discussed more fully in the section on 'Affective illustration and knowledge' later in this chapter (pp. 88–94).

While affective illustrations present a way of feeling about an object, other illustrations present ways of thinking about things. For convenience, these illustrations may be called *interpretive illustrations*. A few words will clarify what I mean by talk of interpretive illustration. A simple example of such representation will be helpful. Perhaps the most familiar sort of interpretive illustration is caricature. An editorial cartoonist may, for example, exaggerate the facial features of a public figure so that he resembles a rat, a bulldog or a pig. Portrayed in this manner, the public figure is represented as contemptible, stalwart or greedy. To represent someone as, say, a pig is to present to audience members an interpretation of the person (in this case, as greedy). In other words, the representation presents a perspective on, or way of thinking about, the individual in question. More generally, in interpretive illustration, the way in which an object is represented presents an interpretation of an object.

One might object that, in a sense, every illustration presents a perspective on some object. A humble vacation snapshot presents a perspective on, say, a cathedral: the perspective that the cathedral is made of stone. I want to distinguish, however, between illustrations which add nothing to how people ordinarily think of an object, and those that do. Even if the line between these types of illustration is not hard and fast, the distinction can still be drawn. Interpretive illustrations are the ones that present perspectives on objects which are not a part of ordinary experience of the objects. As such, interpretive illustrations can change how things are perceived. A vacation snapshot of the cathedral in Rouen probably adds nothing to how people see and think about this church. Monet's paintings of the cathedral, on the other hand, can add something to an audience's conception of the cathedral. Audience members can learn that the appearance of the cathedral varies greatly with time of day and atmospheric conditions, and that its emotional impact on viewers can be enormously various. As a result, Monet's paintings are interpretive illustrations, while the snap-shot is not.

Before investigating the ways in which artworks can demonstrate a perspective, I want to discuss some of the techniques employed in illustrative representation. A variety of such techniques are employed. The use of these techniques makes it possible for such representations to draw attention to features of objects, place them in context, display their consequences and draw comparisons between them. When representations function in these ways, they can put audiences in a position to recognise the rightness of a perspective. Here I will identify six such techniques: amplification, connection, correlation, juxtaposition, selection and simplification. I am not suggesting that this list is anywhere near exhaustive. These techniques are, however, both common and important in the arts. Nor do I suggest that the techniques are exclusive. Indeed, most works of art will employ more than one. Once these techniques have been introduced, a few examples will indicate how each of these techniques can be used to put audiences in a position to recognise the rightness of a perspective.

Selection is, perhaps, the most fundamental of the techniques employed in interpretive illustration. This representational technique is simply the choice of objects, or aspects of objects, for representation. The very selection of objects for representation directs an audience's attention to the object. A work of art can, by judicious use of selection, bring an audience to focus on objects which have been overlooked, or thought unworthy of careful attention. The early novel was important, in part, because it represented aspects of domestic life which had been neglected by artists. Diderot makes this point in his discussion of Richardson's novels. Some early critics of Richardson criticised him for representing mundane events which are experienced every day. According to Diderot, however, although certain events take place daily under our eyes, they are often not observed. As such, part of the value of, for example, *Pamela* is that it opens up perspectives on everyday life. Something similar can be said about the remarkable cityscapes that Thomas Jones executed in Naples in the early 1780s. Painters such as Canaletto focused on grand public buildings and gala events. Jones, in contrast, selected for representation common dwellings and back alleys. His paintings draw attention to signs of decay, shoddy construction and laundry hanging from porches. Only glimpses of great public monuments appear in Jones's works. From the perspective of these paintings, humble objects are the stuff of ordinary life much more than processions on the Grand Canal. Like the monuments in Jones's paintings, the latter are represented as remote from quotidian life. Consequently, Jones's very selection of objects for representation contributes to a perspective on these objects.

Amplification is the second technique employed in interpretive illustration. When amplification is employed, an object is represented as possessing some property to a greater extent, or in a higher degree, than it is normally thought to possess. A simple example of amplification has already been mentioned in passing: the exaggeration of a public figure's facial features in a caricature. More sophisticated instances of amplification are found in a novel such as Joseph Heller's *Catch-22*. No bureaucracy was ever, perhaps, quite so perverse and inefficient as the one that plagues Yossarian. Heller selected some of the most frustrating features of the US Air Force's bureaucracy (and aspects of American society more generally) and amplified them, rendering them more apparent. Amplification is a technique common in all forms of satire. It is found in the paintings and engravings of Hogarth and in the plays of Sheridan. In general, amplification highlights certain properties and thereby draws attention to them. When attention is drawn to the properties, a perspective is presented on the objects which possess them.

The third method of interpretive illustration is simplification. Every object possesses a great many properties. When simplification is used in the representation of an object, some of these properties are down-played or eliminated. Most, perhaps all, interpretive illustration involves a measure of simplification. An illustration that represents all of the properties that an object possesses is scarcely conceivable. Still, simplification is more pronounced in some representations than in others. Both Rupert Brooke and Wilfred Owen represent the First World War, and both employ simplification. Brooke focuses only on the glory of war, while in Owen (in *Dulce et decorum est*, for example) we find only a representation of its horror and brutality. In both cases, the attention of readers is directed towards the features of the war that are not eliminated from the representation. One sub-species of simplification may be called idealisation. Idealisation is simplification that removes all of an object's imperfections. Good examples of the use of this technique are found in the Madonnas of Raphael. These works present the perspective that Mary is flawless.

It is important to note the difference between simplification, as the term is used here, and simplicity. 'Simplicity' and 'complexity' are adjectives that apply to the formal properties of an artwork. A folk song, for example, or a sequence by Hildegard of Bingen is formally simple. Alternatively, these terms characterise the way a work functions. A work may be functionally complex, for example, in that it employs many of the techniques of interpretive illustration. Note that a work of art can be quite formally or functionally complex and yet provide an instance of simplification. On the other hand, an artwork can be formally or functionally simple, and yet not employ simplification.

The next technique to be considered is juxtaposition. When juxtaposition is employed, two or more objects are simultaneously represented. The objects may be represented in close proximity or in other relations, in which they may not have been observed in ordinary experience. Classic instances of juxtaposition are found in Jane Austen's novels. She frequently juxtaposes a superficially engaging but morally flawed character with a type who, though lacking certain social graces, has true worth. Wickham, in *Pride and Prejudice*, represents one sort of character. This type is juxtaposed with the type represented by Mr Darcy. In *Sense and Sensibility* we find the juxtaposition of the character-type represented by Willoughby and the type represented by Colonel Brandon. In *Emma*, Frank Churchill is juxtaposed with Mr Knightley. Similarly, Sophocles juxtaposes Oedipus and Polyneices. Whereas Oedipus has acted in ignorance, his son refuses to withdraw his troops even though he knows that his destruction is prophesied. In the visual arts, juxtaposition is found, for example, in allegorical paintings of the active and contemplative lives. Handel's setting of Milton's *L'Allegro* and *Il Penseroso* similarly juxtaposes representations of the active and contemplative lives.

Correlation, the next technique to be considered, is similar to juxtaposition. Correlation involves the representation of an object in such a way that audiences will see it in relation to a second object. The difference between juxtaposition and correlation is that juxtaposition involves the representation of both objects, while in correlation the second object is not represented. A good example of correlation is provided by Goya's *The Third of May 1808 in Madrid: Executions on Principe Pio Hill*. Here a Spanish patriot is represented in such a way that he resembles and recalls the crucified Christ. His arms are spread in the manner of Christ on the cross, and his hands are marked with stigmata. When someone is represented in this way, viewers are encouraged to see him as having properties in common with Christ: a sacrifice for the good of others, or an innocent victim of oppression. In this way, viewers are presented with a perspective on the patriot.

In literature, metaphors, similes and allegories are often used to correlate a represented object with another. Consider, for example, one of the most familiar metaphors in all of English literature. Juliet represents (among other things) the beloved woman. When, in the course of her representation, we are told that Juliet is the sun, the beloved woman is correlated with the sun. The attention of theatre-goers is drawn to the ways in which Juliet resembles the sun. Just as we revolve around the sun, the lover's life revolves around his beloved. Just as the sun gives us life, and without it we would not exist, the life of the lover depends on the life of the beloved. Similes can function in a similar manner. In *The Rime of the Ancient Mariner*, Coleridge writes that the wedding guest 'listens like a three years' child'. This simile correlates (and draws readers' attention to the resemblance between) the adult spellbound by a narrative and the rapt attention characteristic of children.

Connection is the final technique to be considered. This technique has a great deal in common with certain thought experiments. An early use of this technique is found in Book I of *The Republic*. There, Cephalus suggests that one acts justly if one tells the truth and returns anything with which one has been entrusted. In reply, Socrates considers the case of a man who has been entrusted with a knife by a friend. Socrates suggests that, should the owner of the knife go mad, it would be wrong to return the knife to him. Here we have a representation of a situation where someone returns an object with which he has been entrusted. Connected with this situation is injustice: plainly it is wrong to return the knife. In this way, Socrates presents readers with a perspective on justice: it is not always just to return a person's property.

The technique of connection plays a similar role in many artworks. Plato's use of connection is usefully compared with the use of the same technique by one of his near-contemporaries. In *Oedipus at Colonus*, Sophocles is concerned with the question (among others) of how to treat a man who has committed acts such as parricide and incest. The man might seem to deserve punishment, but Sophocles presents an alternative perspective on this question. He represents a person who is the victim of forces beyond his control and who was ignorant of the consequences of his actions. Sophocles represents a man who has suffered terribly and who feels genuine remorse. He also represents the treatment of such a man by another, morally upright, person. When a parricide is represented in these terms, the persecution of such a man is represented as connected with injustice. Dickens's *Hard Times* affords another good example of interpretive illustrations which employs the technique of connection. Thomas Gradgrind begins the novel by saying, 'Now, what I want is, Facts.... Stick to the Facts, Sir!' Dickens obliges. He represents a society (his own) in which a sort of sterile utilitarianism prevails. Dickens represents this heartless society as inextricably connected with the misery of people such as Gradgrind's daughter, Louisa, shunted into a loveless marriage. He thereby presents a perspective on this society.

Let us turn now to the question of how interpretive illustrations can be used in illustrative demonstration. As we have seen, illustrative demonstration is a matter of putting people in a position to grasp the rightness of a perspective. Interpretive illustrations can, in at least four ways, perform this function. Interpretive illustrations can draw attention to a similarity between two objects and so put an audience in a position to see that a perspective on the objects is right. In other cases, interpretive illustrations direct the attention of an audience to objects, or aspects of objects, which they may have overlooked. Other interpretive illustrations represent things in such a way that their consequences become apparent. Displaying consequences can, in certain circumstances, demonstrate the rightness of a perspective on an object. Still other interpretive illustrations represent objects in a context. Often, the rightness of a perspective on an object becomes apparent once it is placed in context. Illustrative demonstrations do not involve the use of statements. Even when words are employed in such demonstrations, they function more as gestures (say, a nudge that elbows someone into a position to see something) than as statements.

We can begin to understand how an interpretive illustration can demonstrate a perspective when we consider a simple, non-artistic, example of showing. Imagine that two women, Karen and Lana, are out shopping. A hat catches the fancy of Karen and she tries it on. Although she finds the hat appealing, she is not quite certain about it. She has a nagging feeling that it is somehow not quite right. As Karen hesitates, Lana says to her, 'It's the Taj Mahal.' Karen immediately recognises what had made her hesitate about the hat, and sees clearly that it will not do. In comparing the hat to the Taj Mahal, Lana does not state or argue for the conclusion that the hat bears an uncanny resemblance to the great Mogul mausoleum. Rather, her utterance puts Karen in a position to notice this resemblance and to see that the hat is unsuitable. In this way, she demonstrates the rightness of the perspective that the hat is unsuitable.

It is important to note that illustrative demonstration of this sort cannot take place in a vacuum. In the case just discussed, Lana succeeded in demonstrating the rightness of a perspective on the hat only because Karen had a knowledge of the appearance of the Taj Mahal. Similarly, interpretive illustrations in the arts open up perspectives only for suitably equipped audiences. By itself, any interpretive illustration demonstrates nothing. The capacity of any work of art to demonstrate the rightness of a perspective depends crucially on the capacities of an audience. In the absence of the right background knowledge, abilities and values, an interpretive illustration cannot demonstrate a perspective.

Let us turn now to the consideration of how the various techniques of interpretive illustration can be used in illustrative demonstration. Many interpretive illustrations function very much like the comment on the hat. This comment is, in effect, an instance of correlation, so we should not be surprised that some works of art perform a similar function. When metaphors, similes and visual allusions (such as Goya's comparison of Christ and the Spanish patriot) correlate objects, the attention of an audience is drawn to similarities and differences. The very act of making someone aware of a similarity can demonstrate the rightness of a perspective on the relationship between two (or more) objects.

The use of juxtaposition can similarly demonstrate the rightness of a perspective. It can assist audiences in comparing and contrasting represented objects. This can aid in the understanding of the objects. As used by Jane Austen, for example, juxtaposition gives readers the opportunity to understand characters more fully and to estimate more accurately their relative values. When, for example, Wickham and Darcy are juxtaposed, readers are in a position to see clearly the failings of the one sort of character and the true merits of the other. That is, readers are presented with a perspective on certain types of characters. Similarly, Sophocles presents viewers with a moral perspective. When Oedipus and Polyneices are juxtaposed, an audience can see clearly what makes one innocent and the other culpable.

Representational techniques such as amplification and simplification can also play a role in illustrative demonstration. In *Catch-22*, Heller amplifies the inefficiency and perversity of the US Air Force administration and similar bureaucracies (think of the various catch-22s). The excesses of chest-thumping nationalism (the loyalty oaths) and the pretensions of free enterprise (Milo's profiteering) are similarly exaggerated. Heller's readers are prodded into looking again at institutions and practices which may previously have been unquestioningly accepted. From the viewpoint to which Heller leads them, they are in a position to see things which may have hitherto escaped their observation. Something similar happens as a result of Owen's use of simplification. In his poems, readers see only a small part of the First World War. As it is represented, only the brutality and horror of war appear. Owen places readers in a position from which the horror is readily apparent. Even someone inclined to believe that *dulce et decorum est pro patria mori* cannot, while reading Owen, ignore this horror. To be placed where Owen places readers is to be provided with a demonstration of the rightness of a perspective on modern war.

Consider now the use of the technique of connection in illustrative demonstration. Let us begin by considering again the use of connection in *The Republic*. Notice that, in the passage considered above, Socrates does not provide a rational demonstration of the falsehood of Cephalus' position on justice. Rather, he puts readers in a position to note the consequences connected with a perspective on justice. Once readers see that Cephalus' views lead to palpable injustice, they recognise that his is the wrong perspective on human action. Something very similar takes place in *Oedipus at Colonus*. Theatre-goers are placed in a position from which they can see a connection that they might otherwise have overlooked. They can recognise that holding people responsible for unintended and unforeseeable consequences of their actions is connected with unfairness. Oedipus has plainly suffered enough. Having recognised this, it is clear that the right moral perspective is sensitive to factors such as intent and what is reasonably foreseeable. Again, Sophocles does not argue that this perspective is right. Rather, by means of interpretive illustration, he puts audiences in a position to recognise the unacceptable consequences connected with the alternative perspective.

The claim that Dickens's use of interpretive illustration demonstrates something is more controversial. The connection Dickens represents between an unsentimental society and human suffering is a causal connection. In this respect the case from *Hard Times* differs from the other cases just discussed. In these cases, the connection was conceptual. The very concept of justice demands that a just act ought not to result in avoidable or uncompensated harm. Consequently, to show that a moral perspective is connected with such harm is to demonstrate that the perspective is wrong. No conceptual connection exists between rigid utilitarianism and human suffering. One might reasonably ask, therefore, how Dickens's representation of a causal connection provides readers with knowledge. After all, we have no guarantee that the represented connection exists.

The reply to this question is that Dickens's story directs readers' attention to a causal connection experienced in daily life. *Hard Times* provides readers with a lens through which to reinterpret the experience they have already accumulated. Readers do not simply notice a connection between two representations. The representation of a connection draws their attention to a connection in the world. In this way, readers are put into a position where they can recognise the rightness of a perspective on a purely utilitarian approach to life. Once again, an interpretive illustration that puts people in a position to recognise the existence of a connection amounts to a demonstration of the rightness of a perspective. From this perspective, a reader arrives at the recognition of the moral bankruptcy of neglecting the importance of emotion and sentiment, connected as it is with suffering.

This section has provided some understanding of how interpretive illustration can have cognitive value. At best, however, we have only part of the story about the cognitive function of art. We still need to investigate the ways in which the arts can, by employing the two forms of affective illustration, contribute to knowledge. This is the subject of the next section.

Affective illustration and knowledge

Like interpretive illustrations, the affective illustrations of artists can present perspectives. They can direct the attention of audience members and nudge them into a position from where they can recognise the rightness of a perspective on some object or objects. Again, a close analogy between this form of representation, on the one hand, and gestures, on the other, is apparent. In short, affective illustrations can provide illustrative demonstrations. They do so by engaging the affective responses of audience members, which can be good guides to how things are. Affective illustrations can also function simply as testimony. In particular, they can be testimony about emotional experiences familiar to an artist.

Many of the same techniques employed in interpretive illustration can be utilised in extrospective affective illustration to present perspectives. Consider, for example, how amplification can play a role in such representation. Dickens employs amplification in his representations of the Marshalsea (the debtors' prison in *Little Dorrit*) and of the Court of Chancery. These representations are calculated to arouse in the reader indignation and even anger about the conditions under which debtors are imprisoned or lawsuits conducted. Dickens exaggerated the inefficiency and heartlessness of Chancery as a way of generating the intended emotional response. In this manner, he presents a perspective on the court.

Simplification can similarly be used to arouse an emotive response to some object. Wilfred Owen would have diminished the capacity of his poetry to arouse an emotional response had he presented a more nuanced representation of the war in the trenches. As the poems stand, isolating the brutality and suffering, they cannot help but evoke a feeling of horror which is directed towards the First World War. The use of idealisation can obviously play a role in generating emotions directed towards the represented object. After all, a sympathetic attitude is likely towards something represented as without flaws. David's portrait of the assassinated Marat, for example, is calculated to evoke sympathy for the man. Certainly, it is more likely to do so than a less idealised portrayal of the scabrous fanatic.

Juxtaposition is another technique which plays a role in affective illustration as well as in interpretive illustration. Consider, for example, the use of juxtaposition in Caspar David Friedrich's *Monk by the Sea*, an instance of affective illustration. In this painting, a small, solitary figure, in the habit of a monk, his hands raised to his face in a gesture of mourning, stands on a beach. The figure is juxtaposed with a vast, stormy sky and the immensity of a boiling sea. This juxtaposition evokes in many viewers (including Heinrich von Kleist, author of an essay on the painting) a strong feeling of isolation, desolation and eeriness. Many people have a tendency (felt by Kleist among others) to identify with the lone figure and see him as representing humans in an over-awing universe, and the feelings aroused by the painting become directed towards the situation of humans in the world. Viewers are made to consider that the world is mysterious, and to feel some of the disorientation attendant on this perspective. In this way, Friedrich uses affective illustration to present a perspective on the human condition.

Illustrations can generate affective responses to objects by means other than the use of the techniques employed in interpretive illustration. In particular, exemplification plays an important role in some examples of extrospective affective illustration. That is, some works of art generate an affective response by means of the properties they exemplify. These affective responses can be directed towards the object represented by the work. A few examples will illustrate this point. A monumental sculpture (of a Roman emperor, say, or a hero such as Achilles) exemplifies the property of being massive. As such, it may leave viewers awe-struck and overwhelmed. The feeling that the represented person is awe-inspiring or powerful can result. Similarly, a heldentenor's performance of an aria (from one of Wagner's operas, say) can exemplify powerfulness and loudness. The very scale and volume of the performance can send a shiver down the spine of listeners. They are left feeling astonishment, even dismay and dread. Audiences can be left with the feeling that the represented character is intimidating, powerful or terrifying.

The use of exemplification is just one way of using the formal properties of a representation to cultivate feelings about the represented object. Representations can use balance, unity, discordance, garishness, asymmetry and other formal properties to cultivate affects directed towards the objects represented. Since the general point (that illustrations can use the cultivation of affects to present perspectives) has been established, it is not necessary to give examples here. We need to turn to the question of how extrospective affective illustration can be used to provide illustrative demonstrations.

Extrospective affective illustrations provide demonstrations very much as interpretive illustrations do. As we saw in the previous section, 'Interpretive illustration', the very act of providing a perspective can put audiences in a position to recognise the rightness of the perspective. This is as true of the perspectives presented by extrospective affective illustrations as it is of those provided by interpretive illustration. In short, when audiences are made to feel a certain way about an object, they can often gain insight into it. As a result, extrospective affective illustrations can provide illustrative demonstrations.

Extrospective affective illustrations can provide insight into objects (in part) because emotional responses are often good guides to how things are. This is not always true. Emotions can sometimes cloud one's judgement and hinder the acquisition of knowledge. My judgement, for example, was never at its best just after I had received yet another bone-headed memo from our previous Academic Vice-President. I am certain that I made errors while in the grip of the impotent rage that generally ensued. Nevertheless, an object which arouses our approval, for example, is likely to be good or beneficial, while ridiculous objects tend to inspire derision. Similarly, if an object fills us with disgust, then it is probably vile. When artists employ extrospective affective representation, they can take advantage of our emotional responses for cognitive purposes.

Although emotions can cloud judgements, representation of an object that does not arouse an emotional response can have less cognitive value than representation of one that does. Contrast, for example, Dickens's representation of Chancery with a completely dispassionate account. The dispassionate description of Chancery, which excites no emotions in readers, may well have less cognitive value than Dickens's impassioned affective illustration. A clinical description of the court might leave readers thinking that its methods of settling disputes are normal and acceptable. Such an account may state that disputes must be settled in light of all available information. Sometimes, the account may allow, the discovery and presentation of this knowledge takes some time. The dispassionate account may add that the lawyers who argue the cases must be paid. Indeed, as highly trained professionals, they deserve ample remuneration. Such an account of Chancery actually distorts the court more than does Dickens's. A representation that arouses indignation enables readers to form a more accurate conception of the court: that it is the sort of thing about which one is properly indignant.

We have no guarantee that an extrospective affective illustration will provide the truth about some matter. An artwork may arouse in an audience a feeling of distaste for an object which is actually worthy of admiration. We should not conclude that this form of representation cannot show us anything. Any form of representation can be misleading. Rather, we should conclude that, like any representation, an extrospective affective illustration needs to be tested. The audience needs to ask whether the affective response evoked by a representation is appropriate. A decision about the appropriateness of a response has to be made on the basis of other beliefs about the represented object.

It is worth noting that an extrospective affective illustration will not show something to every audience member. An artwork which employs this type of representation can put people in a position to gain knowledge. The work will, however, only be effective if its audience possesses certain beliefs and moral sentiments. Dickens's account of Dotheboys Hall in *Nicholas Nickleby* is a representation of a certain sort of school for boys. It moves many readers to indignation and puts them in a position to recognise that such schools are the proper objects of indignation. It can have these effects only if certain conditions are met. Most importantly, readers must be at least ordinarily disturbed by injustice. *Nicholas Nickleby* will fail to show anything to someone with the character and beliefs of the schoolmaster, Wackford Squeers. Obviously, if a work is to be effective, readers must also have certain beliefs. In this case, they must have beliefs about right and wrong, good and bad.

Let us turn now to the consideration of introspective affective illustration. As we have seen, in such representation, affects themselves are illustrated: experience of such a representation is like experience of some affect. As we saw in the section 'Types of representation' in Chapter 2 (pp. 26–34), an instance of introspective affective illustration is found in, for example, Arnold's *Dover Beach*. This poem represents desolation because it evokes in many readers a feeling of (or like) desolation. Similarly, Handel's aria '*Mie piante correte*' represents surprise and frustration since this is what experience of the work is like. Answers to the questions of why and how experience of introspective affective illustration can be like experience of affects are extremely complex. These questions were touched on in the final section of Chapter 2 (pp. 60–4). Since they are so complex, and perhaps best addressed by psychologists, I will leave them to one side. I can afford to do so since I take the crucial point (that experience of an artwork can be like experience of an affect) to be sufficiently obvious. For present purposes the question is how this form of representation can contribute to knowledge.

Introspective affective illustration can be, for a start, a vehicle of illustrative testimony. Here Emanuel Bach's Fantasia in F# Minor provides a useful illustration. Emanuel Bach was an exponent of the *Empfindsamer Stil*. As such, he regarded music as a way of communicating information about emotions. In the case of the fantasia in question, Bach provides listeners with a clue as to the information he hopes to communicate. At the head of this fantasia, he wrote, 'C. P. E. Bach's feelings'. As noted in the final section of Chapter 2 (pp. 60–4), the experience of this fantasia is like experience of distracted melancholy. In effect, this work is testimony to one of Bach's states of mind, though not one he was necessarily in as he composed the fantasia. A variety of other composers have regarded music as a way of testifying to their emotions. Usually, composers have spoken about the expression of emotion, but the point is the same. This view is commonly associated with romanticism and, indeed, Mendelssohn and Mahler explicitly held the view that a composition can provide insight into the emotions of its composer. The view is not limited to the romantics, however. Even Schoenberg regarded music as a kind of testimony about the emotions of the composer.

An introspective affective illustration can provide testimony about matters other than the emotional life of its author. It can also report information about what it feels like to live in a particular time and place. This point is apparent from reflection on French art of the early eighteenth century. A certain attitude towards life seems to have been quite common during this period. At least in some circles, a languidly sensuous attitude towards life and love seems to have prevailed. In these circles, people apparently felt that a studied elegance, combined with a languorous hedonism, amounted almost (if not entirely) to a virtue. We can know this because of the way in which the art of the period affects us. Experience of a painting by Watteau of a *fête champêtre* (say, *Departure from the Island of Cythera*) has a peculiar affective quality. Experience of such a painting is rather like a feeling of languid decadence. As such, it is testimony to the emotional states of a certain class of persons. A similar point could be made about the *classique* style of music. Experience of a formal, restrained suite by Marin Marais or François Couperin can have much in common with the sensibilities to which I have been referring. As such it can illustrate, and be illustrative testimony of, this state of mind.

The testimony provided by an introspective affective illustration is often much more valuable than semantic testimony. A composer or a poet could simply provide a semantic representation of his feelings or those of other people. He could say, for example, 'I feel rather desolate from time to time' or 'Quite a lot of people nowadays seem to feel a languid insouciance.' These statements do not, however, provide information about what it is like to experience the represented affect. Semantic representations can provide this sort of insight, but only by drawing comparisons. (I might, for example, say: 'You are probably familiar with the helpless feeling of rage and impotence one feels when one answers to moronic administrators. I feel just like that.') Such testimony can be quite informative, but illustrative testimony about the same facts will generally be more valuable. The illustrative testimony provided by an introspective affective illustration provides direct insight into experience of an affect. The difference between semantic and affective representations of experience of an emotion is akin to the difference between reading a review of a concert and hearing a recording of it. The recording, which provides auditors with an experience, will generally be more informative about what experience of the concert was like. This is one reason why a picture (or any other sort of affective illustration) can be worth a thousand words.

Introspective affective illustrations can do more than provide illustrative testimony. They can also provide illustrative demonstrations. Such representations can, for example, demonstrate a perspective on the taxonomy of emotions. By this I mean that an introspective affective illustration can demonstrate something about differences between various affective states. An example will illustrate this point. Someone might think of mourning as a homogeneous phenomenon. One might believe, for example, that mourning is always passionate, bitter and tinged with despair. The experience of music can show listeners that this perspective on mourning is wrong. Consider the following three works: the 'Dead March' from *Saul*, *Trauermusik*, and the second movement of Beethoven's Third Symphony. I suggest that the *Marcia Funebre* of the *Eroica* represents mourning as tied up with distracted and passionate railing against fate. This movement is characterised by large, unrestrained gestures (particularly by the standards of the classical symphony). Consequently, listening to the movement is unsettling. It is, in effect, testimony about one way of experiencing mourning. Experience of the 'Dead March' or *Trauermusik*, however, is quite different. Handel's work is stately and dignified. Experience of the work is like experience of sadness, but a restrained, dignified and resigned sadness. The death of a hero is represented as an occasion of sadness, but also of reflection. The experience of the final movement of Hindemith's work is different again. This experience is akin to experience of an ineffable sense of loss.

Each of these three works is an introspective affective illustration of the experience of mourning and each opens up a perspective on this emotion. Each of the compositions gives listeners a way of thinking about their own experience of bereavement. These works can put listeners in a position to recognise something about this experience. As such, they can function as illustrative demonstrations. In particular, they can show that certain perspectives on the taxonomy of emotions are wrong, while others are more adequate.

Another example of how introspective affective illustrations can demonstrate a perspective is afforded by reflection on certain of Mozart's compositions. As noted in the section on 'Interpretive illustration' earlier in this chapter (pp. 80–8), works such as the Piano Concerto No. 23 (K 488) or the Overture to *Così fan tutti* present a perspective on pleasure. The experience of such works is one of invigorating delight and the music provides an introspective affective illustration of this sort of pleasure. The experience of the music is never monotonous, jejune or cloying. Rather, it is fulfilling and always intellectually satisfying. In this manner, Mozart presents his audience with the perspective that pleasure can be something not at all trivial, but rather a valuable part of human life. He does more, however, than simply present this perspective. He also shows that it is right. When people listen to Mozart's music they can feel for themselves that the delight they experience does not cloy, but is perpetually gratifying. Mozart's music does not simply put listeners in a position to re-evaluate their past experience of pleasure. As they listen, their current experience shows them the rightness of a perspective.

What can be learned from art?

On the basis of the previous sections, I conclude that art is a source of knowledge. Nevertheless, as a form of inquiry, art has its limitations. Art is able to provide insight into some matters, but is of little or no use in the illumination of others. The present section is devoted to a discussion of the scope and limits of artistic inquiry. In particular, I want to indicate that art and the sciences can provide insight into different and complementary areas of inquiry. A discussion of art as a source of moral knowledge is also in order.

We should begin by asking what sort of knowledge works of art can provide. I have already indicated that I believe that artworks can provide propositional knowledge. That is, they can teach us *that* something is the case. For example, in reading *Pride and Prejudice* one learns that first impressions are a poor guide to character, that it is dangerous to delight in making sport of one's acquaintances, and so on. Works of art can also provide non-propositional knowledge, knowledge of how to do something or the ability to recognise something. In particular, an artwork can give audiences the capacity to apply concepts and knowledge of what certain mental states are like. This sort of knowledge cannot be expressed in propositional terms. I will refer to it as *practical knowledge*.

The first way the arts can contribute to practical knowledge is by enhancing the faculty of judgement. In the *Critique of Pure Reason*, Kant distinguished between the understanding and judgement and we may usefully appropriate this distinction. Our understandings are stocked with concepts. Judgement is the faculty that applies these concepts to objects. A judge, for example, may know the definition of slander. That is, he possesses the concept of slander and propositional knowledge about it. Such a judge may nevertheless be unable to tell of a particular utterance whether or not it is slanderous. Nothing is wrong with the understanding of this judge, but his judgement is imperfect. (In other words, the judge lacks a certain sort of practical knowledge.) A brief discussion will indicate how artworks can cultivate judgement and practical knowledge.

Consider the following example. Almost everyone possesses the propositional knowledge that hypocrisy is a vice and that officiousness should be avoided. Even people who know this, however, may not know how to recognise certain acts as hypocritical or officious. A novelist can represent character traits and types of behaviour in such a way that readers become able to recognise that they are, say, officious. I may, like Emma Woodhouse, believe that certain sorts of actions are kindly, justifiable and helpful. In *Emma*, Jane Austen represents these actions in such a way that I may come to see that I was wrong about them. I may realise that, like Emma, I have been officiously interfering in the lives of others. In this case, I do not learn that something is wrong with officiousness. I knew that all along. Instead, I acquire the ability to recognise that the concept of officiousness applies to a range of actions I had hitherto thought unexceptionable. In other words, my judgement has been improved. I know how to do something that I did not previously know. In this way, an artwork can enhance practical knowledge.

Artworks do not only contribute to practical knowledge by improving judgement. A further example will illustrate another way in which artworks can provide practical knowledge. I have already indicated that the 'Dead March' from *Saul*, the second movement of the *Eroica* and *Trauermusik* provide knowledge of the shades of mourning. This knowledge can be characterised in propositional terms: one can know that mourning can be resigned and that it can bitterly rail against fate. Perhaps more importantly, however, listeners can learn what it is like to experience the various shades of mourning, or how different forms of the affect differ. This is practical knowledge and not propositional knowledge. After all, no knowledge of what it is like to experience something can be fully captured in propositional terms. We have, then, another instance of how artworks enhance practical knowledge.

Let us turn now to the issue of the scope and limits of the knowledge which artworks can provide. The first point to make is that some matters are best understood by means of the arts, while others lend themselves to scientific treatment. Theories and rational demonstration are of little use in understanding matters such as the difference between sadness and grief, the forms hypocrisy can assume, and the dangers of a heartless educational system. On the other hand, illustrative demonstration is unlikely to shed much light on matters such as the causes of global warming, whether Homo sapiens is descended from Australopithicus or the motions of celestial bodies. There may, however, be some matters which are illuminated by both the sort of inquiry characteristic of the arts and that employed in the sciences. Perhaps, for example, both Dickens (in *A Tale of Two Cities*) and Lefebvre provide insight into the causes of the French Revolution. Some works employ both illustrative and rational demonstration. Carlyle's history of the French Revolution comes to mind as an example of such a work. Although a work of history, it employs many of the techniques of interpretive and affective illustration to demonstrate perspectives on French history.

It is possible to characterise, in general terms, what sorts of phenomena the arts and sciences help us to understand. As we have seen, the sciences provide rational demonstrations, generally inductive or abductive arguments, for theories. Most of the cognitive work performed by science is done by means of theories. A theory posits the existence of a law (or laws) of nature or, at any rate, law-like regularities. (By the standards of contemporary philosophy of science, this is a somewhat old-fashioned way of talking about science. It suffices, however, for present purposes.) As a result, the sciences are suited to the understanding of law-governed phenomena. Reductionists hold that all phenomena can, in principle, be understood in terms of laws. I do not wish to take a stand on this claim. Even if it is true, we are certainly ignorant of the laws governing many objects. For the foreseeable future we will have to rely on other means of understanding many phenomena.

This is where the arts come in. They will be most able to provide insight into complex, diverse subjects where general laws are elusive or non-existent. Notably, the arts can contribute better than other forms of inquiry to the understanding of such complex phenomena as ourselves, our emotions, our relations to each other and our place in the world. These complex phenomena often appear *sui generis* and cannot be fully understood by subsumption under general laws. We must rely on perspectives, rather than on theories, in understanding these phenomena. A perspective can give us the capacity to discriminate features of complex phenomena and navigate the problems posed by daily life.

The phenomena we understand by means of the arts must be understood one by one. In contrast, when things can be understood by means of theories, a small number of theories will suffice. Some day, perhaps, scientists will develop a single unified physical theory that can explain everything that science can explain. An artwork, however, frequently provides a perspective on only a single object. At most, it presents a perspective on a very specific type of object. While a single law explains the fall of all bodies, a different perspective is needed for each type of character, emotion or human relation. Each sonnet, each sonata, each drawing sheds light on a small corner of reality. While a few scientific theories will suffice, we need a great deal of art.

Let us turn now to the specific question of the relationship between art and moral knowledge. In some ways, this is the most important question to be addressed in this section. Many people have thought that the arts are particularly important as a source of moral knowledge. As purveyors of moral insight the arts have been regarded as edifying. As possible sources of moral error, they have been regarded as potentially pernicious. Works of literature are the most obvious candidates for artworks which can provide moral knowledge. Works with a literary component, such as films and operas, are also good candidates. In this discussion of art and moral knowledge, I will focus on literary art. Some works of visual art (such as some of Goya's paintings, or *Guernica*) are also, however, plausible sources of moral knowledge.

I certainly believe that the arts can contribute to moral knowledge. (Although the existence of moral knowledge is not beyond doubt, for present purposes I will assume that such knowledge is possible.) I am sceptical, however, about some of the more ambitious claims that have been made about the extent of the moral knowledge that art can provide. In particular, I want to examine the suggestion, common in recent years, that works of art, particularly works of literature, are works of moral philosophy. The suggestion that works of art can provide the same sort of knowledge as moral philosophy is extremely dubious. No matter how similar art and philosophy may be qua forms of moral inquiry, some differences certainly exist. At the very least, it is hard to see how the arts can contribute to knowledge of meta-ethical matters. I cannot imagine how any illustrative demonstration could show that moral judgements have (or do not have) truth values. Still, it may seem that artworks and works of philosophy can both contribute to knowledge of normative ethics and that they do so in similar ways.

My views about the limitations on art's contributions to moral knowledge follow from more basic views about types of inquiry. Artworks cannot provide all of the knowledge that moral philosophy can because the arts and philosophy are fundamentally different sorts of inquiry. Rational demonstration is the principal mode of demonstration employed in philosophical inquiry. Moral philosophy, in particular, is essentially the attempt to argue for the truth of moral principles and the correctness of moral theories. (To say that moral theory is correct is just to say that it is composed of true principles.) I suggest that the only way to demonstrate a moral theory is by means of an argument, or rational demonstration. As we have seen, works of art provide illustrative demonstrations of perspectives. I have no doubt that they can show the rightness of perspectives on moral matters. The moral matters that can be illuminated by means of art are, however, specific moral problems and not general moral theories. In short, as sources of moral knowledge, works of art and works of moral philosophy differ in two fundamental respects. For a start, one provides illustrative demonstrations, the other rational demonstrations. As well, artworks can show that perspectives are right, while philosophy can show that moral theories are correct.

In fairness to those who maintain that works of literature can be works of moral philosophy, I should note that a particular conception of moral philosophy is presupposed in the previous paragraph. Moral philosophy, I wrote, is the search for general moral principles and theories. Not everyone accepts this conception of moral philosophy. Moral particularism is the view that this conception of philosophy is mistaken. On this view, the role of moral philosophy is to provide people with guidance about how to act when they find themselves facing specific moral challenges. This guidance is not provided, the moral particularist believes, by general moral principles or theories, applicable in all situations. Rather, the solutions provided by moral philosophy are specific to individual situations. I cannot here resolve questions about the nature of moral knowledge. I should, however, admit that if moral particularism is preferable to a more traditional conception of moral philosophy, the distinction that I find between literature and moral philosophy will be difficult to sustain.

I have already indicated that the difference between literature and moral philosophy corresponds to the more basic distinction between illustrative and rational demonstration. Even if one grants that artworks employ illustrative demonstrations and moral philosophy rational demonstrations, the difference between the two might not seem to be as marked as I have suggested. One might think that artworks, like philosophical essays, are still able to demonstrate the correctness of moral theories. In fact, however, artworks cannot show that moral laws are true or that moral theories are correct. The trouble is that there are limitations on what illustrative demonstrations, such as those found in literature, can show. They can show something about a particular object. (Here the word 'object' is used in a broad sense and applies to sets of objects and properties, including relational properties and types of objects.) An illustrative demonstration can, for example, show that some raven is black. An illustrative demonstration can also show that some perspective is right. An illustrative demonstration can put an audience in a position to see something from some perspective. Once audience members adopt this perspective, it can become clear to them that it is right. An illustrative demonstration cannot, however, show that some law or general principle is true.

An illustrative demonstration is possible when an object can be shown, directly or via a representation, to an audience. I can, for example, show that a raven is black only by producing the bird (or an illustration of the bird). Similarly, when one demonstrates that a perspective on some object is right, the object (or a representation of the object) is presented to the audience. A poem about a raven, for example, might demonstrate the correctness of the perspective that ravens are deeply misunderstood birds. Once the dependence of illustrative representation on the presentation or representation of objects is recognised, it is obvious why an illustrative demonstration cannot show that a law is true. A law is not an object. Rather, it is a generalisation about objects. Since laws are not objects, they cannot be shown to an audience.

Although an illustrative demonstration can show that some raven is black, it cannot show that *all* ravens are black. A series of illustrative demonstrations can reveal that certain ravens are black. Reports of these demonstrations must be marshalled in the form of an argument to demonstrate that all ravens are black. In short, an inductive argument is necessary. This point is perfectly general. Any general principle or law can only be demonstrated by means of an argument. The only demonstrations that can be given of scientific laws, for example, are inductive or abductive arguments. Moral laws are normative and not descriptive, but the demonstration of such a law must be provided by an argument. Like scientific laws, they are generalisations about objects (in this case, actions) and not objects. Consequently, literature, which can provide only illustrative demonstrations, cannot show that moral laws are true or that moral theories are correct.

In spite of everything I have said so far, it may seem that works of literature can have a great deal in common with works of moral philosophy. This is partly so because of the way examples are employed in moral philosophy. Moral philosophers often use little stories or examples. Consider again Plato's story of the borrowed knife in Book I of *The Republic*. Plato is attempting to develop a theory of justice and he tests one possible theory by means of this example. Cephalus suggests that justice is rendering to each person what is his own. Plato then, in effect, tells a little story about a madman who requests the return of a borrowed knife. Once Cephalus' theory is shown to have the consequence that a madman ought to be armed, it is shown to be incorrect. Plato seems to be doing something quite similar to what Sophocles does in *Oedipus at Colonus*. The playwright, like the philosopher, uses an example to make a moral point. Once we consider the story of Oedipus, we can see that people in his position ought not to be punished for their actions. *The Republic* and Dickens's *Hard Times* may seem to make similar contributions to moral knowledge. Dickens, like Plato, is apparently concerned with refuting a moral theory. In particular, Dickens sees himself as refuting a species of crude utilitarianism. He attempts to do so by providing a series of examples of how adherence to this principle has bad moral consequences.

Reflection on the examples of the previous paragraph might lead to the conclusion that literature and moral philosophy are more alike than I have suggested. The only real difference between the two may seem to be that the examples used in literature are developed in much more detail. This may lead some people to the conclusion that the work of moral philosophers (as distinct from that of poets, playwrights and novelists) is really just an inferior sort of literature. At any rate, one might feel that works of literature provide insights that moral philosophy, narrowly construed, cannot. A little reflection, however, reveals important distinctions between the ways in which examples are used by Plato, Mill and other moral philosophers, on the one hand, and by artists such as Sophocles and Dickens, on the other.

For a start, although both literature and moral philosophy make use of examples to make moral points, the examples are used in quite distinct ways. The examples in literature function as parts of illustrative demonstrations. They are used to direct an audience's attention to facts about some specific moral problem. That is, when works of literature use examples to provide moral knowledge, the examples provide a way of viewing and understanding some moral situation. In moral philosophy, on the other hand, examples are used as evidence for moral theories. That is, these examples are used in an effort to provide a rational demonstration of a moral theory. The theories are then used to address moral issues. A few examples will illustrate this distinction.

Sometimes examples are used to shed light on specific moral issues. When I was a boy, I frequently asked my mother for permission to engage in some activity in which boys ought not to engage. I would support my request for permission with the claim that all of my friends were allowed to engage in the activity (hang-gliding, perhaps, or big game hunting). My mother, a wise woman, would reply that the fact that my friends jumped off bridges would be a bad reason for permitting me to do so. My mother thus showed me (could I have but realised it) that I had not given good reasons for thinking that her permission ought to be forthcoming. Her example put me in a position to recognise that the fact that others did something did not prove that I ought to be given permission to do it. Although my mother's use of an example provided me with moral knowledge, it was not part of an argument and it did not provide knowledge of a general moral theory. It did not even present a general position on parental authority. The only knowledge on offer was knowledge about whether parental permission ought to be forthcoming in a specific type of situation.

When examples are used in works of literature to shed light on moral problems, they function in the way my mother's example did. They provide insight into moral problems without resulting in moral principles. Consider, for example, George Eliot's *Middlemarch*, a paradigm of a novel with moral implications. The example of Fred Vincy presents a perspective on the moral value of being self-supporting. The example of Casaubon and Dorothea is used to demonstrate (among other things) a perspective on attempts to control the lives of young people, particularly after one's death. The case of Lydgate is used to demonstrate the rightness of a perspective on the independence of scientists, and the importance of being seen to act rightly. In short, having read *Middlemarch*, sensitive readers have knowledge about how one ought to act and about how to evaluate the actions of others. This knowledge is a kind of practical knowledge, knowledge about how to act and how to look at moral situations. It is not knowledge of a moral theory. The examples in *Middlemarch* do not provide a general account of what makes actions right or wrong.

In order to see that this is the case, reflect that readers might grasp, for example, that people who act as Lydgate does are wrong, but not be in a position to articulate the principle behind this judgement. *Middlemarch* does not show us that Lydgate acts wrongly because his actions do not maximise utility. Neither does the novel demonstrate some deontological moral principle. Instead, it presents a perspective on a certain sort of moral situation. It puts audiences in a position to see that certain actions are right and others wrong. Readers can recognise that these actions are right or wrong without utilising a moral principle.

The example used in Wilfred Owen's poem, *Dulce et decorum est*, functions in a similar way. The poem shows that nothing is sweet and fitting about modern war. One does not need a moral theory to know that nothing is sweet and fitting about young men dying in gas attacks, coughing out their lungs. One just needs the right perspective on the situation. Incidentally, works of visual art can function in very much the same way. The example of the aerial bombing of a Spanish marketplace by fascists, provided by *Guernica*, functions in a similar way. The painting provides a way of looking at the incident. Once audiences look at the bombing from the perspective of *Guernica* they recognise immediately the evil of modern war and the targeting of civilian populations. The example is not used to support a moral theory. Again, one is not necessary.

Examples function quite differently in moral philosophy. Consider, for example, the sort of case used to argue against utilitarianism. In one classic example, terrible race riots and even bloodshed can be avoided if an innocent person is convicted on the basis of fabricated evidence. The utilitarian seems committed to the view that the person ought to be framed since doing so maximises utility. (At any rate, the utilitarian who thinks that each act must be calculated to maximise utility seems committed to this conclusion.) The example is designed to count against this form of consequentialism and play a role in an argument to the effect that some alternative moral theory is correct. In another classic example, Mill asks us to consider an excited mob outside the house of a corn dealer. While in general it is permissible to publish the view that corn dealers are robbers of the poor, one may not trumpet this view to the agitated crowd. Mill uses this example as part of an argument for a particular formulation of his principle of liberty, which specifies when one may interfere with another person's liberty. In general, examples in moral philosophy are used, not to cast light on individual moral problems, but to argue for a moral theory. Mill's example is not a poorly developed work of literature. Rather, it is functioning in a way completely unlike examples given in literature

The different uses which works of literature and philosophy make of examples reflect the different ways in which each contributes to moral knowledge. Moral philosophy can provide knowledge in two ways. At least as it is traditionally conceived, its primary role is to provide knowledge of moral theories. The theories can then be used to acquire knowledge about actual moral problems. The principles of a general moral theory state the conditions under which actions are right or wrong. Three main theories are current. Consequentialists hold that actions are right if they have better consequences than the alternatives. Kantians believe that right actions accord with moral laws. Finally, Hobbes-inspired contractarians maintain that action is right when it does not violate any of the provisions of a contract rational agents would negotiate. Whichever of these positions is correct, moral philosophy contributes to knowledge by providing arguments for a moral theory. Only indirectly, via moral theories, does moral philosophy contribute to knowledge of specific moral problems. Works of literature and other artworks, on the other hand, use examples to directly open up perspectives on specific moral problems.

It could be objected that some artworks function more like moral philosophy than I suggest they can. *Hard Times*, for example, might seem to be a work of literature that provides knowledge about moral theories. One might think that this novel shows that a species of utilitarianism is mistaken. In fact, whatever intentions Dickens may have had, it only provides knowledge about how to regard specific moral problems. In particular, it provides knowledge about the immorality of certain educational policies and the wrongness of coerced marriages. This is, however, the only moral knowledge the novel provides. One cannot learn from *Hard Times* that utilitarianism is less satisfactory than, say, contractarian theories of morality. No utilitarians would defend the practices of Gradgrind or think that any of Dickens's examples count against their theory. Having read *Hard Times*, a reader has no better idea about the theoretical justification of the claim that, say, coerced marriages are wrong. Such marriages could be wrong because they do not maximise utility, or because they violate the provisions of a contract rational agents would negotiate, or for some other reason. When one has the right perspective, one just sees that coerced marriages are wrong.

A work such as *Oedipus at Colonus* might also seem to count against my position. On my view, this play uses the example of Oedipus to put audiences in a position to understand certain moral situations. Once theatre-goers or readers occupy this position they can see that people like Oedipus, who perform bad actions through no fault of their own, ought not to be punished. One might think that audiences can also recognise the truth of a moral principle. According to this principle, information about what can rationally be foreseen is relevant in making moral judgements. In fact, however, the example of Oedipus is not used to argue for any such principle. Rather, the play uses the example to put audiences in a position to see the actions of Oedipus (and people like him) while bearing in mind that he could not rationally foresee the consequences of his actions. When Oedipus is seen from this perspective, audiences see that he ought not to be subjected to further punishment. In effect, the truth of a moral principle (people are not accountable for actions whose consequences they cannot reasonably foresee) is presupposed. Sophocles does not argue for it.

I conclude that works of art do not provide knowledge about the truth of moral principles or the correctness of moral theories. Even so, it is reasonable to suppose that artworks can provide insight into a variety of important matters. A couple of steps remain to be taken, however, before I can say with complete confidence that artworks can have considerable cognitive value. I need to consider several objections to my epistemology of art and show them to be unfounded. I need also to draw attention to some of the added bonuses of a satisfactory epistemology of art.

Replies to objections

My position is immune to many of the standard objections to the view that art has cognitive value, since these are directed against positions quite different from the one advanced here. In particular, objections to the propositional theory of art do not tell against my epistemology of art. Nevertheless, people might, for a variety of reasons, be sceptical about my claims. In the end, these reasons do not, either singly or in combination, undermine the epistemology of art offered in this essay, but this needs to be demonstrated. In this section I will focus on two particularly plausible objections.

The first objection to be considered may be called the *reliability objection*. Versions of this venerable objection can be traced back to Plato, the intellectual ancestor of everyone who is sceptical about the cognitive value of art. A work of art, on my view, can have cognitive value because it is a representation. On Plato's view, artworks are epistemologically suspect precisely because they are representations. According to Plato, artistic representations take us further from reality instead of closer to it. As a result, they are supposed to hinder rather than to assist the search for knowledge. An updated version of Plato's objection can easily be imagined. One could object that any interpretive or affective illustration might be misleading. When I considered (in the section 'Ways to knowledge' in Chapter 3, pp. 65–70) an illustrative demonstration of the colour of my pencil, attention was drawn to the pencil itself, not to a representation of the pencil. As a result, the audience was directly shown something about the pencil. In the same section, I used the example of showing what a *trompe-l'oeil* depicts. In this case, the audience could inspect the *trompe-l'oeil* and determine if the demonstration was right. In general, however, illustrations do not provide direct contact with the objects they represent. (Exemplars are a partial exception to this rule and the reliability objection would not be a serious worry for advocates of the exemplification hypothesis. Introspective affective illustrations may be another exception.) Since illustrations do not directly present objects, it might be thought, any illustrative demonstrations they provide are doubtful.

The reliability objection is genuinely worrisome. It is, perhaps, best understood as asking how we know that the perspective presented by a work of art is right (in the sense of rightness introduced in the section 'Ways to knowledge', above). Works of art can often be extremely compelling and audiences can be moved to believe that the perspectives they present are right when they are actually wrong. We can imagine, for example, a novel by a virulent

Nazi. The author of such a novel could employ many of the techniques of interpretive and affective illustration to present an anti-semitic perspective. Perhaps Jews are represented as engaging in rapacious behaviour. These representations may be calculated to arouse anger and indignation: they are affective illustrations. Perhaps exaggeration and the other techniques of interpretive illustration are similarly employed to present an anti-semitic perspective. Such a perspective is obviously mistaken, but a clever writer may be able to make such a perspective appealing to gullible audience members. Advocates of the reliability objection might take this to undermine the claim that art can have cognitive value in the way I suggest that it has. Perhaps, they may hold, we are no better off than those people who are misled by the imaginary Nazi. In short, the reliability objection claims that we cannot be sure that artistic illustrations present right perspectives, so such illustrations cannot demonstrate anything. The response I will make to the reliability objection can be gleaned from what has already been said, but the objection is a serious one and my earlier remarks should be repeated and amplified.

I should begin by admitting that one can be misled by a work of art. One can be persuaded that an artwork presents a right perspective, believe that one has acquired knowledge from it, but be mistaken. Sometimes works of art are deliberately misleading. In such cases they are propaganda or lies. They can also be inadvertently misleading, as when they are the product of incompetence. Works of art are not, however, the only potentially misleading representations. The representations found in works of science can also be misleading. One might easily read a scientific paper and come to believe that some theory is true. The paper might, nevertheless, be a nest of false data and utterly fail to demonstrate that the theory is correct. We ought not to conclude from this that science cannot provide rational demonstrations. The fact remains that scientific representations are sources of knowledge. Similarly, from the fact that works of art can be misleading, one should not conclude that they can never demonstrate the rightness of a perspective.

The representations employed in the arts are fallible but, like those employed in the sciences, testable. One should never unquestioningly accept that an artwork demonstrates that a perspective is right or that a scientific work demonstrates that a theory is correct. One decides whether a perspective is right, as one decides whether a theory is correct, by submitting it to empirical tests. A scientific theory makes certain predictions about the world. Before I believe the theory, I should check to see if these predictions are accurate. Alternatively, I can consult competent authorities who have checked the predictions. A work of art should be similarly tested. A work of art gives us a way of looking at the world. In order to test the work, we need to look at the world in this way. Audience members need to ask themselves whether the perspective provided by an artwork is supported by their past experience. They may need to seek additional experience before they can decide whether some perspective is right.

A couple of examples will illustrate how perspectives are tested. Jane Austen presents perspectives on first impressions and hypocritical toadies. Enthralled by her imaginative powers, I might uncritically believe that these perspectives are right. This would be a little like believing that some scientific theory is correct because a paper presents data in an accepted manner: they are arranged in neat tables, say. Rather than accepting that Jane Austen presents a correct perspective, I ought to look again at my experience. I should ask myself whether it accords with my experience and whether it helps me to make better sense of the phenomena than alternative perspectives. Jane Austen is a great artist and, more often than not, one can confirm that the perspectives presented in her art are right. By way of contrast, consider again the Nazi's novel. It presents the perspective that Jews are rapacious and untrustworthy. Obviously, one should not just accept that this perspective is right. It must be tested, and testing will reveal that experience does not support the perspective presented by such a novel. Audiences can also rely on others for assistance in the testing of artworks. Part of the critic's role is to test the perspectives presented by artists. The good critic functions rather like the peer reviewers employed by scientific journals.

Frequently, audiences do not need to acquire new experience before they can recognise that the perspective presented by an artwork is right. A good work of art can be convincing just because it enables audiences to reinterpret their past experience. Reading a book, listening to a cantata, or viewing a picture, something can click into place. The experience can be similar to the one people have when they are shown that some trick drawing can be seen as, say, a duck. Certainly, the two cases are somewhat dissimilar. When an artwork provides audiences with a perspective on an object, the object is generally not immediately present. Instead, audience members must usually rely on their memories. Nevertheless, just as people can directly see that a perspective on the drawing is right, audiences can immediately recognise that a perspective presented by an artwork is right. On other occasions, audience members may need to reflect carefully on their past experience before they can recognise that an artwork's perspective is right. In any case, an artwork will not enlighten audience members unless they have had a specific range of past experiences.

Having said this much about how artistic perspectives are shown to be right, another objection may seem to be suggested. The perspectives presented by artworks are shown to be right, not by the artwork, but by experiences that confirm the perspective. This being the case, someone might object that artworks are not, after all, a source of knowledge. The real source of knowledge may seem to be the experience that confirms that the artistic perspective is right. Two points should be made in response to this objection. The first is that, if the objection were right, parity of reasoning would require one to accept that works of science are never a source of knowledge. After all, scientific hypotheses are as much in need of empirical confirmation as any artwork. More importantly, works of art are a source of knowledge in the sense that, without them, a given right perspective may never have occurred to an audience. Works of art, like works of science, contribute to knowledge by interpreting experience. Experience and interpretation are both necessary conditions of knowledge.

The next objection to be considered starts from the claim that great works of art (that is, ones with a high degree of aesthetic value) may not have much cognitive value. I will refer to this as the *value objection*. One might argue that a work presenting a mistaken perspective cannot have much cognitive value. Suppose, for the sake of argument, that a Christian perspective on the world is mistaken. Suppose, that is, that one will tend to form false beliefs if one looks at the world as the product of a beneficent God, at humans as redeemed by God's sacrifice, and so on. On this supposition, works presenting a Christian perspective will not have much cognitive value. Nevertheless, it can scarcely be denied that many supremely great works of art present a Christian perspective on the world. Now, it might be objected, on my view a large part of the total value of an artwork is its cognitive value. A work with little cognitive value should have little total aesthetic value. The greatness of much Christian art is apparently a serious problem for my position. The rightness or wrongness of a work's perspective apparently can have little to do with its value as an artwork.

One could try to support the value objection by holding that works which present conflicting perspectives are both considered valuable. For example, both works of Christian art (Dostoyevsky's *Crime and Punishment*, say) and works presenting an atheist perspective (Butler's *Way of All Flesh*) can be valuable. One can easily think of other pairs of valuable artworks which present conflicting perspectives. Some artworks (*King Oedipus* is one) apparently try to demonstrate that humans cannot control their fates. William Henley, on the other hand, presents the perspective that

> I am the master of my fate,
>   I am the captain of my soul.

Two contrary perspectives cannot both be right. Consequently, works which present conflicting perspectives cannot both provide an illustrative demonstration of a perspective. After all, a wrong perspective cannot be demonstrated. Now, so the objection runs, even though two works present conflicting perspectives they can both be valuable. Apparently, the rightness of an artwork's perspective has little to do with its value.

I have several replies to the value objection. In the final analysis, my defence against the objection must be that artworks are seldom, if ever, great when they have little or no cognitive value. This defence requires a detailed discussion of great works of art. Obviously, I cannot here discuss even a representative sample of great artworks. Even in the absence of such a discussion, however, I can advance several reasons for thinking that the value objection is misguided. The full reply will not be made until the next chapter, where I discuss the evaluation of artworks, but a start can be made here.

My reply to the value objection begins with the reminder that I have explicitly stated (in 'Why art ought to have cognitive value' in Chapter 1, pp. 17–22) that I do not believe that the cognitive value of a work exhausts its value. At the very least, artworks can also have hedonic value. Two works might have equal total value, but differing amounts of cognitive value. Moreover, it might easily be the case that one artwork has more total value than another, but less cognitive value. Artworks which, since they present mistaken perspectives, have little cognitive value can still have a great deal of aesthetic value. All this said, I confess that I do not believe that a work of art will often be great when it has negligible cognitive value. Nor do I believe that two artworks presenting conflicting perspectives will often have equal aesthetic values. Something more must be said in reply to the value objection.

A little reflection will indicate that when a work of art has little cognitive value, we seldom regard it as a great artwork. Consider, for example, *The Importance of Being Earnest*. This play is certainly one of the most delightful comedies in the English language. Despite its enormous hedonic value, however, I do not think that it is a great work of art. (I would say that it has some cognitive value, just not very much. Oscar Wilde was an aesthete, in the narrow and derogatory sense of the term. He held that art has no cognitive value, but his own plays give him the lie since they are often the source of small but perceptive insights into social circumstances.) A little more reflection will indicate that artworks which present mistaken perspectives are seldom thought to be as good as works which present a right perspective. Consider, for example, Robert Heinlein's *Starship Troopers*. In this novel, young men and women defend earth from giant insects. It presents, and tries to demonstrate, the perspective that military service is an inherently ennobling experience and that veterans should rule society. *Starship Troopers* is a bad novel for lots of reasons, but part of what makes it so bad is that its perspective is seriously flawed. Remarque's *All Quiet on the Western Front* and Kubrik's *Full Metal Jacket* also treat military training and service. They are better works of art than Heinlein's partly because their perspectives are (more nearly, at least) right.

Perhaps the most important weakness of the value objection becomes apparent when we recognise that few, if any, perspectives are completely wrong. Consider again *Crime and Punishment*. I assume that this novel does not show that moral value is possible only given the existence of a beneficent God. Nor does it demonstrate that happiness depends on the forgiveness of such a God. On the hypothesis that Christianity is mistaken, these points cannot be demonstrated. Nevertheless, Dostoyevsky's work has considerable cognitive value. The story of Raskolnikov's murder of an old lady and its sequel is packed with moral and psychological insights. I would say that it shows that all persons have equal moral standing, that all persons are capable of evil and so on. Similarly, other works of Christian art can demonstrate the rightness of perspectives on mourning, redemption, forgiveness, charity and other matters. Consequently, even when, on the surface, a work seems to present a mistaken perspective, it will often transpire that the work succeeds in providing an illustrative demonstration of a right perspective.

Cognitive value and the experience of art

Let us turn now to the advantages of the epistemology of art presented in this essay. As I said at the outset of this chapter, I think that my views on art enable me to account for salient features of the experience of art, features that are otherwise inexplicable. The first of these features is the willingness of audiences to experience works of art that arouse in them unpleasant emotions such as fear and sadness. The second is the experience of some works of art as profound.

Writers on philosophy of art have long been puzzled by the so-called paradox of tragedy. This paradox arises from the fact that audiences are willing to view tragedies when they know the experience will be accompanied by sorrow, terror, anxiety and other unpleasant passions. Similarly, a debate has raged about why audiences willingly listen to performances of certain compositions when they report that the experience is distressing. The experience of certain works of visual art can be similarly upsetting. The fact that works of art are often experienced as being profound is also in need of explanation. If art is purely a source of pleasure, it is hard to see what is profound about it. Once one recognises that art is a source of knowledge, one can easily account for both of these features of the experience of art.

Let us consider first the apparent willingness to experience works of art when the experience is unpleasant. Obviously we have a serious puzzle here. If a sensible person willingly chooses to have an unpleasant experience, some explanation is needed. Two broad approaches to this puzzle are available: the *eliminativist* and the *compensatory*. On the eliminativist approach, people do not actually choose to have unpleasant experiences, even when they seem to do so. The eliminativist would hold, for example, that riding a roller coaster is not really terrifying, even if it seems to be. Rather, it is exhilarating. According to the compensatory approach, on the other hand, when people choose to have an unpleasant experience, they receive something that compensates them. The compensationist will not deny, for example, that people do lots of things that cause themselves pain. Even when they have a choice not to do so, they run marathons, climb mountains, attend faculty meetings and so on. Often they do so because they receive compensation. Distance running can, for example, improve one's health and provide a sense of accomplishment. (Why anyone would attend a faculty meeting is less clear.) The compensationist must hold that the benefits of choosing an unpleasant experience can reasonably be expected to outweigh the unpleasantness.

Hume is a classic example of an eliminativist. On his view, the painful emotions aroused by a tragedy are (rather mysteriously) converted into delightful sensations. As a result, the experience of tragedy is not really unpleasant and the fact that sensible people watch tragedies is not puzzling. A representative compensationist holds that audiences have two sorts of responses to tragedies: a direct and a meta-response. The direct response to a tragedy, on this view, is the unpleasant feeling of terror or sorrow. The meta-response is the satisfaction audiences feel when they realise they have the appropriate (direct) emotional response to the suffering of their fellows. The suggestion is that the feeling of satisfaction compensates audiences. It makes it worthwhile to experience the terror and sorrow.

The solution to the puzzle adopted here is a variety of the compensatory approach. The effort to demonstrate that the other solutions to our puzzle are unsatisfactory would take us far beyond the scope of this essay. Suffice it to say that all varieties of eliminativism are subject to a general objection: it does not accord with many people's experience of art. In the experience of many audience members, many artworks do evoke unpleasant emotions. (Though it must be said that the experience of *Othello* and the death of Desdemona is less harrowing than the experience of a real murder.) Compensatory solutions to the puzzle face no similar general objection. My proposal is that, when audiences choose to experience works which they know cause unpleasant emotions, they can be compensated with knowledge. The value of the knowledge gained can outweigh the disadvantages of the unpleasant emotions. If so, nothing is puzzling about the willingness of sensible people to view tragedies when they know unpleasant emotions will result. We already know that explorers and scientists will undergo considerable hardship for the sake of knowledge. Audiences in search of knowledge might do so as well.

In some cases, the painful emotions that accompany the experience of art are simply an undesirable epiphenomenon. In other cases, the knowledge we gain from a tragedy is intimately connected with the unpleasant experiences it evokes. This will be the case when the knowledge gained is knowledge of the evoked emotion. Sometimes we will have no convenient way to acquire some knowledge other than by experiencing works of art that evoke unpleasant emotions. If so, audience members would be wise to gain knowledge of unpleasant emotions by having them aroused by works of art rather than by placing themselves in unpleasant situations in ordinary life. For a start, as already noted, the experience will not be as unpleasant as it is when the similar emotions are evoked in the course of real life. As well, when emotions are experienced in an artistic context, audiences can focus on understanding the emotions. When faced with real tragedy, it will generally be the case that people are too overwhelmed to learn much. In general, audiences can reasonably expect to be compensated with insights when they willingly incur unpleasant emotions by experiencing works of art.

Turn now to the other feature of the experience of art which is in need of explanation. Some works of art are experienced as profound. *King Lear*, Bach's *St Matthew Passion* and Beethoven's late string quartets are examples of such works. *The Importance of Being Earnest*, on the other hand, is not experienced as profound. (Wilde's plays are profoundly amusing, but we are not concerned with the adjectival sense of 'profound'. Rather, we are concerned with a property artworks can possess.) I suggest that artworks can be profound only because they can have cognitive value. Not every artwork with cognitive value is profound, but only works with cognitive value can have this property. Before I can defend this claim, however, something must be said about the property of profundity.

Two sorts of profundity can be identified. The first sort of profundity is possessed by important matters. So, for example, love, death, human fulfilment, redemption, weakness of will, and self-sacrifice are often characterised as profound matters. Notice that a profound matter is not simply an important matter. Profound matters are important, but not all important matters are profound. Healthful exercise, for example, is important, but the need for healthful exercise is not a profound matter. As the term 'profound' is generally used, a profound matter is one that touches on essential aspects of the human condition. It has a moral or metaphysical component. The second sort of profundity is possessed by works (not just artworks) which are about profound matters. So, for example, works which take as their subjects love, death, human fulfilment and so on are potentially profound. Notice that the mere fact that a work is about a profound subject matter does not make it profound. Another condition, still to be identified, must also be met.

Given that profound works of art are about profound subjects, certain conceptions of art have difficulty explaining the profundity of art. Consider, for example, the view that artworks are not about anything and, consequently, not representational. On this view, the profundity of artworks is difficult to explain. The problem is particularly pressing for musical formalists. The musical formalist is a clear case of someone who believes that something can be an artwork, yet not about anything and a representation of nothing. Compositions are, on the formalist's view, simply pleasing patterns of sound. Musical formalists are not the only ones who have difficulty explaining the profundity of art. I will take them as a paradigm case, but, in general, if artworks are not about anything, it is difficult to see what makes them profound.

Formalists are not without a response to this line of argument. They could argue that works of art are about the possibilities afforded by an artistic medium. On this view, musical compositions, for example, are about the possibilities of sound. Works of literature would be about the ways in which words can meaningfully be combined, about narrative possibilities and so on. These possibilities are, one could hold, profound matters. If works of art are about them, artworks can be profound in the second sense of the term.

Unfortunately, for at least three reasons, this line of argument is not satisfactory. For a start, it is not clear that, for example, the possible structure of sound (or any other medium) is a profound matter. If it is not, then we already have a reason for rejecting the formalist's account of profundity. Suppose, however, that it is a profound matter. The formalist then faces another problem. This difficulty is that every musical composition is equally about the possibilities of sound. This is a difficulty since not all compositions are profound. As a result, the formalist cannot explain what makes some compositions profound while others are not. Even if this problem could be overcome, the formalist would still face another. As noted above, the mere fact that something is about a profound matter does not make it profound. Even if sonic possibility is a profound matter, it would not follow that music can be profound. An additional, as yet obscure, premiss would be required to reach this conclusion. The time has come to identify what other condition must be met if a work is to be profound.

My suggestion is that a profound work of art is not merely about profound matters. It also contributes to our knowledge of the profound matter that it is about. If I am right, a great deal can be explained. Consider, for example, Dickens's *Old Curiosity Shop*. This novel is about a variety of profound matters, among them death and filial piety, but it is not a profound work. (Recall Wilde's words: the man must have a heart of stone who can read of the death of Little Nell without laughing.) The novel is not profound because it does not deepen our understanding of the profound matters it addresses. On the contrary, it is almost comically misleading about the important matters it addresses. Similarly, a musical composition can represent, say, the experience of loss without being profound. It will fail to be profound if it is trite or cheaply sentimental and, consequently, fails to provide insight. By way of contrast, a work which contributes to understanding of a profound matter will count as a profound work.

If this is not the explanation of the profundity of some artworks, it is hard to see what the explanation could be. Certainly, the profundity of artworks is inexplicable if they only have hedonic value. Suppose, for example, that an audience can only receive pleasure from Beethoven's late quartets. A little reflection will show that, if this is the case, the works cannot be profound. William Boyce's charming but light-weight 8 *Favourite Symphonies* certainly provide a great deal of pleasure and (almost) nothing but pleasure. For all the pleasure they provide, no one would characterise Boyce's symphonies as profound. In general, things that only provide pleasure are not profound. One pleasure can be more intense than another. (That is, a pleasure can be, in the adjectival sense of the term, more profound than another.) Pleasures can also be more or less enduring, more or less likely to cloy and so on. Some pleasures engage the intellect, while others stimulate the senses. Pleasures, however, simply are not, in themselves, profound. As a result, the property of producing pleasure does not confer another property: the property of profundity. Consequently, if Beethoven's quartets only provide pleasure, they are not profound. They are profound, so they are a source of more than pleasure.

My epistemology of art has, then, some important and welcome consequences. The most important consequences are, however, yet to be reaped. In particular, my position makes it possible to avoid thorough-going relativism about artistic value. The claim that one work of art is better than another makes perfect sense. This advantage of my epistemology of art will be demonstrated in the next chapter. Another advantage of my position is that it can explain why so many people have misgivings about the value of much avant-garde art. The epistemology of art articulated here makes it possible to say with certainty that something has been deeply misguided about much of the art of the past century. I turn to this matter in Chapter 5.

4

EVALUATION OF ART

Relativism and aesthetic value

In Chapter 1, I argued that an artworld ought to define art responsibly. That is, an artworld should accept as artworks only objects which perform some valuable function or functions. Once an artworld establishes the functions of art, questions about the evaluation of art can be posed. The good works will perform the assigned functions well and the poor ones will do so badly. Suppose, for example, an artworld decides that the sole function of art is to provide pleasure. Good artworks will, then, provide a great deal of pleasure, while poor ones will produce very little. (Items that provide no pleasure at all will not be artworks.) An artworld might, however, decide that artworks have a cognitive function. In this case, we get a different answer to questions about what makes art valuable. The short answer is that good artworks are (among other things, perhaps) a source of important knowledge, while bad ones contribute little to knowledge. This chapter provides the long answer. It also indicates how an epistemology of art makes it possible to avoid thorough-going relativism about aesthetic value.

This chapter is divided into three sections. This section demonstrates that, if art is only a source of pleasure, we are condemned to a debilitating relativism about aesthetic value. On the other hand, if art has a cognitive function, some limits can be placed on relativism about aesthetic value. The extent and limits of aesthetic relativism are discussed in the next section. 'Criteria of evaluation' is devoted to stating a few general criteria of aesthetic value.

If aesthetic cognitivism can restrict the scope of relativism about aesthetic value, this is a point in its favour. (When I speak of aesthetic value, I mean the value that something has qua work of art. On my view, this will be the sum of an artwork's hedonic and cognitive value.) I do not believe that judgements about aesthetic value are completely objective. Something is right about the view that *de gustibus non est disputandum*. Nevertheless, almost everyone believes that not every aesthetic judgement is as good as any other. Some artworks are better than others, and some aesthetic judgements are false. (By 'aesthetic judgement', I mean a judgement about the aesthetic value of an artwork.) Milton really is a better poet than Ogilvy, Bach's works are greater than those of Fux, and Jane Austen's novels are superior to Barbara Cartland's. The epistemology of art offered in this essay makes it possible to capture the kernel of truth in aesthetic relativism. At the same time, it can preserve the intuition that this relativism is not thorough-going and that some aesthetic judgements are objectively false. The view that art is simply a source of pleasure, in contrast, is condemned to radical relativism.

We should begin by analysing what is meant, in this context, by talk of relativism. Aesthetic relativism can be formulated in either semantic or ontological terms. However it is formulated, aesthetic relativism is best understood in opposition to aesthetic realism. Let us begin by providing semantic formulations of these positions. According to aesthetic realism, any sentence expressing a judgement about the value of an artwork is true if and only if the artwork possesses certain objective properties. An objective property is one an artwork possesses independently of an audience. The aesthetic realist holds that if a work of art possesses these properties, then not only is the judgement true, but any contrary sentence is false. Furthermore, the aesthetic realist is committed to the claim that the truth values of aesthetic judgements about some work are completely independent of an audience's beliefs and feelings about the work. Aesthetic relativism, on the other hand, is the view that the truth values of judgements about aesthetic value are not determined by the objective features of artworks. Instead, the truth values of such judgements depend, at least in part, on the audiences who make the judgements. A consequence of aesthetic relativism is that two contrary judgements about the value of an artwork can both be true. One judgement can be true relative to some audience members, while a contrary judgement is true relative to others.

Aesthetic relativism and realism can also be formulated as metaphysical theses about the ontological status of aesthetic value. We might be tempted to say that aesthetic value exists only in the mind of the beholder, but this would be a mistake according to realists. They believe that aesthetic value is objective. To say that aesthetic value is objective is to say that artworks can have value independently of whether anyone recognises that they have. According to the realist, objective facts about aesthetic value then determine the truth values of aesthetic judgements. Aesthetic relativists, on the other hand, deny that artworks have objective value. They hold that the value of an artwork depends, to some extent, on the audience which experiences it. In particular, the value of an artwork is determined, at least in part, by the beliefs and preferences of audience members.

As a result, some work may have a given degree of aesthetic value relative to one audience, and a different value relative to another.

The most plausible ontological formulation of aesthetic realism holds that aesthetic value is the result of a capacity which artworks have to affect audiences. The possession of this capacity is supposed to be an objective fact. To treat aesthetic value in this way is to suggest that it is rather like one of Locke's secondary qualities. On Locke's view, secondary qualities (such as colours) supervene on primary qualities (such as extension). That is, redness, for example, exists in an object only because the object's primary qualities can cause in the mind sensations of red. Aesthetic realists can similarly hold that when an artwork has certain primary qualities, it is able to create aesthetic experiences in audiences. Perhaps the analogy between aesthetic value and pain is even closer. No pain is in the needle that pricks a finger, but the needle is still objectively capable of causing the experience of pain. Similarly, the realist will hold, an artwork with aesthetic value has the objective capacity to cause, say, aesthetic pleasure.

Aesthetic relativism can be either modest or thorough-going (or, as I will sometimes say, radical). The thorough-going relativist believes that the aesthetic values of artworks depend entirely on the beliefs and interests of audience members. Alternatively, thorough-going relativism can be characterised as the view that the truth values of aesthetic judgements depend entirely on audience members. Radical relativism entails that any aesthetic judgement is as good as any other. On this view, audience members cannot make mistakes about the aesthetic values of artworks. Each audience member is ideally positioned to determine the value an artwork has for him. Thorough-going relativism is unable to preserve the intuition that, independently of what anyone may believe, the works of Milton and Bach are greater than those of Ogilvy and Fux. According to modest relativism, the aesthetic values of artworks depend only partly on the beliefs and interests of audience members. The values of artworks also depend, in part, on facts about the works. Consequently, not every aesthetic judgement is as good as any other and aesthetic judgements can be false.

When aesthetic relativism and realism are understood in these terms, it is easy to see how to decide which of them is correct. The correct position is the one with the better account of disagreement about the aesthetic values of artworks. According to realists, when audience members differ about the aesthetic value of an artwork, at least one of them is mistaken. Relativists, on the other hand, need not hold that when audience members disagree about the value of an artwork it entails that a mistake has been made. They can hold, on the contrary, that each of the audience members is right. The work has one value relative to one of the audience members, and another value relative to the other.

The problem realists face is that an artwork can have different effects on two (or more) audience members. This difference in effects is attributable to differences between the audience members. In particular, the effect an artwork has on people is influenced by their beliefs, abilities and interests. Apparently, then, when people make judgements about the value of artworks, they are not in a position to judge anything objective. A person's aesthetic judgements seem to be about the effects artworks have on him. If this is the case, conflicting aesthetic judgements are explained by the fact that people are making judgements about different things. If so, radical relativism is correct. Aesthetic realists are aware that artworks have different effects on different people. They do not believe, however, that this fact undermines their position. They typically hold that some audience members are more qualified than others. The fact that blind people cannot detect the colour of some object is not taken as evidence that some object is not objectively, say, red. Similarly, realists will urge, the fact that philistines cannot tell that an artwork is excellent is not evidence that the work is not objectively excellent. The fact is, realists believe, that the philistines are mistaken.

I see no way to avoid some measure of relativism about aesthetic value. This is because there is a profound disanalogy between secondary qualities such as colours and aesthetic value. Something is, say, teal, because it has some objective (primary) qualities. The colour of an object is an objective fact, about which people can be mistaken. Even if an object does not appear teal to an audience, it is nonetheless teal. Aesthetic value, in contrast, is not objective. Aesthetic value is a species of extrinsic value. Something is extrinsically valuable because of what it can do for someone. In particular, an artwork is extrinsically valuable because of certain effects it has on an audience. If an artwork is unable to have these effects on a person, then it has no value for him. Facts about whether an artwork is aesthetically valuable are not independent of the effects that the work can have on audience members. Given that artworks can have different effects on different people, the value of artworks is relative to individuals. Some limits can, however, be placed on relativism if art has a cognitive function. There are some cases where it is possible to say that audience members have made mistakes about an artwork.

If, however, art has only hedonic value, we are condemned to a thorough-going relativism about aesthetic value. If art is valuable only as a source of pleasure, there is only one way for people to evaluate the aesthetic value of an artwork. They can examine the work and note how much pleasure they receive from it, qua artwork. (This may not be the only pleasure they receive. The owner of an artwork may, for example, receive pleasure from the reflection that it is a sound investment.) Pleasure is a subjective state and audience members are the best judges of the degree of pleasure they experience when they contemplate some artwork. This subjectivity of pleasure leads to radical relativism. Frequently, two audience members experience different degrees of pleasure when contemplating the same artwork. One reader, for example, receives a great deal of pleasure from the works of Barbara Cartland, but little from reading Jane Austen. Another reader delights in Austen, but is not at all pleased by Cartland. If the sole function of art is to provide pleasure, and the more pleasure a work affords the better it is, then radical relativism is unavoidable. Relative to the first reader, Cartland's novels are better than Austen's. Relative to the second reader, Austen's novels are better than Cartland's.

One could try to limit this relativism while still holding that art has only a hedonic function. Defenders of a hedonic conception of art could hold that an artwork is better than another if it provides more pleasure to its audience than the other provides for its audience. They could then claim that, say, Jane Austen's novels give her admirers more pleasure than Barbara Cartland's novels give to her fans. They would conclude that Austen's novels are better than Cartland's. This argument is suspect for more than one reason. For a start, one of the premisses is extremely dubious. Cartland's devotees apparently receive a great deal of pleasure from her books. In fact, it is far from obvious that Austen's admirers receive more pleasure from her novels than Cartland-lovers receive from her books. Even apart from this questionable premiss the argument is unsuccessful. Grant for the moment that Austen's devotees received more pleasure from their favoured author than Cartland's fans receive from theirs. The fact remains that Cartland-lovers receive more pleasure from Cartland's novels than they do from Austen's. For them, Cartland's novels are better. Consequently, we are left with radical relativism about aesthetic value.

Advocates of a hedonic conception of art could try to avoid radical relativism by arguing that some audience members are better qualified than others. One could hold, for example, that admirers of Jane Austen have a fineness of discernment greater than that possessed by Barbara Cartland's fans. As a result, the Austen-lovers are able to detect features of, say, *Pride and Prejudice* that elude the Cartland-lovers. Grant that this is so. Perhaps the finely discerning admirers of Austen can even bring the dull Cartland fans to notice the features of *Pride and Prejudice* they have overlooked. If so, they too will experience pleasure when reading it. On this view, Austen's novels really are a source of pleasure. The Cartland-lovers simply do not recognise that this is the case. Consequently, the judgement that a Cartland novel is better than one of Austen's is false. The contradictory judgement seems true only to those who are not able to recognise the truth.

This argument is unsuccessful even if its premisses are granted. Even if the lovers of Jane Austen's novels notice features overlooked by the fans of Barbara Cartland and even if the fans of Cartland can be brought to appreciate these features, we are left with radical relativism. Whether they are less perceptive than Austen's admirers or not, the Cartland-lovers still experience more pleasure when reading her books than they do when they are reading Austen. Consequently, if the novels have only hedonic value, Cartland's novels have more value, relative to the Cartland lovers. Even if the Cartland-lovers come to receive pleasure from Austen's novels, radical relativism is left intact. The fact that Cartland's novels are more valuable for Cartland-lovers remains even if some of the Cartland-lovers become fans of Austen. We are left with the conclusion that, if art has only hedonic value, the value of any artwork is completely relative to individual audience members.

If, however, art has cognitive value, limits can be placed on aesthetic relativism. This is the case because of an important difference between knowledge and pleasure. Pleasure is a purely subjective state of mind. As a result, individuals cannot be mistaken about the amount of pleasure they receive from any object. Suppose I contemplate some object and receive no pleasure. When this is the case, it makes no sense to say that the object has value for me as a source of pleasure. Knowledge differs from pleasure in this respect. Something can be a source of knowledge for me, even though I do not recognise that it is. An artwork might even present a valuable perspective, one capable of enhancing knowledge, even though no one recognises that it does. Something has cognitive value when an audience is able to receive knowledge from it. The aesthetic value of artworks is partly, at least, cognitive value. Consequently, whether a work of art has aesthetic value is, if not an objective matter, at least more than a matter of subjective feeling.

An analogy and an example will illustrate how the evaluation of an artwork's cognitive value is not completely subjective. We can draw an analogy between the function of a tool and the cognitive function of art. Imagine that an audience is presented with a tool with which it is unfamiliar. Audience members may or may not find the tool a source of pleasure. In any case, each member will be able to tell, just by contemplating it, whether it is, for him, a source of pleasure. If it seems to be a source of pleasure for a person, it has hedonic value for him. If another person takes no pleasure in the contemplation of the tool, it has no hedonic value for him. Just by looking at the tool, however, people may not be able to tell whether it is able effectively to perform some function other than that of being pleasing. Similarly, a person can inspect an artwork and his feelings will tell him whether it is, for him, a source of pleasure. The person's feelings will not, however, be equally illuminating about whether the artwork can effectively perform a cognitive function. *Pride and Prejudice*, for example, demonstrates the rightness of valuable perspectives on aspects of human experience. Still, someone might read the novel and not recognise that it does. Such a failure to perceive that

Jane Austen's masterpiece has cognitive value does not entail that the work has no cognitive value. Facts about cognitive value are not as dependent on audiences as are facts about hedonic value.

Even if artworks have cognitive value, the value of an artwork is partially relative to audiences. This is the case since part of the value of an artwork usually is hedonic value. Even the cognitive value of artworks is, however, partly relative to audiences. This modest relativism is a consequence of several factors. Among these is the fact that some perspectives on the world are more valuable for some people than they are for others. Again, an analogy to a tool can help us to see how this can be the case. A particular tool, say a tuning hammer for a harpsichord, is capable of performing some function whether or not anyone recognises that it is. Consequently, when it is evaluated for its capacity to perform this function, the evaluation is not completely relative to an audience's perception. There are objective facts about whether it fits snugly over the tuning pins, has a handle which is comfortably gripped, and so on. If it does fit snugly over the pins and so on, the tuning hammer is valuable. Nevertheless, the tool is more valuable to people who have harpsichords to tune than it is to those who do not. Precisely the same point can be made about artworks. Their capacity to demonstrate a perspective does not depend on the subjective recognition that they can. Still, the value of an artwork depends on the value of the perspective to some audience.

A number of factors will influence an audience's appraisal of the cognitive value of artworks. I will consider three factors that affect aesthetic judgements. The first factor is an audience's ability to comprehend artworks. Audiences who do not understand an artwork will, in general, find it less valuable than audiences who do. The second factor was identified in the previous paragraph: the interests and concerns of audiences. Since all audience members have their own particular concerns and interests, certain perspectives are more valuable to some people than they are to others. Some audience members find certain questions pressing, while others find them unimportant. Audience members are likely to value more highly works which present perspectives on questions of concern to them. Originality is the third factor that affects an audience's evaluation of artworks. All other things being equal, works which offer novel perspectives are more valuable than works that do not.

Each of the factors just identified affects the aesthetic judgements audiences make, and leads to differences of opinion about the value of artworks. The mere fact that these factors are at work does not, however, force us to accept the radical relativity of aesthetic value. When we consider each factor and how it leads to differences of opinion, we have a choice. The first option is to claim that the factor leads audiences to make errors about the aesthetic values of works. The alternative is to claim that a fact affects how much value a work of art has for a particular audience member. If we always opted for the second alternative, we would be left with radical relativism. If we believe that artworks have cognitive value, we can and should frequently take the first option. Only modest relativism results.

The extent of aesthetic relativism

The first factor to be considered is an audience's capacity to understand works of art. To understand a work is to be able to interpret it. Two conditions are satisfied when an audience member understands an artwork. For a start, the audience member is able to recognise what the work represents. The audience member must also grasp what the work testifies about the object or grasp the perspective the work presents on the object. The extent to which an audience understands an artwork will affect its views about the work's aesthetic value. Differences of opinion about aesthetic values which result from a failure to understand a work are not evidence of the radical relativity of value. Indeed, such differences of opinion are not even evidence for modest relativism.

It is easy to see how a failure to understand an artwork can lead audiences to make false judgements about its aesthetic value. If people do not understand a work and do not grasp the perspective it presents, they are unlikely to give a high estimate of its aesthetic value. In spite of this negative judgement, the work may still effectively present an important and original perspective. If it does, the judgement that it has little aesthetic value is mistaken. An analogy between artworks and scientific theories will illustrate how a failure to understand a work leads to error, not to the relativity of value. Imagine that someone fails to understand a scientific theory, while another understands it perfectly. These two people will likely differ about the scientific value of the theory. Faced with the disagreement between them, we would not conclude that the value of the theory is relative to individuals. In spite of the first person's low estimate of the theory's value, it may be extremely valuable. That is, it may enable us to make accurate predictions, explain phenomena and so on. Similarly, a failure to understand an artwork results in a false aesthetic judgement, not in the relativity of value.

A couple of examples will illustrate how failure to understand an artwork can lead to error. One of my friends once read Jane Austen's *Northanger Abbey* without realising that it is a burlesque of Gothic novels. He was quite disappointed by the book and ranked its aesthetic value quite low. Although *Northanger Abbey* is far from being Jane Austen's best novel, my friend's judgement was false. Austen's early novel presents a useful perspective on Gothic romances and the follies of some of their readers. Although someone who is unaware that it is a burlesque will be unaware of this perspective, it is still presented. A mistake I once made will illustrate a similar point. Until recently I was almost completely ignorant about baroque dance and I was inclined to think that it had little aesthetic value. I thought that it was just an amusement for courtiers. Someone who is familiar with the significance of the gestures and steps of baroque dance, on the other hand, knows that it can be a vital and expressive artform. The difference of opinion between me and a person with knowledge of baroque dance should not lead us to be relativists. My judgement about the aesthetic value of, say, a ballet from Lully's *Atys* is simply false. Similar errors arise when critics are exposed for the first time to artworks from alien cultures. Their aesthetic judgements will conflict with those of non-aliens, but this is not an indication that aesthetic value is relative. Rather, when people are ignorant of the artistic styles of some culture, they are unable accurately to estimate the aesthetic values of its artworks.

The second factor affecting aesthetic judgements is a source of a measure of relativism. The aesthetic values of artworks depend, in part, on the interests of critics. This sort of relativity permeates all aspects of life. Two people may agree, for example, that if a bridge is constructed from an island to the mainland, it will effectively perform some function. It will facilitate ease of travel, say, and lead to an influx of tourists. Nevertheless, two people may differ about the value of the bridge. The restaurateur believes that the bridge is valuable, while the poet believes that it is worse than worthless. Similarly, two audience members can understand an artwork, and agree on what it accomplishes, but disagree about whether the work is valuable. Like poets and restaurateurs, audiences have conflicting interests and concerns. These can affect the values works of art have for individual audience members.

When I speak of the interests and concerns affecting the aesthetic judgements audiences make, I have several things in mind. Of these, two are most important. For a start, one can be interested in something in the sense of thinking it important or being curious about it. An interest, in the second sense, is a stake one has in something. One can have an interest, in this second sense, that results from one's needs (an interest in good nutrition, for example) or from one's beliefs (an interest in the success of a political party, say).

In general, one's interests (in both senses) influence what one thinks valuable. People will value something that gives them insight into a matter they are curious about. They will also value whatever promotes that which they need or, as a result of their beliefs, want. This general point applies to artworks. The value an artwork has for the members of a given audience is influenced by their interests. Some audience member may have an interest in understanding some matter, while another does not. In such a case, an artwork which presents a perspective on the matter will have different values for each of the audience members.

Although the interests of audiences will affect the degree of value which artworks have for them, we should not be radically relativist about aesthetic value. Audiences can make mistakes about the aesthetic values of artworks, and (at least sometimes) audiences have shared reference points against which to measure aesthetic judgements. In order to see that this is the case, we need to establish two points. The first is that people can have interests of which they are unaware. I will call such an interest an *objective interest*. Given that audiences have given objective interests, artworks can have some degree of aesthetic value for them, whether they know it or not. The second point is that audiences can have shared objective interests that provide a touch point against which aesthetic judgements can be measured.

An analogy will indicate how people can have objective interests and how the existence of such interests can undermine radical relativism. Some people may have a low estimate of the value of a scientific theory. Nevertheless, given their objective interests, the theory may have value for them. I might, for example, have a low estimate of the theory which states that aerobic exercise promotes good health. I may even believe that exercise has a deleterious effect on health. Nevertheless, given that I have an interest in living a long and healthy life, I have an interest in possessing the information the theory presents. My interest in having this knowledge is objective, since I would benefit from possessing it, regardless of whether I think so. Consequently, the theory has value for me, whether I know it or not. If artworks have cognitive value, they can similarly have value for people independently of their knowledge that the works have value.

An artwork can present a right perspective on some matter about which I am not curious. I may still have an objective interest in knowing about this matter. Under such circumstances, I might judge that the work has little value. In view of my objective interests, such a judgement would be mistaken. Regardless of what I think, the work can have a great deal of value. In general, if audiences have certain objective interests, and artworks can serve those interests, artworks can have aesthetic value independently of the beliefs of audience members. An audience frequently has an objective interest in possessing knowledge that an artwork can provide. Consequently, artworks can have value, in part at least, independently of the beliefs of individuals. If an artwork can have value independently of the beliefs of audience members, radical aesthetic relativism is incorrect.

Although radical relativism is mistaken, sometimes an audience's interests do lead to the relativity of aesthetic value. This is the case since not all interests are shared by all audience members. Members of different societies, for example, often have different interests. This helps explain how the critical opinion of certain artists can change over time. Kipling, for example, is seldom any longer regarded as a writer of the first rank. His works have a lower value for contemporary audiences, in part, at least, because they do not share the same interests and concerns as Kipling's original audience. Kipling addressed, and helped his contemporaries to understand, a number of matters that, since the sun has set on the British Empire, are no longer of much concern. A similar point could be made about some of Orwell's novels. *Animal Farm* is, in large part, concerned with the dangers of Stalinism. As the threat of Stalinism has abated, audiences have less interest in artworks that help them understand it. Consequently, such works will have less value for them. In general, artworks concerned with transient political matters will be less valuable once the problems they address are no longer pressing.

Some interests are both universal and objective and this makes it possible to explain why some artworks are almost universally valued. One of the marks of a supremely valuable work of art is that it addresses matters that serve everyone's objective interests. Every artwork reflects the interests of the artist who produced it as well as the concerns of the artist's community. Some artworks, however, transcend their time and present perspectives on matters of concern to all communities. The plays of Shakespeare spring to mind as obvious examples of such works. They have been found valuable by every age and nation. They will remain valuable for as long as jealousy, avarice, indecision, and other passions which the Bard addresses are met with in human experience and audiences have an interest in understanding them. Similarly, *Pride and Prejudice* will remain valuable for the foreseeable future. The judgement that it is a valuable novel will remain true so long as people have an objective interest in knowing that first impressions are a poor guide to character, that inflexible pride is a failing, and so on.

The third factor affecting audiences' estimates of aesthetic value remains to be considered. Judgements about the value of an artwork are influenced by the degree to which an audience finds the work original. Some audience members may find that an artwork is *passé* and adds little to what other artworks have already achieved. Consequently, the work may have little cognitive value for them. Other audience members may find the same artwork original. For them, it may have considerable value. The freshness that some artwork has for audiences is largely a function of their familiarity with the history of art. (Some audiences may lack a familiarity with some part of the history of art simply because it has not yet occurred.) Given that audience members are familiar with different sets of artworks, it is not surprising that an artwork will seem original to one and stale to another. Nor is it surprising that this will affect the aesthetic judgements audience members make. We should not conclude from this that the values of artworks are radically relative to audiences.

An example will illustrate how the perceived originality of an artwork can affect the work's aesthetic value. Perspective drawing first became common in the fifteenth century. The ability to draw in perspective was a technical development, but the use of this technique also presented a perspective on the world. Simply by employing the new technique, paintings or drawings could present the view that the world is intelligible to humans. At first, the use of perspective in some work of art would have struck the audience as original and exciting. As a result, works drawn in perspective could have a great deal of aesthetic value for early audiences. The mere use of perspective was not enough, however, to make artworks valuable to later audiences. Once audiences had become familiar with the use of perspective, certain works could lose some of their value. (Of course, early examples of perspective would retain all of their historical value. As it happens, many of the first experiments in perspective remain supremely great works of art.)

The perceived originality of artworks introduces a measure of aesthetic relativism, but the extent of this relativism should not be exaggerated. A work could easily be perceived to be original, judged to be highly valuable on this basis, but not have much value. A mathematical example will illustrate this sort of situation. A mathematician may develop a proof for some theorem, not knowing that the proof has already been given. Believing that the proof is original, someone may easily judge that the mathematician's work has a high degree of mathematical value. In fact, of course, the mathematician's result has almost no mathematical value. The value of the proof depends, in large part, on the extent to which it advances mathematical knowledge. Little of its value is owed to the degree to which it appears to someone to advance mathematical knowledge. Art, like mathematics, has cognitive value and a similar point can be made about the value of artworks. The value of an artwork, like the value of a proof, is a function of the extent to which it makes a novel contribution to human understanding. An artwork's value is not a function of the degree to which it seems to do so.

We are now in a position to see why Milton's poems have more value than Ogilvy's, why Bach is a greater composer than Fux, and why Barbara Cartland bears no comparison with Jane Austen. Some artworks are, independently of whether people think that they are, valuable sources of knowledge. Austen, Bach, Milton and other great artists create works of art that contribute to human knowledge. Their works, unlike those of lesser artists, can importantly serve our objective interest in gaining an understanding of important matters. The perspectives presented by other artists are not as valuable, and their works pale by comparison. On the other hand, as we have seen, sometimes judgements about aesthetic value are true only relative to the audiences who make them.

Criteria of evaluation

The evaluation or criticism of any work of art is a complex and difficult undertaking. The process of evaluation is complicated by the fact that art has a hedonic function besides a cognitive one. Even if we ignore art's hedonic function, as I will, evaluation is a complicated matter. Since art criticism is so complex, philosophers can make only a modest contribution to questions about the values of artworks. Philosophy deals with general principles, but the evaluation of artworks is not simply a matter of applying general principles. Familiarity with a particular artform, its history and its techniques will often be of more use than philosophical principles in determining the value of an artwork. Nevertheless, philosophers can provide a few generally applicable criteria of aesthetic value. Most generally, good works of art are sources of valuable knowledge. At a bare minimum, they present right perspectives. More particularly, a few general points can be made about the ways in which good artworks are sources of knowledge.

The most basic criterion of aesthetic value is stated in the *cognitive value principle*. This principle states that works of art with a high degree of aesthetic value can contribute importantly to the knowledge of an audience. (Notice that the principle states what a highly valuable artwork can do, not what it does. Whether a highly valuable artwork actually contributes to knowledge depends, in part, on its audience.) A defence of the cognitive value principle has two parts. The first part of the defence is an argument for the claim that part of the aesthetic value of an artwork is its cognitive value. The second part of the defence argues that only works with a high degree of cognitive value have a high degree of total aesthetic value. The first part of the defence of the cognitive value principle has been provided in Chapters 2 and 3. As we have seen, works of art can convey illustrative testimony and, most importantly, provide illustrative demonstrations of right perspectives. A right perspective assists audiences in acquiring knowledge, while a wrong perspective does not. Something that aids the acquisition of knowledge is valuable. To say that something is valuable is to say that it serves peoples' interests and people certainly have an interest in knowledge. Consequently, artworks can be valuable in so far as they assist in the acquisition of knowledge. The cognitive value of an artwork will be proportional to the value of the knowledge it makes available.

For the second part of the defence of the cognitive value principle, we must think back to the section 'Why art ought to have cognitive value' in Chapter 1 (pp. 17–22). There we noted that humans have a particularly strong interest in the acquisition of knowledge: it is both an intrinsic and an extrinsic good. Certainly, we also have an interest in pleasure and artworks that can provide it have hedonic

126

value. Nevertheless, as I indicated in that section, only works of art that are important sources of knowledge will have a high total aesthetic value. The arts are more valuable as sources of knowledge than they are as sources of pleasure. This is because our interest in understanding matters such as ourselves, our emotions and our relations to each other is so strong. Moreover, although we have sources of pleasure besides the arts, the arts are the only source of some particularly valuable knowledge. Consequently, only those artworks which have cognitive value will have a high degree of aesthetic value. That is, the cognitive value principle is true. This conclusion is confirmed by reflection on the values typically assigned to representative artworks. A work such as *The Importance of Being Earnest*, which is primarily a source of hedonic value, is generally not thought to have a high degree of aesthetic value. Certainly, it has a lower degree of aesthetic value than a work, such as *Pride and Prejudice*, with high degrees of both hedonic and cognitive value.

Other general principles which state criteria of aesthetic value can be inferred from facts about how artworks represent and demonstrate perspectives. Here I will identify three such principles. The first of these can be inferred from the fact that representation in the arts is illustrative representation. Good art will take advantage of the resources afforded by illustrative representation. Good artworks will not be attempts to make statements, a function best performed by means of languages. Another criterion of good art can be deduced from a conclusion reached in the section 'What can be learned from art?' in Chapter 3 (pp. 94–104). There we saw that certain subjects can be effectively investigated by means of art and illustrative demonstration while other matters are suited to scientific investigation. Good works of art will investigate the former. Finally, and most basically, a (third) criterion can be inferred from the fact that artworks have cognitive value only if they affect audiences in a certain way. They can do this only if audiences are able to interpret or understand works. This point leads to the conclusion that good works of art are interpretable. Audiences can grasp what the work demonstrates.

We will find that the three principles just identified state necessary but not sufficient conditions of artistic excellence. A work of art with a high degree of aesthetic value will be interpretable, employ illustrative representation and so on. Nevertheless, an artwork can be interpretable, say, but have very little aesthetic value. Perhaps the work is interpretable, but it presents a wrong or trivial perspective. If so, the artwork likely has little aesthetic value. Still, an artwork cannot have a high degree of aesthetic value if it is uninterpretable. In general, very few sufficient conditions of aesthetic value can be stated. (The cognitive value principle is an exception to the rule.)

Let us begin by considering the suggestion that interpretability is a criterion of artistic excellence. I will call this the *interpretability principle*. In part, this principle follows from the definition of representation given in the section 'What is representation?' in Chapter 2 (pp. 23–5). One of the conditions established by this definition is the recognition condition: something is a representation only if audiences can recognise what is represented. To say that audiences can recognise what is represented is to say that they can (to some extent) interpret the work. Artworks have cognitive (and aesthetic) value qua representations but can only have this value if audiences can interpret them. Consequently, the interpretability principle follows from the fact that artworks have value qua representations.

The interpretability principle is also supported by reflection on the type of representation found in artworks. Artistic representations primarily have cognitive value in so far as they can provide illustrative demonstrations. Such demonstrations are able to put audiences in a position to recognise the rightness of a perspective. A successful illustrative demonstration is adapted to the capacities of audiences, while an unsuccessful one is not. Consider the following example of an unsuccessful illustrative demonstration. I might attempt to demonstrate what cows look like by pointing to an animal on the other side of a fence. If my audience is a child and unable to see over the fence, my demonstration is unsuccessful. A work of art can similarly be unsuccessful, that is, have little aesthetic value, when audiences cannot interpret it. When audiences cannot successfully interpret an artwork, the work cannot put them in a position to recognise the rightness of a perspective. On the other hand, a successful artwork is able to put audiences in a position to recognise the rightness of a perspective. We can easily identify examples of artworks which are aesthetically valuable partly because they are interpretable. One reason why the novels of Jane Austen are so valuable is that any minimally qualified reader finds them readily interpretable. Scarcely anyone who reads *Pride and Prejudice* will doubt for a moment that it presents the perspectives that it is dangerous to delight in thinking ill of others, that obsequious deference to the wealthy is contemptible and so on. Readers are very unlikely to reach the conclusion that the novel supports contrary perspectives.

The interpretability principle does not demand that all audiences be able to interpret an artwork for it to have aesthetic value. The fact that modern audiences cannot understand ancient Greek is no basis for the criticism of Sophocles' tragedies. In such cases, the principle only requires that an artwork be interpretable by a suitably qualified audience. It also requires that audiences be able to acquire the knowledge and abilities necessary for the interpretation of a work. The necessary knowledge may include familiarity with certain artistic conventions. The interpretability principle does not count against the value of Sophocles because people can learn ancient Greek.

The interpretability principle may be thought to have another consequence that it does not have. It does not entail that good works of art are easily interpreted. Some perspectives on human experience are complex and not easily conveyed. Works of art which convey these perspectives may be complex and difficult, and they may demand the careful attention of an informed audience. (Consequently, for all I know, *Finnegans Wake* may be a good novel.) There may even be cases where the obscurity of an artwork plays a role in the presentation of a perspective. For example, the fact that a work of art exemplifies obscurity may contribute to its capacity to present the perspective that some matter is difficult and obscure. In such a case, the obscurity of a work contributes to its aesthetic value. All of this is compatible with the interpretability criterion. This criterion demands only that careful attention to an artwork by an informed audience will be rewarded with comprehension.

As we will see in the next chapter, the failure to satisfy the interpretability principle helps explain the failure of some avant-garde art. With the best will in the world, audiences are simply unable to interpret some works of avant-garde art, including some works of abstract expressionism. The problem is not that audiences have failed to acquire the knowledge of conventions that would make interpretation possible. Rather, the problem is that audiences have no conventions which can be used to interpret some works. If a convention exists, it is a public and communicable rule. Frequently, these rules do not exist even when individual artists and small coteries allege that they do.

A second principle about aesthetic value follows from facts about the sort of representation employed in the arts. According to this principle, artworks with a high degree of aesthetic value exploit the resources of illustrative representation. As we have seen, artistic representation is illustration and not semantic representation. Illustrations are suited to showing an audience that something is the case. Semantic representations, unlike illustrations, are statements suited to telling something to an audience. Valuable works of art show something to an audience. They do not tell. In short, successful works of art employ the sorts of representation employed in illustrative demonstration.

In spite of the fact that works of art are illustrations, some artists attempt to make statements with their artworks. The results are, probably without exception, disappointing. Everyone can think of artworks which are little more than soapboxes from which authors spout their favourite theories. Heinlein's *Starship Troopers* is an example of such a work. In this novel, told in the first person, the narrator frequently expresses his views on a variety of subjects, including democracy and the value of military service. In fact, the whole book is a series of thinly disguised statements of Heinlein's views on these subjects. Discerning readers find such works preachy, didactic and, for this reason, possessed of a low aesthetic value.

The epistemology of art offered in this essay makes it possible to explain why audiences (rightly) judge that didactic works have little aesthetic value. A didactic artwork does not put an audience in a position to recognise the rightness of a perspective. It does not provide an illustrative demonstration. In place of such a demonstration we have only attempts at bare assertion. Even if the work succeeds in making true statements (which will not always be the case) an unsupported assertion has little or no cognitive value. Statements are informative only when there is some reason to believe that they are true. That is, statements are in need of justification, usually by an argument. This is particularly the case when the statements are supposed to be informative about important or controversial matters. Consequently, when artworks are simply vehicles for the statement of an artist's views, they will have little cognitive or aesthetic value.

A final principle of aesthetic evaluation can be inferred from our earlier investigations of representation and demonstration in the arts. It may be called the *suitability principle*. As was noted in the section 'What can be learned from art?' in Chapter 3 (pp. 94–104), certain subjects lend themselves to scientific or philosophical investigation, while illustrative representations are best able to provide insight into other matters. An artwork will have little cognitive value (and so limited total aesthetic value) if it is concerned with matters unsuited to artistic investigation. From this we can infer that, in general, valuable artworks will present perspectives on subjects to which the arts are suited. For example, some artwork might be designed primarily to provide insight into the principles of moral philosophy. As we have seen, this is not a subject suitable for artistic investigation. Consequently, the aesthetic value of the work is likely to be limited.

The suitability principle will be employed, in the next chapter, to help explain the failure of many works of modern art. Some modern artists have attempted to usurp the role of philosophers. They have, for example, created works which they take to address the question, 'What is art?' This is, however, a question that cannot be answered by means of illustrative demonstration. Only argument and conceptual analysis will provide answers to questions about the nature of art. (Of course, reflection on works of art may prompt audiences to reflect on the definition of art, but this is quite another matter.)

A few other general principles about aesthetic value are available, besides those which can be deduced from facts about representation and demonstration in the arts. The first of these criteria is concerned with the subject that an artwork addresses. It may be called the *subject matter principle*. According to this principle, a work has high aesthetic value only if it investigates an important subject. Sometimes a subject is important because it has great practical utility. How to live well is an example of such a subject. Other subjects are important because they are ones about which humans are inherently curious. Metaphysics, Kant would have us believe, is an example of such a subject.

The subject matter principle can be illustrated by reference to the values of scientific theories. The supremely great works of science include those that provide insight into important subjects such as the most basic laws of nature. The value of a theory in a field such as medicine is partly determined by its subject matter. The work of a physician who discovers a cure for cancer, for example, is more valuable than the work of one who discovers a treatment for baldness. This is because cancer is a more important subject than baldness. A similar point can be made about works of art. An artwork that provides insight into an important subject is, *ceteris paribus*, more valuable than one concerned with a matter of little importance.

A few examples will illustrate the applicability of the subject matter principle. *Middlemarch* is a better novel than *Cranford* for lots of reasons. One of them is that George Eliot addresses more important issues than does Mrs Gaskell. Mrs Gaskell's novel is finely observed, and she provides a useful perspective on daily life in provincial, nineteenth-century England. The description of the visit to the old bachelor, with its insight into the gentle, lingering effects of an unprosperous love, is particularly deftly handled. George Eliot, on the other hand, presents a series of perspectives on matters of enduring and pressing concern. These subjects include the impact of technological change and political reform, hypocrisy and sincerity, pedantry and genuine religious feeling, the status of women, the effects of love and infatuation, the force of social mores and a host of others. Similarly, a profound musical composition is, *ceteris paribus*, greater than one that is not. The subjects plumbed in the *St Matthew Passion*, for example, are simply more important than the ones represented in a Boyce symphony. This goes some of the way towards explaining why Bach's work is so much greater.

The subject matter principle states only a necessary condition of high aesthetic value. Having an important subject does not, by itself, make a work of art valuable. Many artworks have important subjects, but treat them in a clumsy, melodramatic or otherwise ineffective manner. The film *Ben-Hur* is a case in point. Forgiveness, friendship and patriotism are all important subjects, but their treatment in *Ben-Hur* makes one cringe. (Mind you, the chariot race scene is magnificent.) By the same token, an artwork that addresses a small point well can have considerable aesthetic value. It can certainly have more value than one that addresses an important subject in an ineffective manner, even if it cannot be supremely great. Consider, for example, Barbara Pym's novels. No one is likely to mistake them for great works of art. They are small works with limited ambitions. They are, however, admirable novels and certainly better than some more ambitious works. Some matters are more important than the social dynamics of an Oxfordshire jumble sale. Still, Barbara Pym investigates such subjects with such an unerring eye and such good humour that her novels have considerable aesthetic value.

Originality is another criterion of aesthetic value. We may formulate an *originality principle*, according to which highly valuable works of art provide hitherto unavailable insights. Here originality is not merely the provision of insights not previously expressed in the arts. Rather, originality is to be understood more generally. The original artwork shows something that was not previously known by any means, artistic or otherwise. Some subjects are already well understood by means of common sense or the sciences, and there is no need for them to be addressed by the arts. An artwork that provides a perspective on such a subject is unoriginal, even if it is the first artwork to do so. Such artworks, which persist in stating the familiar, have little value. The most valuable art helps us understand subjects which puzzle us, which we overlook, or which we avoid. Notice that, although originality is a necessary condition of high aesthetic value, it is far from a sufficient condition. Many original works have little or no aesthetic value. An artwork may present a novel but uninteresting perspective, or one that is original but wrong.

The originality that is a necessary condition of high aesthetic value is originality of perspective. It is not simply technical originality. Technical originality can, by itself, contribute to the value of an artwork. Audiences often delight merely in the virtuosity of an original artistic technique. An original technique is, however, most valuable when it is a means to an end and not merely an end in itself. In particular, original techniques are of most value when they make possible the presentation of new perspectives. The expression of an original perspective in a work of art may depend on the development of a new technique. Consider, for example, the contributions Biber and Paganini made to violin technique. In the one case, the technical development contributed importantly to the aesthetic value of the composer's works. In the other, it did not. Biber's technical originality is at the service of music's cognitive function, but Paganini's originality is an end itself. Biber's use of scordatura, for example, in his *Mystery Sonatas* greatly expanded the expressive possibilities of the violin and contributed to the cognitive value of these compositions. The technical devices employed by Paganini are at least as original as anything used by Biber. The caprices of Paganini's Opus 1 are, however, little, if anything, more than empty show pieces. For all their originality, compared with the *Mystery Sonatas* their aesthetic value is low.

The originality principle is at odds with one of Pope's best-known aphorisms. At root, Pope and I are in agreement. We both believe that art has important cognitive value. Still, we disagree on one point. He held that a successful poem (and, by extension, all valuable artworks) presents a perspective that has oft been thought, but ne'er so well expressed. I think this is wrong. Pope erred in thinking that a thought is independent of its expression. A perspective has not been thought, contrary to what Pope would have us believe, until it has been well expressed. When artists develop new modes of expression they make possible the thinking of new thoughts.

Some artworks present perspectives already familiar from other works. We condemn such works as derivative and, consequently, as possessed of limited aesthetic value. (Recall the analogy to the mathematical proof which has already been provided.) Other works of art are bad because they present perspectives which, although perhaps not previously expressed in art, are commonplace. The section 'Rejected alternatives' in Chapter 3 (pp. 70–80) has already identified a few such perspectives. Artworks that present perspectives on, for example, the consistency of paint or the phenomenological properties of redness have comparatively little aesthetic value. Audiences are generally already perfectly informed on these matters. Much of the visual art of the past hundred years has, however, presented perspectives on these familiar matters.

Someone might object that nothing said in this section is of much use in explaining why works by, say, Bach, Rembrandt, Shakespeare or Henry James are so great. Someone may grant that their works have important cognitive value, that they are interpretable, that they are instances of illustrative representation, and so on. One might even grant that these factors have something to do with the greatness of the works. Nevertheless, someone may object, the greatness of works by, say, Rembrandt, depends crucially on specific facts about individual paintings. I am sympathetic to this objection and I have no desire to take issue with it. Here I have only offered a few very general principles of evaluation. I have already said, and can only repeat, that these principles have a limited utility. The artist and the art historian will have much more to say about evaluation and much of it will be more valuable than anything I have said.

The time has come now to apply the apparatus developed in this essay to the evaluation of an important movement within modern art. When I speak of modern art, I refer to the art which has been created since about the beginning of the twentieth century. Much of modern art is continuous in spirit and method with the art of earlier times. Some of this art is very successful. The modern period has, however, witnessed radical developments in architecture, literature, music and, especially, the visual arts of paintings and sculpture. These radically new works are often referred to as avant-garde. An important part of the avant-garde has been hitherto unknown forms, such as conceptual and performance art. Avant-garde works have led a charmed critical life. Almost no one in academia is prepared to suggest publicly that much of avant-garde art has little aesthetic value. In spite of the reluctance to criticise avant-garde art, the feeling that it is deeply misguided is widespread. The epistemology of art developed in this essay makes it possible to show that this feeling is not without foundation. Something has gone dreadfully wrong in modern art.

5

AVANT-GARDE ART AND KNOWLEDGE

What is avant-garde art?

Over the past hundred years, the most striking development in the arts has been the emergence of the avant-garde style. Many of the most influential artists of the past century have adopted this style. These artists include writers such as Tristan Tzara and composers such as John Cage. The avant-garde style has been most influential in the realm of the visual arts. Notable adherents of the style include Carl André, Marcel Duchamp, Wassily Kandinsky, Jeff Koons, Kazimir Malevich, Piet Mondrian, Barnett Newman, Claes Oldenburg, Mark Rothko, Andy Warhol and many others. Although many people have doubts about the value of avant-garde art, criticism of works in this style has been rare and usually quite unsatisfactory. Often it has failed to rise above ignorant philistinism. This chapter will apply to avant-garde art the general approach to art developed in earlier chapters. The arguments of this chapter will indicate that doubts about the value of much avant-garde art are fully justified. The epistemology of avant-garde art will show that works executed in this style typically can contribute little to knowledge. Since, as I will argue, avant-garde artworks generally have little cognitive value, they generally have little aesthetic value.

This chapter is divided into six sections. This first section identifies the characteristics shared by avant-garde works. As we will see, they have in common a lack of precisely those features that contribute most importantly to the cognitive value of art. Avant-garde art has been characterised by an erosion of illustrative representation and its replacement by semantic representation. Some avant-garde works retain a residue of illustration. They continue to employ exemplification. These works are considered in the next section, which will confirm that artworks can contribute little to knowledge qua exemplars. In 'The semantics of avant-garde art', I consider avant-garde works in which illustrative representation is more thoroughly rejected and replaced by semantic representation. In these works, art becomes the making of statements, with predictably disappointing results. The next section, 'But is it art?', considers the question of whether avant-garde works ought to be accepted as works of art. The question of what to do with bad avant-garde art is addressed in 'Destroying works of avant-garde art'. The final section of this chapter is an envoy, in the poet's sense of the word, for the entire book.

My suggestion that avant-garde artworks constitute a style needs to be defended. The artists I have identified as adherents of the style are seemingly quite diverse. I have lumped together artists associated with dadaism, abstract expressionism, suprematism, pop art, neo-plasticism, conceptual art and a variety of other schools. Before I can defend the suggestion that an avant-garde style exists, I need to say a little more about what I mean by 'style'. A style is simply a category of artworks. Works belonging to the same style share a property or properties. Of course, all artworks share certain properties. Minimally, they possess the property of being artifacts. Some properties, however, are possessed by only some artworks. An artworld can lump together in a category works sharing any contingent property. Artworks in this category may be said to share a style.

Just about any salient contingent properties of artworks can be the basis of the categorisation of selected artworks into a style. Sometimes works that belong to some style share certain formal properties. Artworks in other styles share what may be called representational properties. A couple of examples will illustrate this point. Consider, for example, serialism. The properties shared by works in this style are formal properties. Works of classical dodecaphonic serialism share the property of having the twelve notes of the chromatic scale (from any octave) recur in a fixed order. In other cases, the property shared by works in a given style is a representational property. Consider the romantic style. Works in this style frequently involve the representation of nature. Moreover, they typically represent nature as sublime and beyond human comprehension. Romantic works characteristically make extensive use of affective representation. That is, they engage the passions in presenting their distinctive perspective on nature and the place of humans in the world.

Before proceeding, we need to identify three features of styles. The first is that works from quite different artforms can belong to the same style. So, for example, the paintings of Turner, the compositions of Brahms and the poetry of Wordsworth are all romantic in style. Similarly, the paintings of Mondrian, the writings of Tzara and the music of Cage all belong to the avant-garde style. The second point to note is that a single artwork can belong to two or more styles. So, for example, paintings by Monet and Degas are instances of both impressionism and realism (in the specific, nineteenth-century, sense of 'realism'). Similarly, the paintings of Pollock are equally instances of abstract expressionism and works in the avant-garde style. Abstract expressionism (and constructivism, conceptual art and so on) may be said to be sub-styles of the broader avant-garde style. Finally, properties come in degrees and, consequently, works belong to one style or another to some degree or other. The compositions of Bach, for example, are more fully baroque in style than the somewhat *galant* works of Telemann. Similarly, some works are more fully avant-garde in style than others.

Now we come to the central question to be addressed in this section: what is the property (or properties) shared by works in the avant-garde style? As we have just seen, the properties shared by works in some style can be formal or representational. At first, avant-garde works may seem not to share any salient properties of either sort. After all, minimalist paintings, readymade sculptures, works of abstract expressionism, chance musical compositions, dada poems and conceptual artworks seem to be about as different from each other as one can imagine. As a result, one might be sceptical about the claim that an avant-garde style exists. This scepticism may be reinforced by the impression that many avant-garde artworks do not have any representational properties. A little reflection reveals, however, that avant-garde works do share certain formal and representational properties.

The name of the avant-garde style provides a clue to one property shared by works in this style. Avant-garde works of art are always new and unlike what has previously been produced. One way to put this point is to say that artworks are not avant-garde because they possess some intrinsic property (in the sense introduced in the first section of Chapter 1, pp. 1–4). Rather, a formal property shared by avant-garde works is a relational property (again in the sense of the first section of Chapter 1). In particular, they share the property of being dramatically different from anything previously produced. More precisely, they share the property of differing from all previously produced artworks, except a small set of roughly contemporaneous avant-garde works. Many avant-garde works are quite similar to other avant-garde works which were produced only a short time earlier. The newness of avant-garde art leads to a constant state of flux. Avant-garde artworks must differ from even other avant-garde artworks. Hence the constant succession of sub-styles: futurism, dadaism, surrealism, suprematism, abstract expressionism, pop art, op art, minimalism, conceptual art, neo-geo and so on. (Compare the art of the past century to that of the baroque period. Two baroque musical compositions, composed fifty years apart, are sometimes stylistically indistinguishable.)

This is not the place to investigate the question of why newness has been so highly prized by avant-garde artists. For our purposes, artists' reasons for adopting the avant-garde style are immaterial. Historical and psychological questions about the appeal of newness, as interesting as they are, cannot be answered here. I will simply note that avant-garde artists have had a variety of reasons for adopting the style. Some have been hostile to everything that is old. Other artists have wished to make a political statement. These artists have, for example, wished to criticise the role artworks have played in their society. Others have felt that the expressive possibilities of non-avant-garde art have been exhausted. Some have simply wished to *épater le bourgeois*. (Audiences are often shocked by works they do not understand and they understand illustrative representation.) Still others have enjoyed the feeling of being part of a radical vanguard.

Avant-garde works share another property besides newness or difference from previously produced artworks. They also share a representational property. Contrary to what may often seem to be the case, the avant-garde style does not generally involve a rejection of all representation. Indeed, most avant-garde artworks are intended as in some way representational. This claim may strike some readers as implausible since many paradigm cases of avant-garde artworks are works of abstract art. The claim is less implausible once we recognise that abstract art is distinct from non-representational art. Very few producers of abstract art regard their work as in no way representational. By the same token, very few avant-garde artists accept that their works have only hedonic value. Kandinsky, Mondrian, Rothko and a host of other producers of abstract art all maintain that their works are representational. Newman was a virulent anti-formalist.

Rather than involving the rejection of representation, the avant-garde style involves the abandonment of a certain sort of representation. In particular, the most crucial representational characteristic of avant-garde art is that it forsakes all or many of the resources of illustrative representation. This is true despite the fact that some avant-garde artists (among them Mondrian) see themselves as using illustrations to provide illustrative demonstrations. In some avant-garde works, illustrative representation is not completely abandoned. However, starting with cubism, in the early years of the last century, experience of avant-garde artworks became increasingly unlike experience of objects they represent.

Some avant-garde artworks involve no illustrative representation while others use only some of the resources of illustrative representation. For example, the only form of illustration employed by many avant-garde works is exemplification. Exemplification is frequently the only sort of illustration found, for example, in the works of the constructivists. The use of exemplification, to the exclusion of other forms of illustration, has also been quite common in avant-garde architecture. Other avant-garde works involve a more radical rejection of illustrative representation. A few, it is true, are not representational at all. (The implications of this fact will be considered in the section 'But is it art?', below, pp. 154–9.) More commonly, avant-garde works supplement, or replace, illustration with semantic representation. Representation in some avant-garde works depends on the development of new conventions of representation. Kandinsky's works are examples. Other avant-garde works represent only in conjunction with what is said and written about them. In a few limiting cases, avant-garde works become pure semantic representations.

It may seem easy to think of counter-examples to the claim that avant-garde art involves the abandonment of illustrative representation. Many works by Warhol could be considered as such counter-examples. Consider, for example, his *Brillo Boxes* or *200 Campbell's Soup Cans*. (The former consists of wooden boxes, silk-screened to resemble cartons of Brillo soap pads. The latter is an oil painting of 200 cans of soup. It is just one of many images of soup cans produced by Warhol.) Works by Jasper Johns, such as his paintings of the American flag, might also be thought to count against the claim that illustrative representation does not play an important role in avant-garde artworks. A little reflection will reveal that these and similar works are not the counter-examples they may seem to be.

I do not deny that the works mentioned in the previous paragraph are illustrations. A Warhol picture of a soup can is an illustrative representation of a soup can. This fact about the picture is, however, largely beside the point. No one suggests that it is an artwork qua illustration of soup cans. Warhol's picture may be indistinguishable from an image created by a commercial artist to advertise soup and no one suggests that the commercial image is art. The important feature of a Warhol picture of soup cans is that it is intended to represent something besides soup cans. In particular, it is intended as a representation of facts about images and quotidian life in the modern world. It owes its status as an artwork to its representation of these facts. If it did not represent them, it would no more be an artwork than the work of the commercial artist. The painting is, however, unable to represent these facts by itself. It can only do so in conjunction with a body of discourse (that is, semantic representations). Many of Warhol's pictures are clear cases of avant-garde artworks whose capacity to represent depends crucially on associated semantic representations. Such works are discussed in 'The semantics of avant-garde art', below (pp. 144–54).

The two defining characteristics of avant-garde art (its difference from previous art and its rejection of illustrative representation) are closely linked. Initially, avant-garde artworks differed from earlier art precisely because of the erosion of the role of illustrative representation. Illustration was, until the early years of the twentieth century, characteristic of all, or almost all, art. The easiest and most radical way for art to be new was to give up illustrative representation. Even though the avant-garde is currently the dominant academic style (at least in the visual arts and 'classical' music), the use of illustrative representation is still widespread. The avant-garde style has had little impact on literature, film or the popular arts. Moreover, the most frequently heard music and the most commonly viewed works of visual art are still those that employ illustrative representation. As a result, avant-garde works still seem radically new a century after the style was introduced.

Avant-garde artists were very unwise when they abandoned the use of illustrative representation. For reasons that have emerged in earlier chapters of this essay, artworks have considerable cognitive value when illustrations are used to provide illustrative demonstrations. Valuable artworks are not simply used to make statements. Instead, they make use of the full resources of illustrative representation. In particular, valuable artworks employ forms of illustration besides exemplification. These conclusions will be reinforced by reflection on examples of avant-garde artworks. Works in the style generally have little cognitive value. (Perhaps because avant-garde artworks can contribute little to knowledge, formalism has been common in thinking about the arts for the past century. Critics from Clive Bell to Clement Greenberg believed that artworks have value because their formal properties are a source of enjoyment.) Nevertheless, the view that avant-garde works are important sources of knowledge has also been widely held and this view needs to be considered in detail.

Exemplification and avant-garde art

The exemplification hypothesis (discussed in 'Rejected alternatives' in Chapter 3, pp. 70–80) is currently the most common approach to the epistemology of art. This can be easily explained. Exemplification is the only sort of representation employed in many revered and influential works of avant-garde art and the exemplification hypothesis is able to account for such cognitive value as these works possess. The fact remains, however, that works of art can have very little cognitive value qua exemplars. We have already seen that, when exemplification is the only form of illustration employed by an artwork, it is, at best, a source of knowledge of only rather trivial matters. Only works which employ forms of illustrative representation besides exemplification can have much cognitive or aesthetic value. This conclusion can be supported by consideration of a few examples of the use of exemplification in avant-garde art. The use of exemplification, to the exclusion of other forms of illustration, is quite common in constructivism, op art and International Style architecture. Examples will be considered from each of these movements, beginning with constructivism.

Constructivists such as Naum Gabo said explicitly that art is a means of communication. Indeed, Gabo held that it is the most effective available form of communication. If so, artworks are sources of knowledge. Constructivists other than Gabo were even more explicit about the cognitive value of art and maintained that their artworks are sources of insight into the truth. Constructivists are, however, committed to the view that works of visual art ought not to be pictures of individual things. They also hold that artworks ought neither to express the emotions of an artist nor engage those of an audience. In short, constructivists quite explicitly surrender most of the resources of illustrative representation, including affective illustration. If a constructivist artwork has cognitive value, then it has this value qua exemplar. Constructivists did not speak of their artworks as exemplars. Talk of exemplification came only later in the history of the epistemology of art. Nevertheless, constructivists clearly believed that their artworks have cognitive value in so far as they are objects which possess and refer to their own properties.

Gabo's *Two Cubes (Demonstrating the Stereometric Method)* is a good example of a constructivist work which employs exemplification. This work is a pair of objects. The first is a simple cube, constructed from painted wood. The second object is also constructed from painted wood. It has the base and top of a cube, but it lacks the sides. They are replaced by two intersecting diagonal planes, each extending from one corner of the base and the top to the opposite corner. Gabo's writings on this piece make clear what this work is intended to exemplify. For a start, it exemplifies the property of enclosing space by contrasting the closed cube with the one which has the interior laid bare. Sculptures are three-dimensional and, as a result, enclose space. Most sculptures do not, however, refer to or exemplify the property of enclosing space. As well, *Two Cubes* exemplifies the properties of intersecting planes.

As far as *Two Cubes* goes, it is fully successful. One can learn from this piece that sculptures are three-dimensional. By exemplifying this property, it provides an illustrative demonstration of this feature of sculptures. By exemplifying other properties, the sculpture also effectively demonstrates certain facts about intersecting planes. This is, however, all that an audience can gather from this sculpture. Even if metaphorical exemplification were possible, this work exemplifies its geometrical properties and no others. (In any case, this sculpture is not intended as an exemplification of emotion, so it is not.)

The trouble is that none of what audiences can learn from *Two Cubes* has much value. The fact that sculptures are three-dimensional is not always uppermost in one's mind when viewing a sculpture. The fact remains, however, that the proposition that sculptures are three-dimensional is quite trivial. In fact, it is probably analytic. The geometrical propositions that *Two Cubes* demonstrates are not trivial. However, none of the geometrical knowledge that one can acquire from this work counts as news. School children already possess knowledge of the geometrical propositions *Two Cubes* demonstrates. Moreover, these propositions can only be proven in complete generality by means of rational demonstration. In short, both the suitability principle and the subject matter principle, introduced in the section 'Criteria of evaluation' in Chapter 4 (pp. 126–34), lead to the conclusion that Gabo's sculpture has little cognitive or aesthetic value. Reflection on *Two Cubes* confirms the conclusions about the exemplification hypothesis reached in 'Rejected alternatives', also in Chapter 3 (pp. 70–80). If artworks contributed to knowledge only by means of exemplification, they would have little cognitive value.

Let us turn now to a brief consideration of avant-garde architecture. The principal strand of avant-garde architecture began in the 1920s with the Bauhaus, de Stijl and Charles-Édouard Jeanneret (better known as Le Corbusier). This strand has become known as the International Style. Illustrative representation in avant-garde architecture is almost exclusively exemplification. International Style architecture has primarily used exemplification to represent facts about the construction of modern buildings. Prior to the late nineteenth century, most buildings were supported by their walls. Subsequently, it became possible to construct buildings without load-bearing walls. Instead, buildings could be supported by a steel or concrete grid. Avant-garde architects have deliberately created buildings which represented this method of construction by means of exemplification.

A few examples will illustrate the use of exemplification in avant-garde architecture. An early and famous instance of avant-garde architecture is found in the Schroeder House, designed by Gerrit Rietveld, a member of de Stijl. This house represents the grid construction of the house by exemplifying a grid pattern by means of its sheer surfaces, modularity and stark rectangularity. Bauhaus architects such as Walter Gropius and Ludwig Mies van der Rohe made similar use of exemplification. Walls do not carry loads in grid construction, and it was felt that buildings should exemplify the properties of such construction. This was done by designing buildings whose walls are sheer membranes of stucco or glass, materials that cannot support buildings. Good examples of buildings which exemplify the properties of non-load-bearing walls are found in the model workers' flats that made up the *Weissenhofsiedlung* built for the 1927 Werkbund Exposition.

An interesting and somewhat unusual use of exemplification is found in the Seagram Building in New York designed by Mies. American fire safety codes forbid the use of exposed steel in the construction of buildings. The steel grid of a building must be covered with concrete. Consequently, the actual grid from which the building is constructed cannot be used to exemplify grid construction. Mies circumvented this problem by attaching wide-flange beams to the corners of the building. Although these beams have no structural function, they exemplify grid construction using wide-flange beams. That is, they exemplify the sort of construction that lies beneath the concrete surface. (The exterior beams on the Seagram Building are bronze, so there is a double exemplification. They exemplify the colour of Seagram's distilled products, as well as the building's structural properties.)

As these examples indicate, avant-garde architecture has used exemplification to represent facts about modern construction. As a result, avant-garde architecture is almost exclusively about architecture. Indeed, if a building represents only by means of exemplification of structural properties, it must be about architecture. The trouble is that most of what audiences can learn about buildings from avant-garde architecture is not very interesting. The information that many modern buildings have a grid construction, and that the walls do not bear loads, is commonplace. Even if it were not, this information can be easily conveyed without the construction of buildings that exemplify the properties of modern structures. One could simply state the fact that modern buildings have a grid construction. If more information is required, one could write a textbook on construction techniques. In International Style architecture, we find more examples of avant-garde artworks which do not fare well when judged by the subject matter and suitability principles.

This account of avant-garde architecture might be thought to be unfair. These works frequently exemplify more properties than simply their structural properties. In particular, these works, like other avant-garde works, frequently exemplify the property of newness. I cannot see, however, how the exemplification of this property can confer very considerable cognitive value on avant-garde artworks. An artwork which exemplifies newness provides insight only into the newness that it itself exemplifies. The artwork would be about itself and, in particular, about the ways in which it differs from other artworks. The work is unlikely to do well when measured by the subject matter principle. True, an artwork can, in virtue of its newness, evoke an affective response in an audience. The work of art could, for example, evoke in an audience a feeling of unfamiliarity. If so, however, exemplification is not the only form of representation employed in the work. The work also employs affective illustration.

The avant-garde artworks considered so far in this section mainly exemplify properties of artworks. Not all exemplification in avant-garde art is so restricted. Consider, for example, certain pieces of optical or op art (or perceptual abstraction, as its practitioners often preferred to call it). Works of op art often exemplify the property of being a source of optical illusion. Bridget Riley's *Cataract III*, for example, is an exemplar of an object which is the source of optical bleed. (The painting causes after-images. These after-images lead to the experience of colours that are not present in the painting. This is optical bleed.) Other works of op art exemplify the property of being visually ambiguous. An instance of such a work hangs outside my room in my University's library. (I cannot sit down to work on this book without first seeing it. This may explain a lot.) This painting, *3 Up 3 Down*, by John Dobereiner (do not be surprised if you have never heard of him) consists of parallelograms of colour that can be seen either as vertical or horizontal planes. They resemble either the risers or the treads of a staircase. As such, it is an exemplar of a visually ambiguous object.

Like constructivist works, works of op art are often successful as far as they go. By exemplifying the source of an illusion, such works can provide insight into perception. Audiences can learn from *Cataract III* about the phenomenon of optical bleed. Other canvasses by Bridget Riley and similar perceptual abstractionists are a source of knowledge about other illusions. At the end of the day, however, these works still do not have a great deal of cognitive value. (At least, they do not have much cognitive value qua exemplars. The possibility that they represent in some other, cognitively valuable, way remains open. Riley's paintings, and other non-figurative artworks, could be affective illustrations.) The trouble is that the sources of illusion that these works exemplify are familiar to every student of introductory psychology. Moreover, psychology will be able to provide much fuller information about these illusions. Psychology can, for example, provide some explanation of the illusions in question. Op art is often quite entertaining and attractive, but it is cognitively trivial.

I have considered only a very limited number of works and sub-styles of avant-garde art in this section. Nevertheless, it is fair to conclude that avant-garde artists act unwisely if they restrict their use of illustration to the use of exemplification. The works of art I have discussed are representative in their use of exemplification. Moreover, consideration of these exemplary artworks serves to confirm the previously established conclusion that artworks can have little cognitive value qua exemplars. Only comparatively rarely, however, do avant-garde artists decide to represent only by exemplifying. However, if I am to show that avant-garde art, in general, has little cognitive value, much more remains to be said.

The semantics of avant-garde art

Perhaps because the remnants of illustrative representation (such as exemplification) in avant-garde art can achieve so little, the style has increasingly come to depend on semantic representation. In some cases, this reliance on semantic representation has led to the development of new representational conventions. In effect, new languages have been proposed. The invention of new semantic conventions by avant-garde artists is, however, a little unusual. More commonly, works of avant-garde art represent only in conjunction with existing forms of semantic representation. In fact, avant-garde artworks are frequently completely dependent on artists' statements for their capacity to represent. Finally, in a limiting case, statements are transformed into works of avant-garde art. Some semantic representations are, of course, important sources of knowledge. Art, however, has to do more than make statements if it is to have much cognitive value.

A few avant-garde artists have tried to develop new forms of semantic representation. Kandinsky is probably the most notable of these artists. He was the author of a series of lengthy and influential essays on painting. In these essays, he expresses the hope that a science of art will emerge. This science will only be possible when, as he says, artistic signs become symbols. He seems to mean by this that the elements of paintings (colours and forms) have, or should have, a fixed significance and that what a painting represents is a function of the significance of its elements. In short, Kandinsky calls for the development of a language of painting. He goes to some length to spell out the significance of various colours and shapes, and even to indicate some syntactical rules of this language. If a language of painting (or of any other art) existed, paintings (and other artworks) could conveniently and at will be used to make statements. Artists could forsake the resources of illustrative representation in the knowledge that the full resources of another mode of representation are available.

Little purpose is served in considering proposals such as Kandinsky's. As a matter of fact, no avant-garde artist has succeeded in developing or discovering the rules of a language of painting or any other art. The problem is simply that artworks are not compounded from a finite set of components with fixed meanings. Perhaps more importantly, it is not clear why anyone would want to develop a language of art. We already have many natural and artificial languages and they enable us to state everything that we can imagine stating. (A new language may make possible a new range of statements. Until, however, we know the language, we cannot know what these statements are.) As I have indicated in earlier sections, works of art primarily have cognitive value when they are illustrations that provide illustrative demonstrations. As such, art supplements the sciences and other forms of inquiry that employ semantic representation. Even if a language of art does not exist, however, it is still possible to make statements using works of art. I need to demonstrate that the bulk of avant-garde artworks are being used to make statements and then to show that these works have little cognitive value.

Some avant-garde artworks can be used to make statements because they are conjoined with a body of writing or discourse. Even a casual observer of avant-garde art is aware that the rise of the avant-garde style has been accompanied by the rise of the artistic manifesto and the artist's statement. Artists working in the avant-garde style write far more about their work than do artists working in other styles. This has been true from the very beginning of the avant-garde style, as the various manifestos by the futurists and the surrealists demonstrate. Avant-garde artists are not the only ones who have contributed to this explosion of writing about art. Influential critics, such as Clement Greenberg, have also contributed to the body of writing associated with avant-garde art. The production of this vast literature is no accident. The writings of avant-garde artists, and allied critics, play an important role in their art. I will refer to the remarks with which an avant-garde artwork is conjoined as a *discourse*. When an avant-garde artwork depends importantly on a discourse, I will call it *discourse-dependent*.

Before the rise of the avant-garde style, some artists wrote about art. Painters such as Leonardo, Reynolds and Constable, and authors such as Horace, Tasso, Sydney, Pope, Shelley and Henry James all produced important writings on their art. Generally, however, they wrote about artistic technique. Their writings are, in effect, manuals on how to produce artworks. As a rule, the works of these artists are independent of their writings. Audiences can be ignorant of the writings of these artists and still understand their works. Even if I have never read a word of, say, Shelley's *Defence of Poetry*, I can read, appreciate, enjoy and learn from his poetry. Avant-garde artworks, in contrast, cannot be understood and do not represent except in conjunction with what is said about them.

Without an associated discourse audiences would not even be able to recognise that many avant-garde works are works of art. This is particularly true of certain important instances of performance art. Consider, for example, the influential early works of Chris Burden. One early work consisted of him shooting at an airliner as it took off. (He missed.) In another performance he had himself shot (not mortally). Oldenburg's *Placid City Monument* is also worth considering in this context. In this work, grave diggers were hired to dig and then fill in a hole behind the Metropolitan Museum in New York. Someone who saw these performances might not know what to make of them. Nothing about their contexts (they are not found in galleries or theatres) indicates that they are artworks. Some of Burden's works might be mistaken for acts of terrorism. Fortunately, a great deal has been said and written about these works, and audiences can know that they are being asked to consider works of art.

Here I am most concerned with artworks whose capacity to represent depends on an associated discourse. Discourses on a variety of subjects are conjoined with discourse-dependent artworks. Often, however, the subject of these discourses is the nature of art. Most famously, this sort of discourse is associated with two of the most important of all avant-garde works: Duchamp's *Fountain* and Warhol's *Brillo Boxes*. A great many other instances of such works could be given. Discourses about art are associated, for example, with Bruce Nauman's videos, *Black Balls* (which portrays the artist applying black make-up to his testicles) and the self-explanatory *Walking in an Exaggerated Manner around the Perimeter of a Square*. By themselves, these artworks would not be about the nature of art. Still, in conjunction with a discourse, discourse-dependent artworks succeed in being about (or representing) matters such as the definition of art. We need to ask how a discourse transforms these objects into representations. We also need to ask whether such works are semantic or illustrative representations. We will then be in a better position to evaluate the cognitive values of avant-garde artworks of this sort.

Discourse-dependent artworks are typically not illustrative representations. Frequently, the matters they are about do not admit of illustrative representation. For example, *Fountain* represents something about the nature of art. It is obviously not an illustration of something general about the nature of art. General facts about the nature of art can only be given a semantic representation. We require, that is, a theory about the nature of art. In any case, it is clear that works such as *Fountain* do not represent because experience of the sculpture has something in common with experience of what it represents. That is, *Fountain* is not an illustration. It (and other discourse-dependent artworks) are semantic representations.

The suggestion that an artwork can be used to make a statement may seem to be an odd suggestion from me. After all, in the section 'Visual art and semantic representation' in Chapter 2 (pp. 38–44) I noted that only in rather special circumstances can pictures be used to make statements and I reject the propositional theory of art. I might be expected to have a similar view about sculptures and other works of art. In fact, however, the circumstances are quite special. When a discourse is associated with an avant-garde artwork, it can be used to make a statement. A discourse can transform an artwork into a statement in one of two ways. The first of these ways I call *semantic enfranchisement*. The second involves the creation of what I call *hybrid statements*.

A few words will clarify what I mean by each of these terms. Hybrid statements are a composite of linguistic and non-linguistic elements. Examples of such statements are often seen on bumper stickers. On a bumper sticker, a picture of a dog may be preceded by the phrase 'I love my'. Together, the picture and the phrase combine to form the statement 'I love my dog.' In other cases, hybrid statements contain things (rather than pictures) and phrases. Placing an object in a child's storybook may, for example, complete a statement. I produce another hybrid statement if I say, 'You should use your' and I tap my head. Semantic enfranchisement is the creation of a special convention which transforms some object into a representation. For an example, consider the following case. Imagine that I am a spy and I say to my confederate, 'When you see this pen, it means "The way is clear."' My utterance semantically enfranchises the pen and it can be used to make a statement.

Sometimes the discourses associated with avant-garde artworks transform them into hybrid statements. *Fountain*, for example, in conjunction with a discourse, certainly represents something about works of art. (It represents, say, the fact that even a urinal can be a work of art.) As we have seen, this sculpture is not an illustration. Neither is the work, by itself, a statement. In conjunction with a discourse, however, it forms a hybrid statement. Much that has been said about the work, by Duchamp and others, amounts simply to saying 'is a work of art'. The discourse combines with the sculpture to form a hybrid statement of the fact that *Fountain* is an artwork.

Given its history, *Fountain* is a particularly good example of a discourse-dependent artwork. Originally it was not an artwork at all. Rather, it was simply an object used to test the will of the hanging committee at a 1917 exhibition in New York City. The committee had announced that all artists could display anything at the exhibition, so long as they paid the appropriate fee. Duchamp submitted a urinal, together with the fee, to discover whether anything at all would be accepted. (It was not.) In short, *Fountain* was a prop used in a political act. Only after the piece was rejected did people begin to defend its claim to arthood. Initially, people argued for the arthood of *Fountain* by drawing attention to its formal properties, such as its smooth, lustrous surface. Only later did writers begin to argue that the work is a comment on the nature of arthood. Only then did *Fountain* become part of a statement about the nature of art.

Avant-garde artworks can also be used to make statements because they have been semantically enfranchised by a discourse. Warhol's pictures of Campbell's Soup cans are examples of discourse-dependent artworks which have been semantically enfranchised. As noted in the opening section of this chapter (pp. 135–40), these pictures are illustrations. They are not, however, illustrations of facts about everyday life or mass-produced images. If they were illustrations of such facts, so would be the indistinguishable images of the commercial draughtsman and these manifestly are not. Nevertheless, Warhol's pictures are about the homogeneity of everyday life in the modern world and about mass-produced images. Since they are representations of these matters but not illustrations, they must be semantic representations. By themselves the pictures cannot be used to make statements. They can be so used only because a discourse is associated with them. Audiences who are familiar with the discourse associated with Warhol's works, are able to determine that some picture is about, say, the homogeneity of modern life. The associated discourse simply says that a given artwork makes a specific statement.

Having established that discourse-dependent avant-garde artworks are used to make statements, it is easy to explain why they have little cognitive value. To begin with, we need to address a general question about the cognitive value of statements. The first point to make is that some statements are false and, qua representations, have no cognitive value. (It may be possible to learn something from a statement even when it is false. For example, one may be able to learn that the person who makes the statement is a liar. In such a case, the statement has cognitive value, but not qua semantic representation. I am concerned only with the cognitive value which statements possess qua representations.) Even when a statement is true, it may have little or no cognitive value. At least two classes of true statements have little cognitive value. The first class includes statements about trivial or commonplace matters. The second sort includes statements for which no evidence is available.

A true statement has cognitive value only when its audience has some reason to believe that it is true. In short, the statement needs to be justified. (After all, knowledge is *justified* true belief.) This justification can, in some cases, be provided by the reliability of the person who makes the statement. If I tell my friends that it is raining, they are justified in believing that it is. In other cases, a person's reliability, however great, cannot justify the person's statements. Suppose, for example, I merely state, without providing any justification, that I have witnessed a miracle. No matter how reliable I am, my statement has little or no cognitive value. As Hume argues, no one is so reliable that such testimony ought to be accepted. In general, statements on many topics have little or no cognitive value unless justification for them is provided.

Discourse-dependent artworks generally do not lack cognitive value because they are about trivial or commonplace matters. On the contrary, they are generally statements about important matters such as the nature of art, the role of images in the modern world, mysticism, class struggle, relations between the sexes and so on. The trouble is that statements on these matters are instances of statements which are in need of justification. The mere statement of a view about art, the value of life in the modern world, or the construction of gender has little cognitive value. Since discourse-dependent artworks are simply statements about these matters, they have little cognitive value.

In defence of discourse-dependent artworks, one might urge that they are justified by the associated discourse. An avant-garde artwork could, then, be a source of knowledge about some important and controversial matter. No doubt sometimes the discourses associated with avant-garde artworks justify the statements they are used to make. When this is the case, however, the associated discourse is the item with cognitive value. A great deal of discourse on the nature of art is, for example, associated with *Fountain*. Some of this discourse has contributed importantly to the understanding of arthood. This discourse justifies the statement (one of those *Fountain* may be used to make) that arthood involves acceptance by an artworld. In this case, the associated discourse has cognitive value. Nothing is gained by contemplating the sculpture as well as becoming acquainted with the discourse. (Indeed, this is not an option, since the original work is lost.) Notice the difference between this case and the cases of artworks that are not discourse-dependent. Even after one has read everything written about, say, Rodin's *Thinker*, viewing the sculpture is still valuable. Indeed, one can only discover the full aesthetic value of this sculpture by experiencing it.

A final sort of artwork remains to be considered in this section. In this, the most advanced form of avant-garde art, no special semantic conventions are invented or discovered and artworks do not represent in conjunction with a discourse. Rather, quite simply, statements of natural languages become works of art. I will refer to this sort of work as *pure avant-garde art*. Pure avant-garde artworks have no more cognitive value than other artworks that rely exclusively on semantic representation. Moreover, they lack cognitive value for precisely the same reasons that other such works do.

The evolution of pure avant-garde art can be traced at least as far back as *The Treason of Images* (1928–29) by René Magritte. This work is a painting of a pipe and of the words '*Ceci n'est pas une pipe.*' This work is not yet pure avant-garde art. It is still, in part, an illustration of a pipe. Nevertheless, this painting is significant since the really important part of the work is the statement it makes. Without the painted words, the painting would not represent the fact that paintings are distinct from the objects they depict. It would simply be an illustration of a pipe.

In the 1960s, another stage was reached in the evolution of pure avant-garde art. This stage was reached by people who are usually classified as conceptual artists. Consider, for example, John Baldessari's *Everything Is Purged*. This work consists of a painting of the statement, 'Everything is purged from this painting but art, no ideas have entered this work.' All illustrative representation has been eliminated from this work. Another of Baldessari's works is a painting of the words 'A painting that is its own documentation'. (This painting is particularly interesting since it acknowledges the dependence of avant-garde art on discourse about art.) Baldessari's paintings are not quite pure semantic representations. They are still individual objects. Statements, by way of contrast, can be instantiated in a variety of graphic and phonetic forms. The final step in the transition from art as illustrative representation to art as semantic representation came a little later.

Only in the 1970s did avant-garde art reach its apotheosis. Jenny Holzer's *Truisms* provide excellent examples of pure avant-garde art, or artworks which are nothing but statements. Between 1977 and 1979, Holzer wrote a series of brief aphorisms which were displayed in a variety of forms. *Truisms* is the collection of these aphorisms. The most famous of the aphorisms is 'Abuse of power comes as no surprise.' Other aphorisms include 'Everyone's work is equally important' and 'Romantic love was invented to manipulate women.' The aphorisms were shown on electronic signs in New York's Times Square, London's Piccadilly Circus and in baseball stadiums. They were cast in bronze and carved in marble benches. LED displays were used to display the messages at the Guggenheim Museum in New York and at the Venice Biennale. In perhaps the most modern of the work's incarnations, it was printed on T-shirts. Holzer's *Truisms* represents the final stage in the transformation of statements into artworks. Like any statement, they can have a variety of phonetic or graphic forms. The representation is completely semantic. Nothing remains of illustrative representation.

When artworks are statements, art can sometimes be distinguished from non-art only with great difficulty. Consider, for example, the works of the Guerilla Girls. This group of anonymous female artists (who wear gorilla masks when they appear in public) began work in the spring of 1985 with the first of a series of posters. The first poster named forty-two well-known male artists who allowed their works to be shown in galleries which exhibited few works by women. Subsequent posters named the galleries that show few female artists, the critics who do not write about women's art, and so on. These posters might seem to be political posters, but they have been widely regarded as artworks. (The first thirty were issued in a limited edition boxed set.) Certainly, if statements can be artworks, the Guerilla Girls may be producing art. (I am inclined to say that their works are wonderful political acts, but not art.)

Let us turn now to an assessment of the cognitive value of works of pure avant-garde art. We have already seen, in the discussion of discourse-dependent artworks, that statements, by themselves, generally have little cognitive value. Pure avant-garde artworks, perhaps without exception, are the sort of statements that have little cognitive value. The problem with pure avant-garde artworks is not, in general, that they are false. Certainly, some of them are false. (Many of Jenny Holzer's *Truisms* are far from obviously true. I would be surprised to find that either 'Old friends are better left in the past' or 'Knowledge should be advanced at all costs' is true.) In other cases it is difficult to say what pure avant-garde artworks mean. (Consider, for example, Holzer's 'Stasis is a dream state' and 'You are the past[,] present and future.') Meaningless statements are not even candidate truths. The real problem with pure avant-garde artworks is that, even when true, they contribute little to knowledge. Sometimes they are true but statements of trivialities. Other pure avant-garde artworks may be interesting truths but audiences have no reason to believe them.

Reflection on examples of pure avant-garde art will indicate how this style alternates between triviality and unsubstantiated profundity. Magritte's *Treason of Images* is (as I have noted) not quite a pure avant-garde artwork, but it is a good example of a trivial work. As a matter of fact, just about everyone knows that a picture of a pipe is not a pipe. To the best of my knowledge, no artists have failed to recognise that their paintings of objects are not the objects themselves. Consequently, it is fair to say that the statement that a picture of a pipe is not a pipe is a trivial commonplace. Some of Holzer's *Truisms*, on the other hand, suffer from the other congenital defect of pure avant-garde artworks. Many of them are interesting and anyone who demonstrated that they are true would contribute a great deal to our knowledge. Consider, for example, 'The world operates according to discoverable laws' and 'There is nothing except what you sense.' Let us assume that these statements are true. If Holzer could demonstrate their truth, she would have contributed importantly to human knowledge. (Philosophers have been trying for millennia to demonstrate that these statements are true or false. They are anything but truisms.) Holzer, however, simply asserts them. No matter how reliable Holzer's testimony may be, her assertion does not amount to a demonstration of such statements. They need to be given a rational demonstration. The bare assertion of the statements has little cognitive value.

In general, pure avant-garde art faces a dilemma. Some statements ought to be believed on the basis of the speaker's testimony. However, only testimony about comparatively commonplace and trivial matters ought to be accepted without justification (besides the authority of the speaker). When pure avant-garde art consists of statements of such matters, it has little cognitive value. On the other hand, pure avant-garde art can make statements about interesting matters. In such cases, however, statements have little cognitive value without a supporting demonstration.

Of course, Holzer need not limit herself to simple statements such as those found in *Truisms*. Rather than simply making a statement about, say, causal laws, she could provide a series of connected statements which are designed to establish a position on this subject. Similarly, the Guerilla Girls could produce reasons for their statements. They could go on to develop a systematic position on art and women. In short, these artists could become essayists or philosophers and produce treatises. An artworld could call these treatises artworks. Most people would be inclined, however, to think that doing so stretched the concept of art beyond usefulness.

Perhaps I have been unfair to avant-garde art in regarding it as a species of semantic representation. One could try to defend the avant-garde by arguing that it is a more radical departure from the artistic tradition than I have acknowledged. Perhaps the style, or some of its instances, involves the complete rejection of art as representation. Perhaps many avant-garde artworks are gestures rather than representations. A gesture can provide knowledge without representing anything. Suppose, for example, two people are in a crowded room and one asks the other, 'Who is the Chair of the Philosophy Department?' A gesture of pointing will provide an answer to this question without representing the Chair of the Department. The gesture is used to provide an illustrative demonstration. Perhaps avant-garde artworks function like this gesture. Such works could indicate something to an audience without recourse to representation.

The suggestion that avant-garde artworks are non-representational gestures seems to capture the functioning of some famous works in the style. Consider, for example, Cage's *4' 33"*. This work, four minutes and thirty-three seconds of silence, is intended to draw the attention of listeners to the sounds produced in the world around them. It could be seen as a gesture that reveals something about these sounds to an audience, without representing the sounds. A similar claim could be made about many pieces of performance art. Consider, for example, some of the works of Chris Burden, or Vito Acconci's *Seedbed* (1971). In this work, Acconci masturbated under a platform while fantasising about the gallery-visitors above him. Perhaps this work is a sort of gesture. One could argue that even pure avant-garde works are not really semantic representations. Perhaps the display of one of Holzer's truisms on a stadium scoreboard ought to be regarded as a kind of gesture, not as a statement. Similarly, Tracy Emin's *Everyone I Ever Slept with from 1963–1995* (a tent with over 100 names) could be regarded as a gesture of some sort.

Let us suppose, for the sake of argument, that some avant-garde works are intended as gestures. The trouble with this line of argument is that audiences frequently cannot determine the significance of the gesture made by an avant-garde work simply by examining the work. They must have recourse to an associated discourse. A gesture normally is dependent on the existence of a convention. Only because a convention exists does a shrug express indifference or a nod assent. Obviously, conventions do not exist in the case of every avant-garde work that might be supposed to function like a gesture. Something else must be used to indicate the significance of the gesture made by a work. This function is performed by an associated discourse.

Consider, for example, a work, such as Cage's *4' 33"*, which is plausibly regarded as a gesture. This composition gestures to ambient sounds only against the background of Cage's fairly extensive pronouncements. As such the work seems to be discourse-dependent. The gestural capacities of works of Acconci, Burden, Emin and Holzer seem to be even more dependent on what is said and written about them. Certainly, the matter towards which *Seedbed* or one of Burden's performances gestures is difficult to determine, in the absence of familiarity with an associated discourse. Consequently, these works do not seem to count against the thesis that avant-garde art involves the replacement of illustration by semantic representation, with all the unfortunate consequences that attend this replacement.

But is it art?

The previous paragraph returned to a question, first broached in Chapter 1, about the definition of art. There we saw that anything can be a work of art. It simply needs to be accepted as such by an artworld. At the same time, we saw that artworlds can be given practical reasons for accepting as artworks only works with a limited range of properties. In particular, reasons can be given for restricting the class of artworks to works with cognitive value qua representations. If this restriction is accepted, doubts arise about the arthood of many avant-garde works. For a variety of reasons, many avant-garde works fail to be representations. Consequently, good reasons can be given for saying that these works ought not to be regarded as artworks. These reasons will be rehearsed in this section. This section will also suggest that only works with cognitive value qua illustrative representations ought to be regarded as artworks.

As we saw in the opening section of Chapter 2 (pp. 23–5), something is a representation if and only if three conditions are met. Of these three conditions, I particularly want to recall the intentionality and recognition conditions. A representation, we saw, stands for or is about an object. This aboutness is the essence of representation. In order, however, for something to be about some object, it must be intended to be about it. A representation is also recognisable as standing for an object. Moreover, audience members besides the creator of the representation must be able to recognise what the representation is about. In many cases, avant-garde artworks fail to meet the intentionality and recognition conditions. Consequently, they are not representations and practical reasons can be given for denying that they are works of art.

Let us begin by considering avant-garde works that do not meet the intentionality condition. Many avant-garde works have been produced without any intention to represent. Indeed, some avant-garde works have been produced without many intentions at all. This rejection of intentionality can be traced at least as far back as dadaism. Tzara, the influential dada poet, advocated the use of chance in the production of poetry. He recommended the following as a method of writing poetry. Cut words from a newspaper. Place them in a bag and shake. Draw the words out of the bag one at a time. The order in which the words come out is the order in which they appear in the poem. (I am not certain that Tzara employed this method in the production of his own poems, though in fairness to him they appear to have been produced in this manner.) More recently, computers have been used to take the intention to represent out of the production of poetry. Several internet sites exist where computers generate poetry completely automatically. In some cases, site visitors can choose a few key words that will appear in a poem that is otherwise generated by the computer. In any case, the intention to represent plays no role in the production of computer poetry.

Some avant-garde musical compositions, like some avant-garde poetry, are not the product of an intention to represent. Consider, for example, some of the music of John Cage. Cage flipped coins to determine which notes to include in his *Music of Changes*. Similarly, every performance of *Imaginary Landscape No. 4*, a work scored for twelve radios, is a chance product. The radio dials are scanned up and down and each radio briefly sounds as it hits a station. The sound of each performance is a product of whatever happens to be playing on whatever radio stations can be received. Even Cage's most famous composition, *4' 33"*, is an example of an aleatory or chance composition. The sound of a performance of this work is a collection of chance ambient noises. Cage is not the only composer to produce musical compositions by means of chance, rather than intention. Pierre Boulez and Iannis Xenakis are other notable composers of aleatory music. Playing cards, dice and spatters of paint have all been used in the production of such music.

Objects produced by chance are no more representations than is the piece of rock in the desert that resembles Louis XIV (discussed in 'What is representation?' in Chapter 2, pp. 23–5). They can be beautiful, in the same way that a natural object can be beautiful. Aleatory objects may even prompt people to think about something in a new way. As a result, they may have cognitive value. An artist may, for example, toss some paint over his shoulder and accidentally create a painting that resembles the Sun King. The painting may put an audience in a position to see something about Louis or his characteristics. Even if this happens, however, the painting is not a representation since the intentionality condition is not met. If the class of artworks is limited to representations with cognitive value, the painting is not an artwork. No more are computer- or chance-generated poetry, or aleatory compositions.

Just as some avant-garde works fail to satisfy the intentionality condition, others fail to satisfy the recognition condition. Consider, for example, certain works of abstract expressionism. The paintings of Newman, since he was so adamant that his works are representational, are particularly worth considering.

They are also interesting because Newman often indicated what he intended to represent in a given painting. Starting in the late 1940s, Newman's paintings conformed to a quite distinctive pattern. They generally consisted of solid fields of colour broken by vertical (or, occasionally, horizontal) stripes or (as he called them) zips in a contrasting colour. *Dionysus* (1949) is an early example of a work in Newman's mature style. It consists of a green field trisected by narrow, horizontal bands, one yellow and one orange. Newman wrote, apropos this painting, that his 'image of Bacchus is *luxus*, luxuriousness, a lazy girl lying down in abandon – eating grapes'. Others of his zip paintings were intended to represent religious subjects. These paintings include his series, *Stations of the Cross*, and *Cathedra*. The latter is intended by Newman as a representation of the chair of God. I do not think that Newman intended these paintings as discourse-dependent works (and, consequently, semantic representations). Rather, they were intended as illustrations. Nevertheless, they are not obviously representations of any sort.

Only one method exists for determining whether some work meets the recognition condition. An alleged representation must be presented to qualified audience members and they (or, at least, almost all of them) must agree about what is represented. I have not rigorously employed this method to test the hypothesis that Newman's paintings meet the recognition condition. I can say, however, that without independent knowledge of his intentions, I would never have been able to determine what his paintings are supposed to represent. Many apparently competent audience members seem to share my experience. Erwin Panofsky, the great art historian, for example, was completely bemused by Newman's paintings. Virtually the entire Canadian public was puzzled by *Voice of Fire* when it was purchased by the National Gallery of Canada. Under the circumstances, it is at least doubtful that, say, *Cathedra* is a representation. Consequently, questions can be raised about the arthood of this work. I suggest that similar doubts can be raised about the arthood of many other avant-garde works. Notice that if the recognition condition is not satisfied, neither will the interpretability principle, discussed in 'Criteria of evaluation' in Chapter 4 (pp. 126–34), be satisfied.

Newman and other avant-garde artists (notably Mondrian) share a mistaken view about illustrative representation. They believe that it is possible to illustrate something like luxuriousness, beauty or equality in general without illustrating a particular object which is luxurious, beautiful or equal. (*Dionysius* is not, of course, intended as a representation of a lazy girl eating grapes. It is intended to represent luxuriousness in general.) My argument for this conclusion starts from an ontological premiss: beauty, for example, does not exist independently of beautiful things. If this is the case, it is hard to see how beauty can be illustrated without illustrating something beautiful. My ontological view is, of course, not indubitable. Plato doubts it. Even if I am wrong about the ontological status of beauty, however, beauty in general cannot be illustrated. We have no experience of beauty in general, only experience of particular beautiful things. Now, illustrative representation depends on a resemblance between experience of an object and experience of a representation of the object. Consequently, something like beauty in general cannot be illustrated. To the extent that avant-garde artists intend to represent things in general, they fail to represent and the arthood of their works is open to question.

Perhaps I have unfairly neglected the possibility that avant-garde art employs affective illustration. So far I have proceeded on the assumption that if avant-garde works are illustrations, they are so because experience of these works can resemble visual experience of the objects they illustrate. Perhaps, however, avant-garde works can be illustrations because experience of them can resemble affective experience. This possibility certainly cannot be discounted. Many avant-garde artists state that they intend their works to be about emotions, and audiences report the sort of affective reactions to some avant-garde works that would make affective illustration possible. Such claims have notably been made about abstract expressionism, op art and other sorts of avant-garde art. Peter Halley is a contemporary avant-garde artist who says that some of his paintings are about feelings. These works, in the neo-geo style that revives classical hard-edged abstraction, are, according to Halley, about modern emotions such as being freaked out or feeling a little spacey.

Here I cannot rule out the possibility that some avant-garde works successfully represent affects and count as works of art. Indeed, I have no desire to do so. I believe that some avant-garde works are artworks, even by my own responsible criteria of arthood. These avant-garde works probably owe their arthood to the fact that they are affective illustrations. Nevertheless, reasons can be given for doubting that affective illustration is common in avant-garde art. If so, many avant-garde works cannot owe arthood to the fact that they are affective representations.

The first reason is that affective illustration is difficult, if not impossible, without the illustration of something besides affects. As noted in 'Types of representation' in Chapter 2 (pp. 26–34), extrospective affective illustration is impossible without the representation of an object towards which an affect is directed. Avant-garde works, since they employ few of the resources of illustrative representation, usually cannot illustrate objects, such as persons, places and things, towards which affects are directed. Consequently, introspective affective illustration is the only sort we can expect to find in most avant-garde works. That is, such works can only represent the affects themselves, independently of their relations to objects. Even this sort of representation often depends on the representation of objects other than the represented affect. Experience of a lyric poem, for example, is often able to resemble experience of an affect because of the way some object is represented. Consider again *Mariana*. It can represent despair in part because experience of Tennyson's representation of the situation of Mariana has an affective element. Even in instrumental music, introspective affective illustration is aided by the representation of movement (and the moving body this representation presupposes).

Affective illustration is possible without the representation of objects. As noted in the final section of Chapter 2 (pp. 60–4), the experience of the formal properties of music can resemble experience of emotions. The experience of a balanced, graceful composition can resemble experience of serenity, while experience of unstable music can resemble experience of distracted melancholy. Perhaps, similarly, experiences of non-figurative avant-garde paintings and sculptures can resemble experiences of various affects. So, for example, experience of a painting with a particular jarring combination of colours may resemble experience of being freaked out. I expect that some such resemblances make possible affective illustration by some avant-garde works. These works ought to be regarded as works of art.

Nevertheless, affective illustration is probably less common in avant-garde works than artists intend. I have two reasons for thinking this. For a start, I am impressed by the fact that audience members frequently report quite different responses to a single avant-garde work. The same work may, for example, be described as a representation of inner turmoil, of inner peace and of several other dramatically different affects. When this happens, one can reasonably doubt whether the recognition condition has been satisfied. Of course, audiences differ about what affects are represented by some of the greatest works of instrumental music. I still want to say that works of instrumental music can be affective illustrations. The difference is that large segments of an audience agree about what is represented in great musical works, while differences of opinion about avant-garde works are widespread. Very few listeners believe, for example, that Mozart's Symphony No. 40 in G Minor (K 550) contains a representation of carefree insouciance. Although audiences are not unanimous about what this work represents, the consensus is that this work is about dark emotions. I believe that less consensus exists about what is represented in avant-garde works. This is, however, an empirical claim and it may be false.

If the claim is not false, its truth is easily explained. One of the factors that makes possible affective representation in music is not available to works in the avant-garde style. Experience of an artwork is influenced by an audience's knowledge about a style. In the context of one style, certain formal properties will appear outré and bizarre. In the context of another style, the same properties will seem unremarkable. Jarring harmonies are, for example, experienced quite differently in classical and romantic music. In the context of one style, such harmonies are shocking, in the context of the other they are expected. Affective illustration is possible in music (in part) because audiences and composers are familiar with the clearly established conventions of various musical styles. Shared stylistic conventions, employed by artists and familiar to audiences, constitute the factor missing in the avant-garde style. The absence of this factor makes affective representation in avant-garde works even more difficult. This is the second of my reasons for scepticism about the existence of widespread affective illustration in avant-garde art.

When audiences are presented with an avant-garde work they are frequently ignorant of the work's stylistic conventions. To a certain extent, audiences are inevitably ignorant of these conventions of avant-garde art since they are constantly changing. As a result, audiences are likely to be bewildered by avant-garde works. They simply will not know how to experience the formal properties of many avant-garde works. Some combination of colours may seem to be jarring, but perhaps in some avant-garde sub-style it is not intended to be jarring. Consequently, when audiences do not know how to experience works, these works cannot be affective illustrations. The recognition condition is not met. Unless these works represent in some other way, if artworks ought to be representations with cognitive value, these works ought not to be endowed with arthood.

Even if affective representation plays a role in some avant-garde works, we saw in 'The semantics of avant-garde art' earlier in this chapter (pp. 144–54) that some avant-garde works employ only semantic representation. One might reasonably wonder whether these semantic works ought to be accepted as works of art. If members of an artworld want to accept them as works of art, they are free to do so. Avant-garde works which employ only semantic representation generally have, however, little cognitive value. In fact, they possess so little cognitive value, and so little aesthetic value, that an artworld might very well want to discourage production of such works. One way to discourage the production of more such works is to refuse to accord them arthood. With any luck at all, avant-garde artists will return to the production of works that make full use of the resources of illustrative representation. In any case, an artworld can be given good practical reasons for not accepting some avant-garde works as artworks.

Destroying works of avant-garde art

Suppose I am right and many avant-garde artworks have little aesthetic value. Suppose, moreover, that many people come to share this opinion. A pressing question then arises about what to do with all the unvalued art. More specifically, there is a question about whether the destruction of artworks is ever permissible. This is not merely an academic question. Calls have been heard for the destruction of such avant-garde works as André's *Stone Field* (thirty-six glacial boulders arranged in a triangle in a Hartford, Connecticut, churchyard). I believe that these calls will become more common as museums awaken to the fact that they are saddled with a great deal of very bad art. Already some avant-garde works have been deliberately destroyed. The most celebrated of these is Richard Serra's *Tilted Arc*, destroyed in 1989. Any suggestion that artworks may be destroyed is usually condemned and dismissed as philistinism, vandalism or both. The destruction of artwork is also condemned as a violation of artists' rights. Under some conditions, however, the destruction of an artwork is unobjectionable. This will come as welcome news to those who share my opinion of much avant-garde art.

A couple of preliminary points are necessary before I begin to argue that the destruction of art can be permissible. The first point concerns the status of the works whose destruction is mooted. The previous section raised doubts about the arthood of many avant-garde works. If these doubts are well-founded, then any strictures against the destruction of artworks do not apply to some avant-garde works. If no reasons could be given for thinking that a sheet of rusted metal is an artwork, no one would cavil at putting it out with the rubbish. When I say that the destruction of some avant-garde works is permissible, I do not want it to be permissible for the reason that they are not artworks. Consequently, for the purposes of this section, I will assume that all of the candidates for destruction are works of art.

The second preliminary point is that questions about whether some artwork may be destroyed cannot be answered simply by reflection on proprietary matters. The destruction of an artwork, without its owner's permission, is wrong in most circumstances. The ownership of an artwork does not, however, carry with it the right to dispose of the work. Suppose, for example, that I buy the *Portrait of Ginevra de' Benci* from the National Gallery of Art in Washington. Suppose that the gallery had a legal right to sell it and I certainly possess legal title to the work. I would still act wrongly if, on a whim, I destroyed the painting. The law in many jurisdictions recognises that the destruction of artworks in private hands is wrong. For example, it is illegal in many places to destroy architectural works that have been designated as heritage buildings. A consequentialist principle justifies these laws and the wrongness of destroying the da Vinci. Some works are so valuable to humanity that restrictions on what anyone may do to it are justified. This point raises the larger question of whether someone ever owns an artwork. After all, ownership of something is the right to dispose of it freely. This matter cannot be resolved here. For now, the important point is that questions about whether an artwork may be destroyed are not questions about ownership.

The destruction of many artworks is certainly wrong under most circumstances. Regardless of the criteria of arthood selected by a responsible artworld, most artworks have value and, thus, contribute to human well-being. The injunction against destroying works of art is simply a special case of a more general imperative. *Ceteris paribus*, one should not destroy things that contribute to human well-being. When it is wrong to destroy some artwork, for the same sort of reason it is wrong to vandalise public buildings, kill whales or deface scenes of natural beauty. Sometimes, however, the *prima facie* case against destroying something can be overcome. This is the case when the preservation of something valuable requires that something else of value be sacrificed. When not all value can be preserved, difficult calculations must be made. Such calculations are difficult because things are valuable in different ways. Still, these calculations can be made. On some of them, the destruction of artworks, including avant-garde artworks, is justified.

A few examples will illustrate the general point that the destruction of valuable things is sometimes justifiable. A tree, for example, may have value as a thing of natural beauty. Still, under some circumstances felling the tree is justifiable. I may, for example, need to use the timber to build a house to protect myself from the elements. Similarly, freedom of speech and assembly are valuable, but they may be restricted under some circumstances. In time of war or other emergency, for example, certain basic civil liberties can justifiably be suspended. In such a case, survival of a society is considered more valuable than preservation of certain freedoms.

Consider now the question of whether a work of art may be destroyed. One can easily imagine circumstances under which even good artworks could unobjectionably be destroyed. Consider, for example, the following variation on the classic lifeboat problem. Someone is adrift in a lifeboat full of Rembrandts. The only way to prevent the lifeboat from sinking, and ruining the paintings, is to throw some of the pictures overboard. The occupant of the boat, an art historian, makes a quick calculation of the relative aesthetic values of the paintings. The best available evidence suggests that a couple of portraits, fortunately rather heavy, are relatively poor. The art historian tosses them over the gunwale. Plainly, he does not act wrongly in consigning these pictures to the deep. Or suppose that a group of terrorists is barricaded in a lovely Norman church. Suppose, moreover, that only by destroying the church can the terrorists be prevented from killing thirty children. One would not, in these circumstances, act wrongly in destroying the church. Indeed, one would act wrongly if one did not.

Two conclusions can be drawn from these examples. Both cases show that artworks may be destroyed when more of value is lost by not destroying them. The second example also shows that non-aesthetic considerations may be weighed when deciding whether to destroy an artwork. What holds for artworks in general applies equally to avant-garde works. Under circumstances similar to those described in the previous paragraph, tossing Pollocks into the ocean, or blowing up the Seagram Building, is unobjectionable. In neither of the examples, however, is an artwork destroyed qua artwork. In the first case, paintings are destroyed qua ballast and in the second a building is being destroyed qua redoubt. The interesting question is whether a work of art may be destroyed just qua work of low aesthetic value.

I suggest that the answer to this question is that artworks may legitimately be destroyed simply because they are bad. The aesthetic value of an artwork can be so low that it is not able to outweigh the cost of the work's upkeep. Imagine that some museum owns a painting of indisputably low aesthetic value. For hundreds of years, say, no one has ever thought that this artwork rises anywhere close to mediocrity. When a curator hangs the painting in the museum cafeteria, diners complain that they are being put off their food. (This happened once at the Art Gallery of New South Wales in Sydney.) When the museum attempts to sell the painting, no bids are received. Finally, in despair, the museum staff attempt to give away the painting, but no one is willing to take it off their hands. If the painting is returned to the vault, it will occupy much-needed storage space. (The museum has made other unwise investments.) Effort must be expended to keep the painting warm and dry. Tax dollars will be expended. Under such circumstances, a curator decides that the painting has so little value that it is not worth preserving. He leaves it in the dumpster in the lane behind the gallery. In doing so, he does not act wrongly. Nor does anyone act wrongly who destroys bad art under comparable circumstances. Many avant-garde artworks are so bad that they cannot justify their own preservation. The destruction of these works is permissible.

This conclusion faces several possible objections. I will begin with what might be called the historical interest objection. Even when a work possesses little aesthetic value, it may possess historical interest or value. As an object of historical interest, it may be wrong to destroy an object. Consider, for example, a piece of rudely decorated pre-Columbian peasant pottery. No one will ever confuse it with good art. Nevertheless, it would be wrong to destroy such a work.

It can provide insight into interesting aspects of daily life in past cultures. Similarly, one might argue, no matter how little aesthetic value many avant-garde works possess, future generations may be curious about what has passed for art in our time. That is, avant-garde artworks possess historical value. Indeed, the lower the aesthetic value of these works, the higher the historical value may be. The more bizarre an avant-garde artwork, the more historical fascination it may hold for a future artworld. In short, an estimate of the aesthetic value of an artwork can never, by itself, justify the work's destruction.

A great deal can be said for the historical interest objection. Questions about whether the destruction of an artwork is justifiable are concerned with its total value, not just its aesthetic value. While something may possess little aesthetic value, it may have value in another way, perhaps as an object of historical interest. Another work may possess value as, say, a windbreak. These other sorts of value must be taken into consideration. Even so, however, works of art may sometimes be unobjectionably destroyed. The total value, aesthetic and non-aesthetic, of an artwork may still not be sufficient to outweigh the costs of its preservation. Some future artworld may be mildly amused by an exhibition of some avant-garde sculpture. This mild amusement may not, however, be unable to outweigh the ennui a contemporary audience suffers daily from exposure to the banal piece of public art. In any case, clearly the mere fact that something has or will have historical value is not sufficient to show that it may not be destroyed. If it were, nothing ought to be destroyed. In ten thousand years, a glass given away (with a minimum purchase) at a service station may be of enormous historical interest. Surely, however, I may throw one away if I please. Perhaps we ought to document the works we destroy, or preserve a representative sample of avant-garde works. But the fact that they have historical interest is not enough to protect them from destruction.

Another objection to my view may be called the argument from contrast. According to this argument, we are only able to apprehend the virtues of good art because we can contrast it with poor art. Perhaps if only masterpieces existed, we would grow insensitive to their greatness. Since it is obviously undesirable that audiences lose the capacity to appreciate great art, the argument concludes, one ought not to destroy bad art.

I am completely unpersuaded by the argument from contrast. I do not believe that audiences can apprehend the virtues of good art only if they are familiar with the vices of bad art. One need not have suffered agony in order to experience pleasure. Even if a contrast is required, some neutral state will probably suffice. Similarly, one need not experience the worst art in order to appreciate the best. If a contrast is required, mediocre art will suffice. Even if, however, we grant the initial premiss of the argument from contrast, its conclusion does not follow.

Perhaps a weaker conclusion can be inferred. Perhaps it is wrong to destroy all bad art. A few bad pieces would be able to provide the necessary contrast. The remainder could be destroyed. One might doubt whether even this weaker conclusion follows. After all, new bad art will always be created.

According to another version of the argument from contrast, avant-garde artworks could be useful to future generations of art teachers. They could, for example, provide valuable exemplars of what artists ought not to produce. One could hold that it is not enough to preserve some bad art. Rather, it may seem, we ought to preserve representative examples of all the ways in which art can be bad. Now, avant-garde art certainly goes wrong in ways never before seen in the history of art. (Nowhere else has illustrative representation been so comprehensively rejected.) One might conclude that avant-garde works ought to be preserved. Again, however, the argument fails to prove that all avant-garde art ought to be preserved. So long as representative samples are preserved, and others are documented, future art teachers will have all the resources they need.

A further objection starts from the premiss that any destruction of artworks violates artists' rights. Serra, for example, has claimed that the destruction of *Tilted Arc* violated his rights. I am uncertain about precisely what rights are supposed to be violated by the destruction of an artwork. When artists have sold or given away a work, their property rights are not violated by its destruction. Perhaps, however, the right to freedom of expression is violated by the destruction of artworks. One could argue that destroying an artwork is tantamount to interfering with freedom of the press or like stopping someone from speaking in public. Perhaps conditions must be met before freedom of expression is permitted. Perhaps, for example, permission to hold a rally or erect a sculpture in a public place must be obtained. But, one might argue, once these conditions are met, a rally cannot be stopped or an artwork destroyed simply because some people do not approve of what is being expressed. Since restrictions on freedom of expression are wrong, one might conclude, the destruction of artworks is wrong.

The argument from artists' rights is not without force, but it does not demonstrate that all destruction of art is wrong. Without a doubt, everyone ought to be allowed to express himself in art. People ought even to be permitted to create bad art. One cannot, however, validly infer from this that artists have the right to have their art preserved for them. Consider, for example, the following parallel case. A political party has the right to print a pamphlet and place it in my mailbox. I would be wrong to destroy this pamphlet before it has been distributed. Once it has been placed in my mailbox, however, I am free to destroy it. Even if everyone throws away the pamphlet, no wrong has been done. (At least, this is true most of the time. I might act wrongly if I destroyed what I had reason to believe is the last copy of an historically important pamphlet.) Similarly, if an artist sells or gives me a painting, I may (under some circumstances) destroy it. If I own a piece of lousy op art, I may burn it in my back yard.

A fourth argument against the destruction of art is a slippery slope argument. One might argue that the destruction of artworks is always wrong because it may lead to the destruction of other works. Perhaps if museum curators get into the habit of destroying bad art, they may find the habit hard to break. Perhaps they will end up destroying art that is not bad, but merely inconvenient for some reason. (A similar argument is often made against assisted suicide.) The destruction of artworks may also lead society to devalue the arts. This may have the result that further works are destroyed, ones that ought to be preserved. Obviously, this would be an unfortunate outcome and can be taken as grounds for refraining from the destruction of all artworks.

The slippery slope argument is difficult to assess without a better idea about the probability that the destruction of some artworks will lead to the devaluation of art and so the destruction of other, valuable, works. Nevertheless, the preservation of bad artworks could have worse consequences than its destruction. I do not doubt that the proliferation of bad avant-garde art has led to a fall in public esteem for the arts. In many quarters, even in educated circles, artists are regarded as charlatans. If the low standing of artists and the arts has not led to the destruction of artworks, this has only been good fortune. Certainly, widespread contempt for avant-garde art has made cultural spending an attractive target for cost-cutting governments. If bad avant-garde artworks (and, to be fair, bad works in other styles) lower the public's opinion of the arts, we have another reason to destroy them.

Perhaps the most trenchant argument against the destruction of bad artworks is an epistemological argument. The view that bad works of art may be destroyed presupposes that bad works are distinguishable from good ones. Now, one might argue, we have no completely reliable way to decide which works of art are good and which are bad. Since we have no completely reliable test of aesthetic value, one might conclude, we ought not to destroy any artworks lest we destroy good ones. This argument becomes even more worrisome when we consider that, in some cases, estimates of the aesthetic merit of works have changed over time. For many years, for example, one could scarcely give away the works of Lord Leighton (mainly because they are not avant-garde). Now, however, they are recognised as masterpieces. In some cases, the value of an artwork has not been widely recognised for some years. The merits of Van Gogh's paintings, for example, were not initially recognised.

This epistemological argument is worrisome. Certainly, errors can be made about the aesthetic value of artworks. At the very least, this possibility is reason to employ the utmost caution before destroying artworks. The epistemological argument does not, however, prove that art ought never to be destroyed simply because it is bad. I have two reasons for thinking this. For a start, I am not unduly pessimistic about the ability to distinguish good art from bad. True, false judgements about artworks abound. Some works are undervalued and some (among them many avant-garde works) are absurdly overvalued. Nevertheless, it is possible to know that certain artworks are good and others very bad. (The guidelines offered in 'Criteria of evaluation' in Chapter 4 (pp. 126–34) should be of assistance.) Only because artworks can be known to have aesthetic value is art a worthwhile enterprise. Even if all decisions about the destruction of artworks involve some uncertainty, however, artworks may sometimes be destroyed. Any moral decision involves some measure of uncertainty. This is not a reason for refusing to make moral decisions. Nor does a small measure of uncertainty about an artwork's value constitute grounds for refusing to make a decision about its destruction.

Any decision to destroy a work of art should not be taken lightly. The act of destroying a work of art, even a bad work of art, is not to be compared with, say, throwing away a useless kitchen appliance (an electric wok, say, or an inefficient fish-slice). A work of art, even a bad one, has a cultural significance lacked by most kitchen appliances. Since art is so important to a culture, artworks should be accorded a measure of respect and protection not extended to kitchen appliances. It does not follow that artworks ought never to be destroyed. Artworks are important because they can serve human interests. When the preservation of an artwork ceases to serve human interests, it may be destroyed. Some works of art are so bad that they are simply not worth preserving. A disproportionate percentage of avant-garde works fall into this class.

Envoy

In the early eighteenth century, Joseph Addison noted that, 'It is impossible for us, who live in the latter ages of the world, to make observations in criticism, morality, or in any art or science, which have not been touched upon by others. We have little else left us but to represent the common sense of mankind in more strong, more beautiful, or more uncommon lights.' Three centuries later, saying something startlingly new about the arts or criticism of the arts is even more difficult. Here I have tried to follow Addison's advice and represent as strongly as I can humanity's common sense. Almost everyone has the belief that works of art can have great value. Equally many people believe that artworks are not, like the products of vintners and upholsterers, simply valuable as sources of pleasure. Artworks can be a source of something many people find more valuable than pleasure. As Sir Joshua Reynolds noted, 'the natural appetite or taste of the human mind is for Truth'. This is the appetite which works of art can, however temporarily, satisfy. Although this has long been abundantly clear to many reflective people, how art caters to the taste for truth has been less clear. I hope that this essay has contributed to the understanding of how art contributes to knowledge.

NOTES

PREFACE

The passage from Dylan Thomas is quoted in R. W. Beardsmore, 'Learning from a Novel', *Royal Institute of Philosophy Lectures*, 1973, vol. 6, p. 32.

DEFINITIONS OF ART

When I say that an earlier generation of writers on the epistemology of art assumed that works of art have cognitive value, I have in mind Theodore Meyer Greene, *The Arts and the Art of Criticism*, 2nd edn, Princeton, Princeton University Press, 1952. Greene held (p. 233) that, 'It is only in periods of cultural and spiritual decadence, ... that the "aesthete" (in the narrow and derogatory sense) has made his appearance and proclaimed that art is *reducible* to aesthetically agreeable patterns of sound and color.' Greene did not accept that works without cognitive value can be genuine art.

The approach to the definition of art adopted here has been influenced by T. J. Diffey and Arthur Danto. Diffey first held that works of art are those adopted by an artworld. See 'The Republic of Art', in his *The Republic of Art and Other Essays*, New York, Peter Lang, 1991. This essay was first published in *British Journal of Aesthetics*, 1969, vol. 9, 145–56. From Danto I have taken the idea that an artworld confers arthood by means of theories, but I speak of guidelines instead of theories. Danto presents his view in a number of places, including *The Transfiguration of the Commonplace*, Cambridge, Mass., Harvard University Press, 1981, and *The Philosophical Disenfranchisement of Art*, New York, Columbia University Press, 1986. The best general discussion of definitions of art is Stephen Davies, *Definitions of Art*, Ithaca, Cornell University Press, 1991.

I am not the first to use Plato's *Euthyphro* to provide insight into definitions of art. See Melvin Rader, 'Dickie and Socrates on Definition', *Journal of Aesthetics and Art Criticism*, 1974, vol. 32, 423–4.

THE RELATIVITY OF ARTHOOD

For the views of Royal Cortissoz on Duchamp and other avant-garde artists, see 'The Post-Impressionist Illusion', in his *Art and Common Sense*, New York, Charles Scribner's Sons, 1913.

DEFINING ART RESPONSIBLY

Richard Wollheim is among those who have complained that institutional definitions of art (of which my perspectival definition is an example) are suspect because they divorce questions of arthood from questions of value. See *Painting as an Art*, London, Thames and Hudson, 1987, p. 15. Wollheim is also an example of someone who objects to institutional definitions on the grounds that the artworld does not hold meetings where arthood is conferred. See *Painting as an Art*, p. 16.

George Dickie believes that something is an artwork when it is created by a recognised artist for presentation to an artworld. I have his view in mind when I talk about how it would be misguided to accept guidelines which classify as artworks items that have been so produced. It would be unfair to attribute to Dickie the view that such guidelines ought to be adopted. Nevertheless, such a guideline captures the spirit of his version of the institutional definition of art. See *The Art Circle*, New York, Haven, 1984, p. 80f.

The principal point on which Danto and I differ concerns how guidelines (or theories) succeed each other. I have Danto in mind when, towards the end of this section, I reject the view that sets of guidelines succeed each other with Hegelian inevitability.

WHY ART OUGHT TO HAVE COGNITIVE VALUE

The quotation from Horace is taken from *The Art of Poetry*, trans. Thomas Howes, ed. Albert S. Cook, Boston, Ginn and Company, 1892, p. 25.

WHAT IS REPRESENTATION?

My assertion that private representations cannot exist (embodied in the recognition condition) relies on Wittgenstein's argument (in the *Philosophical Investigations*, trans. G. E. M. Anscombe, Oxford, Basil Blackwell, 1967) against the possibility of a private language.

TYPES OF REPRESENTATION

The account of representation given in this section is fundamentally at odds with Goodman's influential account, presented most fully in *Languages of Art*, Indianapolis, Hackett, 1976. He maintains that resemblance has nothing to do with representation in the arts. This is not the place to refute Goodman's position, but it has recently been subjected to a number of telling criticisms. See, for example, Flint Schier, *Deeper into Pictures*, Cambridge, Cambridge University Press, 1986 and Dominic Lopes, *Understanding Pictures*, Oxford, Oxford University Press, 1996.

THE REPRESENTATION OF TYPES

The passage from Aristotle is found in *Poetics*, trans. Preston H. Epps, Chapel Hill, University of North Carolina Press, 1970, p. 18 (1451 b). There Aristotle says that 'poetry is something more philosophic and of more serious import than history; for poetry tends to deal with the general, while history is concerned with delimited particular facts'.

When I refer to Anthony Trollope I have in mind his statement that his intention was to teach 'by representing to [his] readers characters like themselves, or which they might liken to themselves'. *An Autobiography*, London, Oxford University Press, 1950, p. 146.

VISUAL ART AND SEMANTIC REPRESENTATION

Many people have held the view that pictures can serve as statements. See Søren Kjørup, 'George Inness and the Battle at Hastings, or Doing Things with Pictures', *The Monist*, 1974, vol. 58, 216–35; David Novitz, *Pictures and Their Use in Communication*, The Hague, Martinus Nijhoff, 1977; Marcia Eaton, 'Truth in Pictures', *Journal of Aesthetics and Art Criticism*, 1980–1, vol. 39, 15-26; Carolyn Korsmeyer, 'Pictorial Assertion', *Journal of Aesthetics and Art Criticism*, 1985, vol. 43, 257–65; Morris Weitz, *Philosophy of the Arts*, Cambridge, Mass., Harvard University Press, 1950, pp. 147ff.; and Otto Neurath, *International Picture Language*, London, Kegan Paul, Trench, Truber & Co., 1936, p. 20. Novitz is responsible for the suggestion that context can enable pictures to function as statements. See *Pictures and Their Use in Communication*, p. 93.

The influential definition of information to which I refer is given by Fred Dretske, *Knowledge and the Flow of Information*, Cambridge, Mass., MIT Press, 1981, p. 44.

The picture of the boxer is discussed in Wittgenstein's *Philosophical Investigations*, p. 11n. Novitz also notes that transforming pictures into propositions is difficult. 'The problem is that there is no way way of knowing what is to count as a correct translation of, say, a cow-in-a-field-picture. The sentence "The cow is in the field" is just one among many possible candidates, for one could also use sentences like "This is a cow in profile" or "A cow is eating clover", and so on indefinitely.' *Pictures and Their Use in Communication*, p. 86.

The concept of syntactical repleteness is introduced by Nelson Goodman, *Languages of Art*, pp. 229f.

REPRESENTATION IN LITERATURE

My suggestion that literal meanings are the only meanings is influenced by Donald Davidson, 'What Metaphors Mean', in his *Inquiries into Truth and Interpretation*, Oxford, Clarendon Press, 1984.

The *Dilbert* strip to which I refer was published on 17 July 1997.

REPRESENTATION IN MUSIC: I

For an excellent survey of the arguments against the existence of a language of music, see Stephen Davies, *Musical Meaning and Expression*, Ithaca, Cornell University Press, 1994, ch. 1.

Carroll Pratt is one source of the suggestion that musical works '*sound* the way moods *feel*'. *The Meaning of Music: A study in psychological aesthetics*, New York, Johnson Reprint Corporation, 1968, p. 203. Pratt, in the same work (pp. 185ff.), anticipates some of the points I make in this section about the relation of musical movement to bodily movement. Roger Scruton has noted the connection between music and dance. He holds that, 'There is no doubt in our feeling that the object of this [musical] imitation is a human life, presented somehow through the music.' See 'Notes on the Meaning of Music', in Michael Krausz (ed.) *The Interpretation of Music*, Oxford, Clarendon Press, 1993, p. 199. Kendall Walton is another writer who remarks on the connection between music and dance. See 'Listening with Imagination: Is music representational?', *Journal of Aesthetics and Art Criticism*, 1994, vol. 52, p. 50. This article is also the inspiration behind the passage where I speak of the importance of listening with imagination.

Jenefer Robinson is the author of a notable article on musical representation: 'Music as a Representational Art', in Philip Alperson (ed.) *What is Music?* University Park, Pa., Pennsylvannia State University Press, 1994, 165-92. Peter Kivy, *Sound and Semblance:*

Reflections on musical representation, Princeton, Princeton University Press, 1983, is, perhaps, the most important work on representation in music.

REPRESENTATION IN MUSIC: II

Geoffrey Madel is among those who hold that the objects of emotional responses to music are the properties of music. See 'What Music Teaches about Emotion', *Philosophy*, 1996, vol. 71, 63–82.

The example of Hindemith's *Trauermusik* is taken from Jan Zwicky, 'Trauermusik', *Brick: A Literary Journal*, 1996, vol. 53, p. 62. Zwicky might not agree with the use I make of the example.

WAYS TO KNOWLEDGE

For a discussion of the cognitive value of testimony, see C. A. J. Coady, *Testimony*, Oxford, Clarendon Press, 1992.

REJECTED ALTERNATIVES

A classic statement of the propositional theory of art is found in Morris Weitz, *Philosophy of the Arts*, Cambridge, Mass., Harvard University Press, 1950, ch. 8. At times Martha Nussbaum seems committed to the theory. She writes that, 'The claim is that only the style of a certain sort of narrative artist ... can adequately *state* certain important truths about the world' (emphasis added). *Love's Knowledge*, New York, Oxford University Press, 1990, p. 6. Notice that Nussbaum believes that certain sorts of artworks make statements that cannot otherwise be made.

The exemplification hypothesis can be traced back to essays by Charles W. Morris, 'Esthetics and the Theory of Signs', *Journal of Unified Science*, 1939–40, vol. 8 , 131–50 and 'Science, Art and Technology', *Kenyon Review*, 1939, vol. 1, 409–23. Most of this section is directed against the version of the hypothesis adopted by Nelson Goodman and Catherine Z. Elgin. The view that the cognitive value of art is to be explained by means of exemplification is presented, though never very systematically, in a variety of Goodman's works. See *Languages of Art* and *Ways of Worldmaking*, 2nd edn, Indianapolis, Hackett, 1978. See also Nelson Goodman and Catherine Z. Elgin, *Reconceptions in Philosophy and Other Arts and Sciences*, Indianapolis, Hackett, 1988; Elgin, *With Reference to Reference*, Indianapolis, Hackett, 1983; and Elgin, 'Understanding: Art and science', in Peter A. French, Theodore E. Uehling, Jr. and Howard K. Wettstein (eds) *Midwest Studies in Philosophy*, vol. 16, Notre Dame, Indiana, University of Notre Dame Press, 1991, 196–208. With one exception, the examples of exemplification used in this section are found in these works. The exception is Malevich's *Red Square*. It is taken from Kenneth Dorter, 'Conceptual Truth and Aesthetic Truth', *Journal of Aesthetics and Art Criticism*, 1990, vol. 48, 37–51.

INTERPRETIVE ILLUSTRATION

For Diderot's views on Richardson, see *Thoughts on Art and Style*, trans. Beatrix L. Tollemache, New York, Burt Franklin, 1971, p. 274.

The passage from Plato's *Republic* to which I refer is found at p. 331c.

AFFECTIVE ILLUSTRATION AND KNOWLEDGE

The example of the hat that looks like the Taj Mahal is taken from John Wisdom, *Paradox and Discovery*, Oxford, Basil Blackwell, 1965, p. 3. Wisdom's example was brought to my attention by James Jobes, 'A Revelatory Function of Art', *British Journal of Aesthetics*, 1974, vol. 14, 124–33.

For the views of Mendelssohn, Mahler and Schoenberg on music and emotion, see the selections from their writings in Sam Morgenstern (ed.) *Composers on Music: An anthology of composers' writings from Palestrina to Copland*, n.p., Bonanza, 1956.

WHAT CAN BE LEARNED FROM ART?

The passage from Kant's *Critique of Pure Reason* to which I refer is found at A132/B171ff.

A version of the race riot example is found in Kai Nielsen, 'A Defense of Utilitarianism', *Ethics*, 1972, vol. 82, 113–24. The corn dealer example is found in the first paragraph of Chapter III of Mill's *On Liberty*.

Martha Nussbaum is someone who appears to believe that literature is a branch of moral philosophy. She writes that 'certain literary texts ... are indispensable to a philosophical inquiry in the ethical sphere: not by any means sufficient, but sources of insight without which the inquiry cannot be complete'. Martha Nussbaum, *Love's Knowledge*, pp. 23–4.

REPLIES TO OBJECTIONS

Plato argues against the cognitive value of art in Book X of the *Republic*.

COGNITIVE VALUE AND THE EXPERIENCE OF ART

David Hume adopts an eliminativist approach to the paradox of tragedy. Susan L. Feagin is the advocate of the compensatory account. See Hume, 'Of Tragedy' and Feagin 'The Pleasures of Tragedy' in Alex Neill and Aaron Ridley (eds) *Arguing About Art*, New York, McGraw-Hill, 1995.

The discussion of the profundity of art was prompted by a debate about the profundity of music initiated by Peter Kivy. 'The Profundity of Music', an excerpt from his *Music Alone* (Ithaca, N.Y., Cornell University Press), and essays by Jerrold Levinson ('Musical Profundity Misplaced') and Aaron Ridley ('Profundity in Music') are included in *Arguing About Art*. I believe that Levinson makes the most useful contribution to this debate and his views have influenced mine.

RELATIVISM AND AESTHETIC VALUE

For discussions of aesthetic realism, see John McDowell, 'Aesthetic Value, Objectivity and the Fabric of the World' and Philip Pettit, 'The Possibility of Aesthetic Realism', in Eva Schaper (ed.) *Pleasure, Preference and Value*, Cambridge, Cambridge University Press, 1983. See also my 'Aesthetic Antirealism', *Southern Journal of Philosophy*, 1997, vol. 35, 119–34. In this section I suggest that aesthetic relativism is preferable to aesthetic realism (and vice versa) if it has the better explanation of disagreements about aesthetic value. This claim is influenced by Crispin Wright, *Truth and Objectivity*, Cambridge, Mass., Harvard University Press, 1992. Wright says that if realism about some matter is correct, then statements about the matter possess 'cognitive command'. When a class of statements possesses cognitive command, and people disagree about the truth values of statements in the class, someone is in error.

CRITERIA OF EVALUATION

When I refer to Pope, I have in mind *The Essay on Criticism*, l. 298.

WHAT IS AVANT-GARDE ART?

When it comes to the evaluation of avant-garde art, I find a kindred spirit in Derek Matravers. See his 'Why Some Modern Art is Junk', *Cogito*, 1994, vol. 8, 19–25.

EXEMPLIFICATION AND AVANT-GARDE ART

For a good discussion of constructivism and its use of exemplification, see David Herwitz, *Making Theory/Constructing Art*, Chicago, University of Chicago Press, 1993, chs 2 and 3.

THE SEMANTICS OF AVANT-GARDE ART

For Kandinsky's writings on painting, see Kenneth C. Lindsay and Peter Vergo (eds) *Complete Writings on Art*, London, Faber and Faber, 1982. 'The Language of Colors and Forms' is the title of section 6 of *On the Spiritual in Art* (vol. 2, p. 161). In *Point and Line to Plane*, Kandinsky states that 'the new science of art can only come about provided that signs become symbols' (vol. 2, p. 540). He seems to mean by this that pictorial elements should have a fixed significance.

Herwitz provides a good discussion of the relationship between avant-garde artworks and discourses. (He does not, however, believe that the dependence of an artwork on a discourse is a failing.) Herwitz holds that avant-garde works often serve and provide examples of theories (or, in my terminology, discourses). He writes, for example, that Mondrian's '[w]ords are required to get the audience to take the sermon in the art'. *Making Theory/Constructing Art*, p. 108.

The passage by Newman is quoted in Thomas B. Hess, *Barnett Newman*, New York, Walker, 1969, p. 55. For a reproduction of Baldessari's *Everything Is Purged...* see Lucy R. Lippard, *Six Years: The dematerialization of the art object from 1966 to 1972*, New York, Prager, 1973, p. 58. For information on the Guerilla Girls, see Susan Tallman, 'Guerilla Girls', *Arts Magazine*, 1991, vol. 65, no. 8, 21–2.

BUT IS IT ART?

For Halley's views on art and emotion, see Matthew Collings, *It Hurts: New York art from Warhol to now*, London, 21 Publishing, 1998, p. 158.

DESTROYING WORKS OF AVANT-GARDE ART

This section draws upon material from my 'Destroying Works of Art', *Journal of Aesthetics and Art Criticism*, 1989, vol. 47, 367–73.

ENVOY

The passage from Joseph Addison is found in his remarks on Pope's *Essay on Criticism*, first published in *The Spectator*, No. 253. The remark of Sir Joshua Reynolds is found in his *Fifteen Discourses Delivered in the Royal Academy*, London, J. M. Dent, n.d, p. 104.

BIBLIOGRAPHY

Addis, Larry, *Of Mind and Music*, Ithaca, N.Y., Cornell University Press, 1999.

Beardsley, Monroe C., *Aesthetics*, New York, Harcourt, Brace and Co., 1958 (chs 8 and 9).

Beardsmore, R. W., 'Learning from a Novel', *Royal Institute of Philosophy Lectures*, 1973, vol. 6, 23–46.

Bender, John W., 'Art as a Source of Knowledge: Linking analytic aesthetics and epistemology', in John W. Bender and H. Gene Blocker (eds) *Contemporary Philosophy of Art*, Englewood Cliffs, N.J., Prentice Hall, 1993.

Carroll, Noël, 'Moderate Moralism', *British Journal of Aesthetics*, 1996, vol. 36, 223–38.

——, 'Art, narrative, and moral understanding', in Jerrold Levinson (ed.) *Aesthetics and ethics: Essays at the intersection*, Cambridge: Cambridge University Press, 1998.

——, 'Art and Ethical Criticism: An overview of recent directions in research', *Ethics*, 2000, vol. 110, 350–87.

Collingwood, R. G., *The Principles of Art*, Oxford, Clarendon Press, 1938.

Currie, Gregory, 'Realism of Character and Value of Fiction', in Jerrold Levinson (ed.) *Aesthetics and ethics: Essays at the intersection*, Cambridge, Cambridge University Press, 1998.

Davenport, Edward A., 'Literature as Thought Experiment (On Aiding and Abetting the Muse)', *Philosophy of Social Sciences*, 1983, vol. 13, 279–306.

Day, John Patrick, 'Artistic Verisimilitude (I)', *Dialogue*, 1962, vol. 1, 163–87.

——, 'Artistic Verisimilitude (II)', *Dialogue*, 1962, vol. 1, 278–304.

Depaul, Michael R., 'Argument and Perception: The role of literature in moral inquiry', *Journal of Philosophy*, 1988, vol. 85, 552–65.

Diffey, T. J., 'What Can We Learn from Art?', *Australasian Journal of Philosophy*, 1995, vol. 73, 202–11.

Dorter, Kenneth, 'Conceptual Truth and Aesthetic Truth', *Journal of Aesthetics and Art Criticism*, 1990, vol. 48, 37–51.

Eaton, Marcia, 'Truth in Pictures', *Journal of Aesthetics and Art Criticism*, 1980–1, vol. 39, 15–26.

Elgin, Catherine Z., *With Reference to Reference*, Indianapolis, Hackett, 1983.

——, 'Understanding: Art and science', in Peter A. French, Theodore E. Uehling, Jr. and Howard K. Wettstein (eds) *Midwest Studies in Philosophy*, vol. 16, Notre Dame, Indiana, University of Notre Dame Press, 1991.

——, 'Relocating Aesthetics: Goodman's epistemic turn', *Revue Internationale de Philosophie*, 1993, vol. 47, 171–86.

Elliot, R. K., 'Poetry and Truth', *Analysis*, 1966–7, vol. 27, 77–85.

Freeland, Cynthia A., 'Art and Moral Knowledge', *Philosophical Topics*, 1997, vol. 25, 11–36.

Gaskin, Richard, Critical notice of *Truth, Fiction and Literature*, by Peter Lamarque and Stein Haugom Olsen, *British Journal of Aesthetics*, 1995, vol. 35, 395–401.

Goodman, Nelson, *Languages of Art*, Indianapolis, Hackett, 1976.

——, *Ways of Worldmaking*, 2nd edn, Indianapolis, Hackett, 1978.

Goodman, Nelson and Catherine Z. Elgin, *Reconceptions in Philosophy and Other Arts and Sciences*, Indianapolis, Hackett, 1988.

Graham, Gordon, 'Value and the Visual Arts', *Journal of Aesthetic Education*, 1994, vol. 28, 1–14.

——, 'Learning From Art', *British Journal of Aesthetics*, 1995, vol. 35, 26–37.

——, 'The Value of Music', *Journal of Aesthetics and Art Criticism*, 1995, vol. 53, 139–53.

——, 'Aesthetic Cognitivism and the Literary Arts', *Journal of Aesthetic Education*, 1996, vol. 30, 1–17.

——, *Philosophy of the Arts*, London, Routledge, 1997.

Greene, Theodore Meyer, *The Arts and the Art of Criticism*, 2nd edn, Princeton, Princeton University Press, 1952.

Hagberg, G. L., *Art as Language*, Ithaca, Cornell University Press, 1995.

Hepburn, Ronald W., 'Art, Truth and the Education of Subjectivity', *Journal of the Philosophy of Education*, 1990, vol. 24, 185–98.

Hermerén, Göran, 'Art and Life: Models for understanding music', *Australasian Journal of Philosophy*, 1995, vol. 73, 280–92.

Hirst, Paul H., 'Literature and the Fine Arts as a Unique Form of Knowledge', in his *Knowledge and the Curriculum*, London, Routledge and Kegan Paul, 1974.

Hospers, John, *Meaning and Truth in the Arts*, Chapel Hill, University of North Carolina Press, 1946.

Hursthouse, Rosalind, 'Truth and Representation', in Oswald Hanfling (ed.) *Philosophical Aesthetics*, Oxford, Blackwell, 1992.

Jobes, James, 'A Revelatory Function of Art', *British Journal of Aesthetics*, 1974, vol. 14, 124–33.

Kjørup, Søren, 'George Inness and the Battle at Hastings, Or Doing Things with Pictures', *The Monist*, 1974, vol. 58, 216–35.

Korsmeyer, Carolyn, 'Pictorial Assertion', *Journal of Aesthetics and Art Criticism*, 1985, vol. 43, 257–65.

Lamarque, Peter and Stein Haugom Olsen, *Truth, Fiction and Literature: A philosophical perspective*, Oxford, Clarendon Press, 1994.

Langer, Susanne K., *Philosophy in a New Key*, Cambridge, Mass., Harvard University Press, 1951.

——, *Feeling and Form*, London, Routledge and Kegan Paul, 1953.

Levinson, Jerrold, 'Messages in Art', *Australasian Journal of Philosophy*, 1995, vol. 73, 184–98.

Lyas, Colin, *Aesthetics*, London, UCL Press, 1997, ch. 9.

Madel, Geoffrey, 'What Music Teaches about Emotion', *Philosophy*, 1996, vol. 71, 63–82.

Martin, Graham D., 'A New Look at Fictional Reference', *Philosophy*, 1982, vol. 57, 223–36.

Mellor, D. H., 'On Literary Truth', *Ratio*, 1968, vol. 10, 150–68.

Morgan, Douglas N., 'Must Art Tell the Truth?', in John Hospers (ed.) *Introductory Readings in Aesthetics*, New York, The Free Press, 1969.

Morris, Charles W., 'Science, Art and Technology', *Kenyon Review*, 1939, vol. 1, 409–23.

——, 'Esthetics and the Theory of Signs', *Journal of Unified Science*, 1939–40, vol. 8, 131–50.

Novitz, David, *Pictures and Their Use in Communication*, The Hague, Martinus Nijhoff, 1977.

——, 'The Trouble with Truth', *Philosophy and Literature*, 1995, vol. 19, 350–9.

Nozick, Robert, 'Goodman, Nelson, on Merit, Aesthetic', *Journal of Philosophy*, 1972, vol. 69, 783–5.

Nussbaum, Martha C., *Love's Knowledge*, New York, Oxford University Press, 1990.

——, *Poetic Justice*, Boston, Beacon Press, 1995.

O'Hear, Anthony, *The Element of Fire: Science, art and the human world*, London, Routledge, 1990.

Osborne, Harold, 'Interpretation in Science and in Art', *British Journal of Aesthetics*, 1986, vol. 26, 3–15.

Putnam, Hilary, 'Literature, Science, and Reflection', in his *Meaning and the Moral Sciences*, Boston, Routledge and Kegan Paul, 1978.

Reid, Louis Arnaud, 'Art and Knowledge', *British Journal of Aesthetics*, 1985, vol. 25, 115–24.

Robinson, Jenefer, 'Music as a Representational Art', in Philip Alperson (ed.) *What is Music?* University Park, Pa., Pennsylvannia State University Press, 1994.

——, 'L'Éducation sentimentale', *Australasian Journal of Philosophy*, 1995, vol. 73, 280–92.

Ryle, Gilbert, 'Jane Austen and the Moralists', in his *Collected Papers*, vol. 1, London, Hutchinson, 1971, 276–91.

Scheffler, Israel, *Symbolic Worlds: Art, science, language, ritual*, Cambridge, Cambridge University Press, 1997.

Sesonske, Alexander, 'Truth in Art', *Journal of Philosophy*, 1956, vol. 53, 345–53.

Sirridge, M. J., 'Truth From Fiction?', *Philosophy and Phenomenological Research*, 1975, vol. 35, 453–71.

Skinner, Quentin, 'Ambrogio Lorenzetti: The artist as political philosopher', *Proceedings of the British Academy*, 1986, vol. 72, 1–56.

Stolnitz, Jerome, 'On the Cognitive Triviality of Art', *British Journal of Aesthetics*, 1992, vol. 32, 191–200.

Tilghman, Benjamin, *Wittgenstein, Ethics and Aesthetics*, Basingstoke, Macmillan, 1991.

Walsh, Dorothy, 'The Cognitive Content of Art', *Philosophical Review*, 1943, vol. 52, 433–51.

——, *Literature and Knowledge*, Middletown, Conn., Wesleyan University Press, 1969.

Walton, Kendall L., 'What is Abstract about the Art of Music?', *Journal of Aesthetics and Art Criticism*, 1988, vol. 46, 351–64.

——, 'Listening with Imagination: Is music representational?', *Journal of Aesthetics and Art Criticism*, 1994, vol. 52, 47–61.

Warner, Martin, 'Literature, Truth, and Logic', *Philosophy*, 1999, vol. 74, 29–54.

Weitz, Morris, 'Does Art Tell the Truth?', *Philosophy and Phenomenological Research*, 1942–3, vol. 3, 338–48.

——, *Philosophy of the Arts*, Cambridge, Mass., Harvard University Press, 1950, ch. 8.

Wilson, Catherine, 'Knowledge and Literature', *Philosophy*, 1983, vol. 58, 489–96.

Young, James O., 'Artworks and Artworlds', *British Journal of Aesthetics*, 1995, vol. 35, 330–7.

——, 'Evaluation and the Cognitive Function of Art', *Journal of Aesthetic Education*, 1995, vol. 29, 65–78.

——, 'Inquiry in the Arts and Sciences', *Philosophy*, 1996, vol. 71, 255–73.

——, 'Relativism and the Evaluation of Art', *Journal of Aesthetic Education*, 1997, vol. 31, 9–22.

——, 'Defining Art Responsibly', *British Journal of Aesthetics*, 1997, vol. 37, 57–65.

——, 'The Philosophical Disenfranchisement of the Commonplace', in Arto Haapala, Jerrold Levinson and Veikko Rantala (eds) *The End of Art and Beyond*, Atlantic Highlands, N.J., Humanities Press, 1997.

——, 'Art, Knowledge, and Exemplification', *British Journal of Aesthetics*, 1999, vol. 39, 126–37.

——, 'The Cognitive Value of Music', *Journal of Aesthetics and Art Criticism*, 1999, vol. 57, 41–54.

——, 'Representation in Literature', *Literature and Aesthetics*, 1999, vol. 9, 127–43.

Zwicky, Jan, *Lyric Philosophy*, Toronto, University of Toronto Press, 1992.

INDEX